Contemporary

European

Architects

Volume III

Philip Jodidio

Contemporary European Architects

Volume III

TASCHEN

Page 2 · Seite 2
Rem Koolhaas: Grand Palais, Lille, 1990–94
Photo: © Arnaud Carpentier

This book was printed on 100% chlorine-free bleached paper in accordance with the TCF-standard

© 1995 Benedikt Taschen Verlag GmbH
Hohenzollernring 53, D-50672 Köln

Edited by Angelika Muthesius, Cologne
Text edited by Silvia Krieger, Cologne
Design: Frank Schwab, Schwäbisch Gmünd
Cover Design: Angelika Muthesius, Cologne; Mark Thomson, London
French translation: Jacques Bosser, Paris
German translation: Franca Fritz, Heinrich Koop, Cologne

Printed in Italy
ISBN 3-8228-9264-5

Contents
Inhalt
Sommaire

Pragmatic Utopias
European Architects in the 1990s

Pragmatische Utopien
Europäische Architekten in den 90er Jahren

Les utopies pragmatiques
Architectes européens des années 90

A sculpture by Santiago Calatrava shows
a direct relationship to his Lyon-Satolas TGV
station.

Diese Skulptur von Santiago Calatrava steht
in direkter Beziehung zu seinem TGV-Bahnhof
Lyon-Satolas.

Sculpture de Santiago Calatrava, qui n'est pas
sans liens avec la gare de TGV de Lyon-Satolas.

The 1990s have been marked by a series of rapid transformations in the very nature of European architecture. When the political and economic euphoria which presided over the late 1980s gave way to recession, a series of new priorities emerged to dictate the flow of limited resources. The explosion of transportation and communications has, for example, been a leading factor in the emerging architectural forms of the 1990s. Another has been the continuing emphasis placed on culture by public authorities in almost every European country. Although the private sector has often participated actively in the large projects carried out recently, some governments have led the way in difficult economic times towards an expanding recognition of the importance of quality architectural design. Public facilities can thus be retained as a third category of ongoing interest.

Despite the growing pains of the European Community, it has become increasingly difficult to examine architecture on a country by country basis. This is due to the international character of some underlying trends, but also to the cosmopolitan nature of the architects themselves. The most visible figures of the current scene might be a Dutch architect who works in France, a Spanish engineer based in Zurich who builds in Lyon, or an Italian globetrotter who creates an airport in the bay of Osaka. Despite the flamboyant personalities of some, much of their theoretical analysis is clearly dependent on factors beyond their control. New styles are evolving from the necessity to use inexpensive materials and to respect budgets more rigorously than in the past. Notwithstanding the apparent contradiction in terms, today's architectural utopias are pragmatic, and the increasing ability of "quality" architects to come to terms with the economic aspects of their art is one reason that their influence is on the rise.

Transport & Communication
No project is more emblematic of the resurgence of transportation and communication in architecture than the extraordinary new Kansai airport built by the Italian Renzo Piano on an artificial island in the bay of Osaka. Despite the examples of Dulles Airport in Washington, D.C., or the

Die europäische Architektur der 90er Jahre ist geprägt von einer Reihe rascher und tiefgreifender Veränderungen. Als die politische und ökonomische Euphorie der späten 80er Jahre einer allgemeinen Rezession wich, begannen sich neue Prioritäten durchzusetzen, die den Fluß der nunmehr begrenzten Geldmittel bestimmten. Zu diesen, für die Entwicklung der Architektur bestimmenden Faktoren gehört zum Beispiel die explosive Entwicklung in den Bereichen Transport und Kommunikation, aber auch der ungebrochen hohe Stellenwert der Kultur bei den verantwortlichen Stellen der meisten europäischen Länder. Obwohl der private Sektor an den Großprojekten der letzten Jahre häufig aktiv beteiligt war, zeigten einige Regierungen trotz wirtschaftlich schwieriger Zeiten ein gestiegenes Interesse an qualitativ hochwertigem architektonischem Design. Daher können öffentliche Einrichtungen als dritter Faktor ungebrochenen architektonischen Interesses genannt werden.

Ungeachtet der wachsenden Probleme innerhalb der Europäischen Union wird es immer schwieriger, architektonische Entwicklungen nach Ländern getrennt zu betrachten. Dies liegt zum einen am internationalen Charakter einiger aktueller Entwicklungen, zum anderen an der kosmopolitischen Einstellung vieler Architekten. Zu den bekanntesten Figuren der heutige Szene zählen ein niederländischer Architekt, der in Frankreich arbeitet, ein in Zürich ansässiger spanischer Ingenieur, der in Lyon baut, sowie ein italienischer Globetrotter, der einen Flughafen in der Bucht von Osaka entworfen hat. Obwohl es sich z.T. um extravagante Persönlichkeiten handelt, ist ein Großteil der theoretischen Analysen dieser Architekten von Faktoren abhängig, die außerhalb ihres Einflußbereichs liegen. Neue Stilrichtungen entwickeln sich, weil es notwendig ist, preiswerte Materialien zu verwenden und die vorgegebenen Budgets rigoroser eingehalten werden müssen als in der Vergangenheit. Trotz des offensichtlichen Widerspruchs in sich sind die heutigen architektonischen Utopien pragmatischer Natur, und die wachsende Fähigkeit sogenannter »erstklassiger« Architekten, sich mit den wirtschaftlichen Aspekten ihrer Kunst zu arrangieren, ist ein Grund dafür, daß ihr Einfluß zunimmt.

Les années 90 ont été marquées par une série de transformations rapides de la nature même de l'architecture européenne. La récession succédant à l'euphorie politique et économique de la fin des années 80, de nouvelles priorités sont apparues. Il s'agissait alors de tirer le meilleur parti de moyens dorénavant limités. L'explosion des transports et des communications s'est imposée comme l'un des facteurs majeurs de l'émergence des nouvelles formes architecturales des années 90, un autre étant l'intérêt porté au développement culturel par les autorités publiques de pratiquement tous les pays européens. Bien que le secteur privé ait souvent activement participé à de nombreux grands projets récents, il faut reconnaître que certains gouvernements ont ouvert la voie à une reconnaissance grandissante de la qualité architecturale, en dépit des difficultés du moment. Les équipements publics sont ainsi devenus une catégorie architecturale d'importance.

Malgré les difficultés croissantes de l'Union Européenne, il est devenu de plus en plus difficile d'étudier l'architecture en Europe sur une base strictement nationale. C'est à la fois la conséquence du caractère international de certaines grandes tendances, et d'un nouveau cosmopolitisme des architectes. Les acteurs les plus en vue de la période sont ainsi un architecte néerlandais qui travaille en France, un ingénieur espagnol installé à Zurich et construisant à Lyon, ou un globe-trotter italien qui crée un aéroport dans la baie d'Osaka. Quelle que soit la flamboyance de la personnalité de certains de ces créateurs, une bonne partie de leur analyse théorique ressort à l'évidence de facteurs qui leur échappent. De nouveaux styles naissent ainsi de la nécessité d'utiliser des matériaux bon marché, et de respecter les budgets avec plus de rigueur que par le passé. Les utopies architecturales d'aujourd'hui sont pragmatiques, et la capacité croissante des architectes «de qualité» à prendre en compte les aspects économiques de leur art, est l'une des raisons du développement de leur influence.

Transports et communication

Aucun projet n'est plus emblématique de la résurgence des transports et des communications dans le champ

TWA Terminal building at John F. Kennedy Airport (1956–62), both by Eero Saarinen, until about ten years ago, few countries took the architecture of their airports very seriously. Like railway stations, airports were anonymous points of transition where architecture mattered less than simply moving people in and out with as little fuss as possible. The rapid development of the Asian economies and their reliance on world-wide air transport have been one factor in this change of attitude. In fact, the idea of locating the airport on the sea in the Kansai (Kyoto-Osaka) area was first proposed in 1971, as a response both to the density of local construction and to the need to keep flights landing or taking off 24 hours a day despite strict noise regulations. The resulting structure is a feat of engineering and architecture which has few equals in history. An island, 4.37 kilometers long and 1.27 kilometers wide was quite simply created on the 18 meter deep sea bed, requiring the use of no less than 180 million cubic meters of landfill. This 511 hectare island, a "platform born at the juncture of the sea and the sky," was the object of an international competition in November 1988 which brought together 15 groups of architects and builders, including such well-known names as Norman Foster, Ricardo Bofill, I.M. Pei, Kazuhiro Ishii, Jean Nouvel, Kiyonori Kikutake, or Bernard Tschumi. The winner, Renzo Piano, designed a "megastructure" 1.7 kilometers long as the main passenger terminal. As large as this building seems, in the imagination of the architect, it was only part of a much bigger ring with a diameter of 16.4 kilometers, tilted at an angle of 68.2° to the surface. The terminal was imagined as that portion of the ring that is exposed above ground. The roof of the completed building measures no less than 90 000 square meters, covered by 82 400 identical ferrite type stainless steel panels, whose weather resistance is close to that of titanium. Despite numerous difficulties, including the ongoing "problem of differential settlement" which simply means that parts of the artificial island are settling faster than others, the Kansai project is no doubt exemplary of the kind of international cooperation which such huge projects will engender in the future. Together with the Italian architect, the French group Aéroports de Paris

Transport und Kommunikation

Kein Projekt ist typischer für die Wiederentdeckung von Transport und Kommunikation im Rahmen der Architektur als der außergewöhnliche neue Kansai Airport, den der Italiener Renzo Piano für eine künstliche Insel in der Bucht von Osaka entwarf. Obwohl Eero Saarinen mit dem Dulles Airport in Washington, D.C. oder dem TWA Terminal am John F. Kennedy Airport (1956–62) herausragende Beispiele geschaffen hatte, maßen bis noch vor zehn Jahren die wenigsten Länder der architektonischen Gestaltung ihrer Flughäfen große Bedeutung bei. Ebenso wie Bahnhöfe betrachtete man Flughäfen als anonyme Durchgangsstationen ohne architektonischen Reiz, deren einziger Zweck darin bestand, eine möglichst große Anzahl von Menschen reibungslos durch sie hindurchzuschleusen. Der rasche Aufschwung der asiatischen Wirtschaft und ihre Abhängigkeit von einem weltweiten Transportnetz spielten eine entscheidende Rolle bei der Änderung dieser Einstellung. Schon 1971 dachte man darüber nach, einen Flughafen für die Region Kansai (um Kioto und Osaka) ins Meer zu bauen – als Antwort auf die hohe Bevölkerungsdichte dieser Region und die Notwendigkeit, trotz strikter Lärmschutzgesetze rund um die Uhr Starts und Landungen durchführen zu können. Das entstandene Bauwerk ist eine architektonische und technische Meisterleistung, die in der Architekturgeschichte ihresgleichen sucht. Auf dem nur 18 Meter tiefen Meeresgrund entstand mit Hilfe von 180 Millionen Kubikmetern Schüttmaterial eine künstliche Insel von 4,37 km Länge und 1,27 km Breite. Dieses 511 Hektar große Areal – »eine Plattform, entstanden am Übergang von Himmel und Meer« – war im November 1988 Gegenstand eines internationalen Architekturwettbewerbs, an dem 15 Gruppen von Architekten teilnahmen, darunter bekannte Namen wie Norman Foster, Ricardo Bofill, I.M. Pei, Kazuhiro Ishii, Jean Nouvel, Kiyonori Kikutake und Bernard Tschumi. Der Gewinner, Renzo Piano, entwarf den Passagierterminal als eine 1,7 km lange »Megastruktur«. Dieses riesige Bauwerk bildet in der Vorstellung des Architekten jedoch nur einen kleinen Teil eines wesentlich größeren Rings mit einem Durchmesser von 16,4 km, der in einem Winkel von 68,2 Grad zur

architectural que l'extraordinaire aéroport de Kansai qu'a édifié l'Italien Renzo Piano sur une île artificielle dans la baie d'Osaka. Malgré les exemples de Dulles Airport à Washington D.C. et du terminal TWA de John F. Kennedy Airport (1956–62), tous deux œuvres d'Eero Saarinen, peu de pays se sont préoccupés sérieusement de l'architecture aéroportuaire, jusqu'à il y a une dizaine d'années. Comme les gares de chemin de fer, les aéroports étaient des lieux de transit anonymes, pour lesquels l'architecture n'avait guère pour fonction que d'aider les passagers à se déplacer avec le minimum d'embarras. Le développement rapide des économies asiatiques et leur dépendance des liaisons aériennes internationales a beaucoup contribué à ce changement d'attitude. L'idée de créer un aéroport sur la mer dans la région de Kansai (Kyoto-Osaka) fut initialement proposée en 1971, pour répondre à la fois au problème de la densité urbaine locale et au besoin de faire atterrir ou décoller les avions 24 heures sur 24, malgré la réglementation anti-bruit. L'édifice né de ce défi est le triomphe de l'ingénierie et de l'architecture. Il n'a que peu d'équivalents dans l'histoire. Une île de 4,37 km de long sur 1,27 de large a tout simplement été créée sur des fonds marins de 18 m de profondeur, grâce au déversement de 180 millions de m³ de remblais. Cette «plate-forme au point de rencontre de la mer et du ciel», de 511 ha, a fait l'objet d'un concours international en novembre 1988, qui a vu se confronter 15 équipes d'architectes et d'entreprises de travaux publics, avec des participants aussi célèbres que Norman Foster, Ricardo Bofill, I.M. Pei, Kazuhiro Ishii, Jean Nouvel, Kiyonori Kikutake, ou Bernard Tschumi. Le vainqueur, Renzo Piano, proposa pour le terminal passagers principal, une «mégastructure» de 1,7 km de long. Si grand ce bâtiment puisse-t-il paraître, il n'est, dans l'esprit de l'architecte, que la partie émergée d'un anneau de 16,4 km de diamètre, incliné à 68, 2° par rapport à la surface du sol. Son toit ne mesure pas moins de 90 000 m². Il est recouvert de 82 400 panneaux identiques d'acier inoxydable à la ferrite, dont la résistance aux éléments est proche de celle du titane. Malgré de multiples difficultés, dont le récurrent «problème de tassement différentiel» (certaines parties de l'île artificielle se tassent

Top: Façade of Kansai Airport, a 1.7 kilometer long "megastructure" built by Renzo Piano in the Bay of Osaka. Bottom: Rail station at Kansai Airport with its specially designed trains.

Oben: Fassade des Kansai Airport in der Bucht von Osaka, einer 1,7 Kilometer langen »Mega-struktur« von Renzo Piano. Unten: Bahnhof des Kansai Airport mit seinen speziell angefertigten Zügen.

Ci-dessus: Façade de l'aéroport de Kansai, bâti-ment géant de 1,7 km de long construit par Renzo Piano dans la baie d'Osaka. Ci-dessous: Gare de chemin de fer de l'aéroport de Kansai, dont les trains ont été spécialement conçus.

Page 10/11: The new airport at Chek Lap Kok Island, Hong Kong, designed by Sir Norman Foster to accommodate 35 million travellers per year in its first phase.

Seite 10/11: Der von Sir Norman Foster entworfene, neue Flughafen auf der Insel Chek Lap Kok bei Hongkong soll jährlich 35 Millionen Passagiere abfertigen können.

Page 10/11: Le nouvel aéroport de Chek Lap Kok, à Hong Kong, conçu par Sir Norman Foster. Dans sa première phase, il accueillera chaque année 35 millions de voyageurs.

(Paul Andreu) developed the basic concept; Nikken Sekkei was responsible for the foundations, the first and second floors; Bechtel and Fluor Daniel of the United States acted as general contractors; and Watson of Great Britain and Eiffel of France as subcontractors. Another huge Asian project is the new airport at Chek Lap Kok currently being built by Sir Norman Foster, which is intended to handle upwards of 40 million passengers a year before the end of the decade. Confirming the trend, the new Seoul Metropolitan Airport (Fentress Bradburn/BHJW), located on Yong Jong Do Island in the Yellow Sea, 50 kilometers west of Seoul, is also due for completion in the year 2000.

The rebirth of the train station
Although airports of the past never underwent the kind of architectural transformation being wrought at this moment by Asian ambitions coupled with Western architectural talent, railway stations used to aspire to palatial dimensions. According to Jean-Marie Duthilleul, head architect of the French national railways (SNCF), it was a combination of factors including the devastation of the Second World War and the rise of the airplane, heralding the end of an era of great European train stations built between the late 19th century and the 1930s. Duthilleul is presently heading an effort in France to give stations back some of the excitement they lost when it was decided that underground, anonymous spaces would do for a type of transport which seemed to be doomed by the airborne competition. In fact, the TGV (Train à grande vitesse) lines in which the French government has invested heavily in the past decade have brought about a transformation not only in station architecture, but also in the property development which accompanies the creation of the new, high-speed lines. The most significant example of this trend has occurred along the Eurostar line which links Paris and London via the Channel Tunnel. Duthilleul's group has revamped the formerly sinister Gare du Nord into a friendly, efficient point of departure. He is also responsible for the new Lille-Europe station at the heart of the so-called Euralille development.

It was thanks to the political clout of former Prime

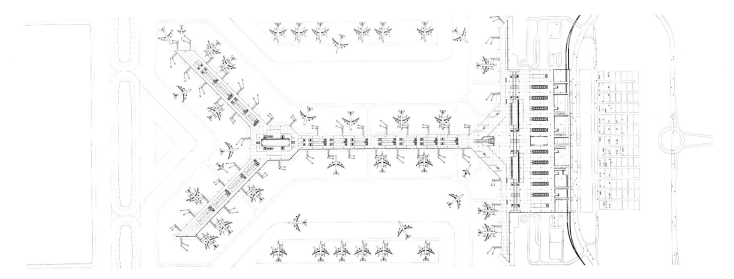

Erdoberfläche geneigt ist. Den Passagierterminal hatte Piano als den überirdischen Teil des Rings vorgesehen. Die Dachkonstruktion des Gebäudes umfaßt 90 000 m², bedeckt mit 82 400 identischen Blechen aus ferritischem, nichtrostendem Stahl, dessen Wetterbeständigkeit Titan ähnelt. Trotz diverser Schwierigkeiten – wozu auch das andauernde »Problem der unterschiedlichen Setzung« zählt (einige Teile der künstlichen Insel setzen sich schneller als andere) – ist das Kansai-Projekt ein typisches Beispiel für die Art von internationaler Kooperation, in der solch riesige Bauten in Zukunft realisiert werden. Das Grundkonzept entstand in Zusammenarbeit von Piano und der französischen Gruppe Aéroports de Paris (Paul Andreu); Nikken Sekkei zeichnete verantwortlich für die Fundamente sowie die ersten beiden Stockwerke; Bechtel und Fluor Daniel aus den USA traten als Hauptauftragnehmer auf, und die britischen bzw. französischen Firmen Watson und Eiffel als Nebenauftragnehmer. Ein weiteres Großprojekt im asiatischen Raum ist der neue Flughafen von Chek Lap Kok, der momentan unter der Leitung von Sir Norman Foster entsteht und nach seiner Fertigstellung 1999 jährlich 40 Millionen Fluggäste abfertigen soll. Diese Entwicklung bestätigt auch der neue Seoul Metropolitan Airport (Fentress Bradburn/BHJW), der auf der Insel Yong Jong Do, 50 km westlich von Seoul, im Gelben Meer entsteht; die Bauarbeiten werden voraussichtlich im Jahr 2000 abgeschlossen sein.

Die Wiedergeburt des Bahnhofs

Im Gegensatz zu den Flughäfen, die erst in letzter Zeit solch massiven architektonischen Veränderungen unterworfen sind (dank asiatischer Ambitionen und westlichem architektonischem Talent), bewiesen Bahnhöfe schon immer einen Hang zu verschwenderischen Dimensionen. Laut Jean-Marie Duthilleul, dem Chefarchitekten der Französischen Staatsbahn (SNCF), wurde den großen, europäischen Bahnhöfen, die in der Zeit zwischen dem Ende des 19. Jahrhunderts und den 30er Jahren entstanden, eine Kombination aus diversen Faktoren zum Verhängnis. Dazu zählten u.a. die Verwüstungen des Zweiten Weltkriegs und der Aufstieg des Flugzeugs als Verkehrs- und

plus vite que d'autres…), cette réalisation est sans aucun doute exemplaire du type de coopération internationale que des projets aussi énormes engendreront dans l'avenir. En collaboration avec l'architecte italien, la société française Aéroports de Paris (Paul Andreu) a développé le concept de base. Nikken Sekkei a conduit les travaux pour les fondations, le premier et le deuxième étages. Les groupes américains Bechtel et Fluor Daniel ont été choisis comme maîtres d'œuvre, et les entreprises Watson (Grande-Bretagne) et Eiffel (France) comme sous-traitants.

Un autre projet asiatique géant est celui du nouvel aéroport de Chek Lap Kok, à Hong Kong, actuellement construit par Sir Norman Foster, qui pourra recevoir jusqu'à 40 millions de passagers par an, avant la fin de la décennie. Confirmant cette tendance, le nouvel aéroport de Séoul (Fentress Bradburn/BHJW), situé sur l'île de Yong Jong Do en Mer Jaune, à 50 km à l'ouest de la capitale coréenne, devrait également être terminé pour l'an 2000.

La renaissance des gares

Si les aéroports n'avaient jamais connu de mutations architecturales aussi nettes que celles auxquelles les poussent aujourd'hui les ambitions asiatiques relayées par les meilleurs talents architecturaux d'Occident, ce n'est pas le cas des gares, qui affichèrent longtemps des prétentions palatiales. Selon Jean-Marie Duthilleul, architecte-en-chef de la Société Nationale des Chemins de Fer Français, la combinaison de plusieurs facteurs, dont les destructions de la seconde guerre mondiale et l'essor de l'aviation, condamna les grandes gares européennes construites entre la fin du XIXe siècle et les années 30. Duthilleul anime actuellement l'effort pour redonner aux gares françaises un peu du lustre qu'elles perdirent lorsqu'il fut décidé que des espaces souterrains et anonymes seraient bien suffisants pour un mode de transport qui semblait condamné par la concurrence aérienne. Le TGV dans lequel la France a massivement investi au cours de ces dernières années, a provoqué de profondes transformations, non seulement dans l'architecture des nouvelles gares, mais également à travers les opérations immobilières qui les accompagnent. L'exemple le plus

Minister Pierre Mauroy, the mayor of Lille since 1973, that his blighted northern city was included at the last moment in the route to London in the place of Amiens. Suddenly, Lille was to find itself only one hour from Paris by train, and two hours from London. Lille-Europe would become an obligatory point of passage for some 30 million passengers a year. Significantly, Margaret Thatcher and François Mitterrand signed the agreement to build the TGV-tunnel link in the Lille mayor's office in January 1986. The Rotterdam office of architect Rem Koolhaas (OMA) was chosen to oversee the development of the multi-use Euralille complex, combining the train station, a 155 000 square meter commercial center, two office towers and a 50 000 square meter convention center, in November 1988. Koolhaas, who has become a true "star" of international architecture, was quick to grasp the significance of this massive urban development project. "The underlying notion," he said, "is that you don't look at distance anymore, but at the time it takes to go from one place to another. 60 to 70 million people now live within 90 minutes of each other. By the sheer fluke of geography, Lille is the transplanted heart of a virtual community." Rather than being based on more traditional definitions of place, the architecture and development of the future could thus depend on the location of nodal points in the web being created by new forms of transport and communications. Euralille is all the more significant of a new trend in that Koolhaas called on other well-known architects such as Jean Nouvel and the 1994 Pritzker Prize winner Christian de Portzamparc to make up his design team.

Although the influence of the French projects may only be peripheral in this instance, the English end of the Eurostar line is marked by another significant piece of architecture, Nicholas Grimshaw's extension to Waterloo Station in London. In the desolate South Bank area where car and rail traffic have all but excluded pedestrians, Grimshaw's long curved snake of a building brings a touch of color and light in the great tradition of Paxton or Eiffel. This "gateway to Europe" is intended to handle upwards of 15 million passengers a year, and to have a life of a century. Again, the ambition and scale of this effort herald a

Transportmittel. Duthilleul steht an der Spitze einer Gruppe, die sich darum bemüht, den französischen Bahnhöfen wieder etwas von ihrem verlorenen Flair zurückzugeben, das verlorenging, als man den Beschluß faßte, daß unterirdische, anonyme Räumlichkeiten für ein Transportmittel genügen mußten. Tatsächlich bewirkte das Schienennetz des TGV, in dessen Ausbau die französische Regierung im vergangenen Jahrzehnt intensiv investierte, nicht nur eine Veränderung der Bahnhofsarchitektur, sondern auch der Grundstückserschließung, die mit der Einrichtung neuer Hochgeschwindigkeitsstrecken einherging. Das herausragendste Beispiel für diese Entwicklung ergab sich im Zusammenhang mit dem Eurostar, der Paris durch den Kanaltunnel mit London verbindet: Duthilleuls Gruppe polierte den ehemals tristen Gare du Nord zu einem freundlichen, effizienten Ausgangspunkt für Reisen auf. Darüber hinaus zeichnete er für den neuen Bahnhof Lille-Europe inmitten des Bebauungsplans des Euralille-Komplexes der Stadt Lille verantwortlich.

Dank des politischen Einflusses des ehemaligen französischen Premierministers Pierre Mauroy, Lilles Bürgermeister seit 1973, führte man die Strecke im letzten Moment über Lille (statt über Amiens) nach London. Plötzlich lag Lille nur noch eine Stunde Zugfahrt von Paris und zwei Stunden von London entfernt, und der Bahnhof Lille-Europe bildet in Zukunft eine Durchgangsschleuse für jährlich schätzungsweise 30 Millionen Passagiere. Bezeichnenderweise unterschrieben Margaret Thatcher und François Mitterrand 1986 den Vertrag zum Bau des Kanaltunnels im Büro des Bürgermeisters der Stadt Lille. Im November 1988 beauftragte man das Rotterdamer Büro des Architekten Rem Koolhaas (OMA) mit der Überwachung der Bebauungspläne des Mehrzweckkomplexes Euralille, das einen Bahnhof, ein 155 000 m² großes Einkaufs- und Dienstleistungszentrum, zwei Bürogebäude und ein Kongreßzentrum umfaßt. Koolhaas, der inzwischen zu einem »Star« der Architekturszene avancierte, erkannte schnell die Bedeutung dieses gewaltigen Städtebauprojekts: »Die Grundidee beruht darauf, daß Distanzen uninteressant werden und nur noch die Zeit zählt, die man benötigt, um von einem Ort zum anderen zu gelangen.

significatif est celui de la liaison Paris-Londres, via le tunnel sous la Manche: Eurostar. L'équipe de Duthilleul a magistralement transformé l'ancienne et sinistre gare du Nord en un point de départ fonctionnel et accueillant. Elle est également responsable de la nouvelle gare Lille-Europe, au cœur du complexe Euralille.

C'est grâce à la puissante protection de l'ancien premier ministre, Pierre Mauroy, maire de Lille depuis 1973, que cette sombre cité du Nord a figuré, en dernière minute, sur le parcours du TGV vers Londres, au lieu d'Amiens. Brusquement, Lille se retrouvait ainsi à une heure de Paris par le train, à deux heures de Londres, et la nouvelle gare Lille-Europe allait devenir le point de passage obligé de 30 millions de voyageurs par an. Margaret Thatcher et François Mitterrand signèrent d'ailleurs l'accord sur la construction de la liaison TGV et le tunnel sous la Manche à la mairie de Lille, en janvier 1986. C'est l'agence de Rotterdam de l'architecte Rem Koolhaas (OMA) qui fut choisie en novembre 1988 pour superviser le développement du complexe Euralille qui combine la gare, un centre commercial de 155 000 m², deux tours de bureaux et un centre de congrès de 50 000 m². Koolhaas, l'une des grandes «stars» de l'architecture internationale, comprit tout de suite la signification de cet énorme projet urbain. «L'idée sous-jacente, dit-il, est que vous ne pensez plus en termes de distances, mais au temps nécessaire pour vous rendre d'un point à un autre. 60 à 70 millions de personnes vivent maintenant à 90 minutes maximum les unes des autres. Par un simple hasard géographique, Lille est aujourd'hui le cœur transplanté d'une communauté humaine virtuelle.» Plutôt que continuer à s'appuyer sur des définitions plus traditionnelles du lieu, l'architecture et le développement du futur pourraient ainsi dépendre de la localisation de points nodaux nés des nouvelles formes de transports et de communication. Euralille est d'autant plus représentatif de cette nouvelle tendance que Koolhaas a fait appel à d'autres architectes très connus pour constituer son équipe de conception: Jean Nouvel et le Prix Pritzker 1994, Christian de Portzamparc.

Bien qu'en l'occurrence l'influence des projets français soit sans doute lointaine, le terminus londonien de la ligne

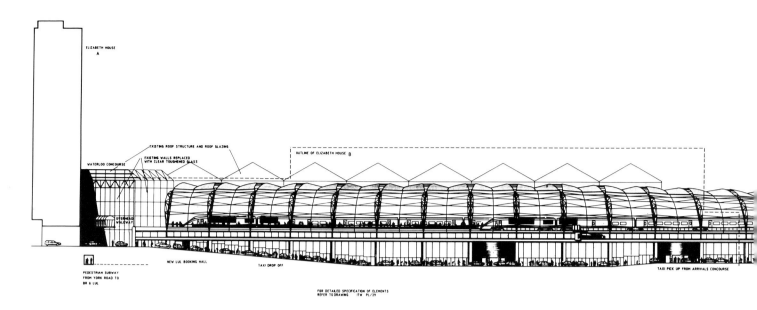

new type of architecture, even if British Rail has fallen
years behind in the construction of the very high speed rail
lines which give breath to the Eurostar project. The
prospect of a renewal of the South Bank complex
may well be speeded now that the Waterloo terminal is
operational, giving the whole area a concentration of
cultural and communications facilities unparalleled in London. The message here, as in the Euralille complex, may
be that good architects are now considered a commercial
asset, capable not only of respecting a budget, but of
inciting public or even official interest to a greater extent
than more ordinary practitioners.

   The idea of a new type of architecture designed to meet
the needs of evolving transportation nodes is confirmed by
the remarkable bird-like structure designed by the Spanish
engineer Santiago Calatrava for the Lyon-Satolas station,
where the south-bound TGV lines meet the Lyon airport.
120 meters long, 100 meters wide and 40 meters high,
this "bird" is made of 1 300 tons of steel, resting on two
concrete arches. Although the suggestion of flight evoked
by the building may recall Eero Saarinen's TWA Terminal,
Calatrava's imagery is more dramatic, confirming his place
as one of the most creative contemporary architect/
engineers, in the spirit of Italian Pier Luigi Nervi or the
Swiss bridge designer Robert Maillart.

Technology and inspiration
Transportation and communication have also come to
inspire structures which do not function as part of a visible
architectural complex, but rather as elements in the growing, invisible network of electronics. Such is certainly the
case of Sir Norman Foster's Torre de Collserola, described
by the City of Barcelona as a "monumental technological
element" when he won the competition in May 1988.
This 288 meter high telecommunications tower dominates
the city, recalling that the architectural history of the city
did not stop with the towers of Gaudi's Sagrada Familia.
Foster, whose architectural practice is amongst the most
successful in Europe, indeed seems to be at his best
when he is facing a technical problem that enables him to
use all of his considerable ingenuity. He points out with

Heute leben 60 bis 70 Millionen Menschen in 90 Minuten
Entfernung zueinander. Nur wegen seiner geographischen
Lage wird Lille zum transplantierten Herz einer virtuellen
Gemeinde.« Demzufolge könnten Architektur und Städte-
bau in Zukunft immer seltener anhand von traditionellen
Definitionen eines Ortes verwirklicht und in zunehmendem
Maße von Knotenpunkten im Netz neuentwickelter Kom-
munikations- und Transportformen abhängig werden. Euro-
lille ist aber auch bezeichnend für einen neuen Trend, der
sich darin äußert, daß Koolhaas andere bekannte Architekten wie etwa Jean Nouvel und den Pritzker-Preisträger des
Jahres 1994, Christian de Portzamparc, zur Verstärkung
seines Teams engagierte.

   Obwohl sich der Einfluß französischer Bauprojekte
sicher nicht bis über den Kanal erstreckt, ist die englische
Endstation der Eurostar-Strecke ein weiteres Beispiel zeitgenössischer Architektur: Nicholas Grimshaws Erweiterungsbau für den Londoner Bahnhof Waterloo Station.
Dem trostlosen Gebiet der South Bank, wo Auto- und Zug-
verkehr nahezu sämtliche Fußgänger vertrieben haben,
verleiht Grimshaws langgestrecktes, leicht gekrümmtes
Bauwerk einen Hauch von Farbe und Licht und erinnert
damit an die Tradition großer Baumeister und Ingenieure
wie Paxton oder Eiffel. Dieses »Tor nach Europa«, das einmal über 15 Millionen Reisende jährlich passieren werden,
soll von seinen Dimensionen her die nächsten einhundert
Jahre ausreichen. Auch hier kündet das Ausmaß des Bau-
vorhabens von einem neuen Architekturtypus – selbst
wenn die British Rail Jahre mit der Verwirklichung der
Hochgeschwindigkeitstrecken im Rückstand ist, die das
A und O des Eurostar-Projektes bedeuten. Da der Bahnhof
Waterloo Station nun betriebsbereit ist, wird auch die
Sanierung der South Bank sicherlich zügiger voranschrei-
ten, wodurch das gesamte Areal eine Konzentration kultu-
reller und kommunikativer Einrichtungen erfährt, die in
London ihresgleichen sucht. Wie beim Euralille-Komplex
gilt auch hier, daß ein guter Architekt mittlerweile als wirt-
schaftlicher Gewinn betrachtet wird, da er sich nicht nur
an ein vorgegebenes Budget halten kann, sondern auch
mehr Publikum anzieht bzw. das Interesse der Öffentlichkeit in einem viel stärkeren Maße auf das Bauwerk lenkt.

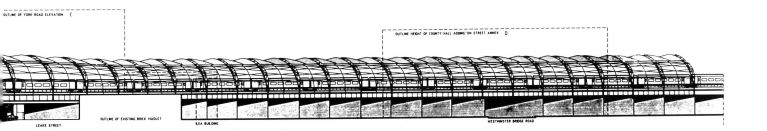

OUTLINE OF YORK ROAD ELEVATION C · OUTLINE HEIGHT OF COUNTY HALL ADDINGTON STREET ANNEX D · LEAKE STREET · OUTLINE OF EXISTING BRICK VIADUCT · ILEA BUILDING · WESTMINSTER BRIDGE ROAD

Eurostar se signale par une autre réalisation architecturale d'importance, l'extension de Waterloo Station, par Nicholas Grimshaw. Dans ce quartier désolé de la South Bank (rive sud) où la voiture et les voies de chemin de fer ont réussi à exclure les piétons, le long bâtiment serpentin de Grimshaw apporte une touche de couleur et de lumière qui rappelle la grande tradition de Paxton ou d'Eiffel. Cette «porte de l'Europe» devrait voir passer jusqu'à 15 millions de voyageurs par an pendant un siècle. Là encore, l'ambition et l'échelle de l'effort annoncent un nouveau type d'architecture, même si British Rail a pris un retard de plusieurs années dans la construction des voies à grande vitesse, qui donneront à Eurostar tout son intérêt. Les perspectives de rénovation de l'ensemble de la South Bank pourrait s'accélérer maintenant que le terminal de Waterloo est opérationnel. Cette concentration d'équipements culturels et de transports est sans équivalent à Londres. Ici, comme pour Euralille, la moralité est que les bons architectes sont enfin appréciés pour leur valeur commerciale, puisqu'ils sont capables non seulement de respecter un budget, mais de séduire (plus aisément que des praticiens moins doués) le public et même les responsables officiels.

L'idée d'un nouveau type d'architecture conçu pour répondre aux besoins de modes de transport en pleine évolution est confirmée par la remarquable construction en ailes d'oiseau imaginée par l'ingénieur-architecte Santiago Calatrava pour la gare de TGV de l'aéroport de Lyon-Satolas. Avec ses 120 m de long, 100 m de large et 40 m de haut, cet «oiseau» qui repose sur deux arcs de béton a nécessité 1 300 tonnes d'acier. Même si cette suggestion d'envol évoque le terminal de la TWA d'Eero Saarinen, le geste de Calatrava est plus spectaculaire. Il confirme ainsi qu'il est un des architectes-ingénieurs les plus créatifs de ce temps, dans la lignée de l'Italien Pier Luigi Nervi ou de l'ingénieur créateur de ponts, le Suisse Robert Maillart.

Technologie et inspiration
Les transports et les communications peuvent également inspirer des constructions qui ne font pas partie d'ensemble architecturaux, mais des réseaux de plus en gigan-

The elevation above shows the great length of the extension to Waterloo Station in London by Nicholas Grimshaw. Below, a photo showing the juncture between the new and old sections of the station.

Der Aufriß oben verdeutlicht die enorme Länge des Anbaus der Waterloo Station in London von Nicholas Grimshaw. Die Abbildung unten zeigt die Verbindung zwischen den alten und neuen Teilen des Bahnhofs.

L'élévation, en haut, montre la très grande longueur de l'extension de Waterloo Station, à Londres, réalisée par Nicholas Grimshaw. En dessous, la liaison entre la partie ancienne et la partie nouvelle de la gare.

pride that a conventional tower this height would require a supporting shaft 25 meters in diameter, whereas the Torre de Collserola has a 4.5 meter diameter "hollow slip-formed reinforced concrete main shaft" which reduces to a minuscule 300 mm at the base of the upper radio mast.

Where Foster seeks to display his technical prowess overtly, the Swiss architects Herzog & de Meuron have taken an opposite tack for their Signal Box in the Basel train yards. Rather than affirming the validity of the "high-tech" stereotype, they question it with a thoroughly ambiguous structure clad in copper. Although the cladding may serve to obviate electromagnetic interference which could be hazardous for the sophisticated switching and signal equipment housed within, it also gives the whole a sculptural quality or a mystery heightened by the fact that the six floors of the building are not made apparent from the exterior.

Monuments to culture

Despite a well-deserved reputation for careful spending, The Netherlands have actively promoted the construction of remarkable culturally oriented buildings in the past few years. Rotterdam is very much a case in point. It is a city which has adopted contemporary architecture openly where others have remained reticent. Indeed, it is no accident that one of the most surprising new cultural buildings in Holland is the Rotterdam Kunsthal designed by native son Rem Koolhaas. Opened on October 31, 1992, the Kunsthal now is a part of the Museum park including the nearby Boymans-van Beuningen (1929–35, Adrianus van der Steur) and the Netherlands Architecture Institute (NAI) designed by Jo Coenen. The Kunsthal sits at the end of a park designed by Koolhaas with the late French landscape architect Yves Brunier. Although this pleasant park with its long line of stream-worn stones and arched bridge leads directly to the NAI building, there was clearly little consultation between the architects, a pattern which is unfortunately often repeated when well-known practitioners share a common ground. Capable of organizing about 25 exhibitions a year on subjects ranging from the design of compact cars to the court culture of Indonesia, the

Die Idee eines neuen Architekturtypus, der auf die Bedürfnisse immer größerer Verkehrsknotenpunkte abgestimmt ist, wird von der außergewöhnlichen, vogelähnlichen Konstruktion des spanischen Ingenieurs Santiago Calatrava für den Bahnhof Lyon-Satolas bekräftigt, wo die nach Süden führende TGV-Strecke mit dem Flughafen von Lyon zusammentrifft. Dieser 120 Meter lange, 100 Meter breite und 40 Meter hohe »Vogel« besteht aus 1300 Tonnen Stahl, die von zwei Betonstützpfeilern getragen werden. Obwohl der Entwurf Assoziationen an einen zum Flug ansetzenden Vogel erweckt und dadurch an Eero Saarinens TWA Terminal erinnert, wirkt Calatravas Konzept jedoch expressiver. Hiermit bekräftigte er seinen Ruf als einer der kreativsten Architekten/Ingenieure unserer Zeit – ganz im Geiste des Italieners Pier Luigi Nervi oder des Schweizer Brückenbauers Robert Maillart.

Technologie und Inspiration

Transport und Kommunikation dienten ebenfalls als Inspirationsquelle für Konstruktionen, die nicht Teil eines sichtbaren architektonischen Komplexes ausmachen, sondern Elemente des wachsenden, unsichtbaren elektronischen Netzwerks darstellen. Dazu zählt in erster Linie Sir Norman Fosters Torre de Collserola, der von der Stadt Barcelona als »monumentales technologisches Element« beschrieben wurde, als Foster im Mai 1988 die Ausschreibung gewann. Dieser 288 Meter hohe Fernmeldeturm beherrscht die Stadt und erinnert daran, daß die Architekturgeschichte Barcelonas nicht mit den Türmen von Gaudis Sagrada Familia endete. Foster, der zu den erfolgreichsten europäischen Architekten zählt, läuft zur Höchstform auf, sobald er mit einem technischen Problem konfrontiert wird. Der Architekt vermeldet mit Stolz, daß ein konventionellerer Entwurf eines Turms von dieser Größe einen Säulenschaft mit einem Durchmesser von 25 Metern erfordert hätte, wohingegen der Torre de Collserola einen »hohlen, in Gleitbauweise errichteten Stahlbetonschaft mit einem Durchmesser von 4,5 Metern besitzt«, der sich am Fuße des oberen Antennenmasts auf winzige 30 cm verjüngt.

Während Foster die überragende Technologie seines

Page 16: The bird-like form of the Lyon-Satolas
station by Santiago Calatrava visible in the
drawing recalls Calatrava's sculpture reproduced
on page 6.

Seite 16: Die Vogelform des TGV-Bahnhofs
Lyon-Satolas von Santiago Calatrava
(Zeichnung links) erinnert an die Skulptur auf
Seite 6.

La forme d'oiseau de la gare de Lyon-Satolas
par Santiago Calatrava visible sur le dessin,
rappelle la sculpture de l'architecte reproduite
page 6.

tesques de la communication électronique. C'est le cas
de la Torre de Collserola, de Sir Norman Foster. Elle fut
présentée par la ville de Barcelone comme «un monument
technologique», lorsque l'architecte britannique remporta
ce concours, en mai 1988. Cette tour de télécommunications domine la ville du haut de ses 288 m, et prouve que
l'histoire architecturale de celle-ci ne s'est pas arrêtée
avec les tours de la «Sagrada Familia» de Gaudi. Foster,
dont le portefeuille de clientèle est l'un des plus pres-
tigieux d'Europe, semble être particulièrement à l'aise
lorsqu'il se retrouve confronté à un problème technique
qui lui permet de déployer sa considérable inventivité. Il
fait remarquer avec fierté qu'une tour conventionnelle de
cette hauteur aurait exigé un mât de 25 m de diamètre,
alors que sa «Torre», ne possède qu'un axe creux de
béton armé monté en coffrage glissant de 4,5 m de
diamètre, qui se réduit à un minuscule 30 cm à la base du
mât d'antenne supérieur.

Si Foster cherchait à afficher ouvertement sa maîtrise
technique, les architectes suisses Herzog & de Meuron
ont choisi la démarche opposée pour leur Poste
d'aiguillage de la gare de Bâle. Plutôt que d'affirmer le sté-
réotype «high-tech», ils le questionnent avec une structure
gainée de cuivre, profondément ambiguë. Bien que cette
couverture ait pour fonction d'éliminer les interférences
électromagnétiques qui pourraient contrarier les équipements de signalisation et d'aiguillage sophistiqués qu'elle
contient, elle confère à l'ensemble une qualité sculpturale,
voire mystérieuse, soulignée par le fait que les six niveaux
du bâtiment sont invisibles de l'extérieur.

Les monuments de la culture
Même si leur réputation d'économie est bien établie,
les Pays-Bas ont activement encouragé, au cours de ces
dernières années, la construction d'une poignée de remarquables édifices culturels. Rotterdam en est une bonne
illustration. Cette ville a ouvertement pris le parti de
l'architecture contemporaine, alors que d'autres sont
restées plus réticentes. Il n'est donc pas étonnant que l'un
des plus surprenants édifices culturels néerlandais soit le
Kunsthal de Rotterdam, conçu par l'un de ses concitoyens,

A TGV train moving through the station at over
300 kilometers per hour.

Ein TGV-Zug fährt mit mehr als 300 km/h durch
den Bahnhof.

Le TGV traverse la gare à plus de 300 km/h.

Kunsthal is certainly a flexible building, although certain typical Koolhaas touches like the broad metal grating on the floor of one double height gallery area have met with the outright disapproval of female visitors wearing high heels or skirts. As the architect admits, "I'm not interested in fetishizing detail ... I'm not interested in resolving a meeting between a metal frame and a wooden panel ..." The Kunsthal is also a symphony of unusual juxtapositions, with a path large enough for a car cutting directly through its center, and materials ranging from corrugated plastic to travertine marble. By comparison, the NAI building, opened on October 23, 1993 seems far more solid and functional in a traditional sense, despite its cantilevered, sharply angled design. An independent national museum, the NAI houses more than one million documents (the Berlage, Oud and Rietveld archives amongst others) and is the largest architecture institute in Europe. Its architect was chosen after a closed competition in 1988 with five others including Koolhaas and Luigi Snozzi from Locarno, one of Coenen's mentors and the only foreign participant. As Jo Coenen says of his own building, "The four building sections represent the four functions: entrance hall with foyer and auditorium, museum (exhibition halls), archives and library-reading room with offices below." Furniture designed by Borek Sípek in the entrance foyer confirms that this complex is very much in the current style. The whole of the Museum park, with the very active and diverse Boymans–van Beuningen represents Rotterdam's concerted effort to wrest cultural leadership in The Netherlands from Amsterdam.

Another remarkable Dutch museum was opened on October 29, 1994. Although the basic design is that of the Italian Alessandro Mendini, perhaps better known as one of the founders of the Memphis Group with Ettore Sottsass, and as editor of the magazine *Domus* from 1980 to 1985, than for his architecture, the new Groninger Museum is divided into separate pavilions devoted to its very diverse collections, and each area was entrusted to a different architect: Mendini for the central, 30 meter high, gold laminate covered tower, the French designer Philippe Starck for the applied arts, Michele de Lucchi

Werks offen präsentiert, wählten die Schweizer Architekten Herzog & de Meuron für ihr Basler Stellwerk einen völlig anderen Weg. Anstatt den Eigenwert eines »High-Tech«-Stereotyps zu unterstreichen, hinterfragen sie diesen mit ihrer bewußt vieldeutigen, mit Kupfer verkleideten Konstruktion. Diese Kupferhülle schützt nicht nur vor elektromagnetischen Störungen, sie verleiht dem Bauwerk auch eine rätselhafte, an eine Skulptur erinnernde Ausstrahlung, die noch verstärkt wird durch die Tatsache, daß die Geschoßaufteilung (sechs Geschosse) von außen nicht erkennbar ist.

Kulturmonumente

Trotz ihrer wohlverdienten Reputation einer sparsamen Nation haben die Niederlande in den vergangenen Jahren den Bau herausragender kulturpolitischer Bauwerke aktiv gefördert. Insbesondere die Stadt Rotterdam zeichnete sich durch ihr Engagement für zeitgenössische Architektur aus. Es überrascht dann auch nicht, daß einer der verblüffendsten neuen Kulturtempel der Niederlande, die Rotterdam Kunsthal, von dem in Rotterdam geborenen Architekten Rem Koolhaas errichtet wurde. Die am 31. Oktober 1992 eröffnete Kunsthalle liegt am Ende des von Koolhaas und dem verstorbenen französischen Landschaftsarchitekten Yves Brunier entworfenen Museumspark, der auch das nahegelegene Museum Boymans-van Beuningen (1929–35, Adrianus van der Steur) und das Niederländische Architekturinstitut (NAI) von Jo Coenen umfaßt. Obwohl dieser hübsche Park mit seiner langen Reihe wettergegerbter Steine und den Bogenbrücken direkt auf das NAI-Gebäude zuläuft, gab es offensichtlich nur wenig Kontakt unter den beteiligten Architekten, was leider häufig passiert, wenn bekannte Architekten am selben Ort arbeiten. Die Kunsthalle ist ein sehr flexibles Bauwerk, in dessen Räumen pro Jahr etwa 25 Wechselausstellungen ausgerichtet werden – von der Hofkultur Indonesiens bis hin zum Kleinwagendesign. Allerdings stießen einige für Koolhaas typische Details, wie das breite Metallgitter auf dem Boden einer erhöhten Galerie, insbesondere bei weiblichen Besuchern mit hohen Absätzen oder Röcken nicht gerade auf Begeisterung. Koolhaas gab zu: »Ich inter-

Rem Koolhaas. Inauguré le 31 octobre 1992, il fait partie du Museum Park – aussi dessiné par Koolhaas et l'architecte-paysagiste français récemment disparu, Yves Brunier – qui comprend également le musée Boymans-van Beuningen (1929–35, Adrianus van der Steur), et l'Institut d'Architecture des Pays-Bas (NAI), signé Jo Coenen. Bien que ce parc agréable, aux longs cheminements de galets et au pont en arc, mène directement au bâtiment du NAI, il est évident qu'il n'y a guère eu de consultation entre les architectes, schéma qui se produit malheureusement souvent lorsque deux praticiens de renom se partagent un même terrain. Capable de recevoir environ 25 expositions par an, sur des thèmes allant du design des voitures compactes à la culture de cour en Indonésie, le Kunsthal est un édifice tout de polyvalence. Certains détails typiques du style Koolhaas, comme les grilles de métal à large espacement sur le sol de l'une des galeries hautes, sont peu appréciés des visiteuses en jupes ou talons hauts. Comme l'admet l'architecte: «Je ne suis pas sensible à la fétichisation du détail... Je ne m'intéresse pas à la solution du problème de la jonction entre un cadre métallique et un panneau de bois...» Le Kunsthal est aussi une symphonie de juxtapositions inhabituelles, avec un passage de la largeur d'une voiture permettant d'accéder directement à son centre, et des matériaux allant du plastique ondulé au travertin.

Par comparaison, le NAI, inauguré le 23 octobre 1993, semble beaucoup plus «solide» et fonctionnel, au sens traditionnel, en dépit de ses anguleux porte-à-faux. Musée national indépendant, le NAI abrite plus d'un million de documents (les archives Berlage, Oud et Rietveld, entre autres) et constitue le plus vaste institut de ce type en Europe. Son architecte a été choisi, en 1988, à l'issue d'un concours restreint, qui vit également s'affronter Koolhaas et Luigi Snozzi, de Locarno, l'un des mentors de Coenen et seul participant étranger. Comme le dit Jo Coenen de son propre édifice: «Les quatre sections du bâtiment représentent les quatre fonctions: hall d'entrée avec foyer et auditorium, musée (halls d'exposition), salles d'archives et de lecture, et bureaux aux niveaux inférieurs.» Le mobilier du foyer d'entrée, dessiné par Borek Sípek, signale que ce NAI est bien dans l'air du temps. Actif et diversifié,

for the archeology and history of Groningen, and, most surprising of all, the Austrian group Coop Himmelblau for the visual arts from 1600 to 1950. It was a gift from Nederlandse Gasunie (Dutch Gas Company) of 25 million florins to the city for the company's 25th anniversary in 1987 that made the project possible. The northern Dutch city of Groningen, capital of the province of the same name, has a population of about 160 000 people. The generosity of Gasunie, unusual in The Netherlands where only 1 % of museum revenue usually comes from corporate donations, was undoubtedly due to the fact that vast reserves of natural gas were discovered here in 1961. The Groninger Museum is situated in the middle of the Verbindingskanaal, like some contemporary version of the Egyptian temple of Philae, and the bridge which goes through the museum now links the central train station to the downtown area. This very fact suffices to guarantee that close to two million people a year will go directly past the entrance of the new structure. In itself, this fact is significant in the context of the radical options of Mendini and the Groninger's director Frans Haks. As Mendini says, "I think that a museum nowadays has a similar role to that of the church in past centuries. It is a place for relaxation with respect to the rapid passage of time – This also coincides with the intention to free museums, at last, from the rhetoric and the elitist paternalism of art." Both Haks and Mendini clearly believe that fewer distinctions should be made between the visual arts, design and architecture, and their efforts are intended to prove the viability of a complete symbiosis. Joyous in its debauchery of colors and forms, the Groninger Museum is nonetheless resolutely connected to the city and to the history of architecture, reaching back to Egypt and forward to the surprisingly disjointed pavilion by Coop Himmelblau. This despite Mendini's self-proclaimed effort to create internal spaces which "alienate" the visitor, and despite the building's apparent connection to design styles which had their heyday in the 1980's if not before. It should be pointed out that the flamboyant architecture of Mendini, et al does not correspond to a very significant art collection. The inaugural show, dedicated to none other than Mendini himself,

essiere mich nicht dafür, das Detail zum Fetisch zu erheben ... Ich interessiere mich nicht für den Übergang zwischen einem Metallrahmen und einer Holztäfelung ...«. Die Kunsthalle stellt auch eine Sammlung ungewöhnlicher Gegensätze dar: Eine mitten durch das Gebäude führende Schneise ist so groß, daß ein Wagen direkt bis zum Mittelpunkt der Halle vordringen könnte; darüber hinaus fanden beim Bau die unterschiedlichsten Materialien Verwendung – von Wellkunststoff bis zu Travertin. Das Gebäude des NAI, das 1993 eröffnet wurde, erscheint dagegen sehr viel solider und auf traditionelle Weise funktionell, ungeachtet seines vorkragenden, spitzwinkligen Designs. Als unabhängiges nationales Museum beherbergt dieses größte Architekturinstitut Europas über eine Million Dokumente (u. a. die Archive von Berlage, Oud und Rietveld). Jo Coenen konnte den für dieses Gebäude 1988 ausgeschriebenen geschlossenen Architekturwettbewerb für sich entscheiden, zu dem noch fünf weitere Architekten eingeladen waren, u. a. Rem Koolhaas und Luigi Snozzi, einer von Coenens Mentoren und einziger ausländischer Teilnehmer. Coenen beschreibt sein Bauwerk so: »Die vier Gebäudebereiche repräsentieren seine vier Funktionsbereiche: Eingangshalle mit Foyer und Auditorium, Museum (Ausstellungshallen), Archive und Leseraum mit den darunterliegenden Verwaltungsräumen.« Die von Borek Sípek entworfenen Möbel in der Eingangshalle bestätigen den Eindruck, daß es sich hierbei um ein Gebäude in einem ausgesprochen modernen Stil handelt. Der gesamte Museumspark mit seinem aktiven und vielseitigen Museum Boymans-van Beuningen repräsentiert Rotterdams konzertierte Bemühungen im Wettstreit mit Amsterdam um die kulturelle Vormachtstellung in den Niederlanden. Im Oktober 1994 konnte in Groningen ein weiteres außergewöhnliches Museum eröffnet werden. Obwohl der italienische Architekt Alessandro Mendini – eher bekannt als Mitbegründer der Memphis Group (zusammen mit Ettore Sottsass) oder als Herausgeber der Zeitschrift »Domus« (1980–85) – für die Gesamtkonzeption verantwortlich zeichnete, ist das Groninger Museum in verschiedene Pavillons unterteilt, die die sehr unterschiedlichen Sammlungen beherbergen. Jeder dieser Bereiche wurde

le complexe du Museum Park, Boymans-van Beuningen compris, illustre les efforts de Rotterdam pour ravir à Amsterdam son leadership culturel.

Une autre institution néerlandaise remarquable à plusieurs égards s'est ouverte le 29 octobre 1994. La conception générale du nouveau musée de Groningue est due à l'architecte italien Alessandro Mendini, plus connu pour avoir fondé, avec Ettore Sottsass, le Memphis Group, et édité le magazine Domus de 1980 à 1985, que pour son œuvre architecturale. Mendini l'a divisé en pavillons indépendants consacrés aux diverses collections et confiés à des architectes différents: Mendini pour la tour centrale de 30 m de haut, recouverte d'un placage laminé doré, le designer français Philippe Starck pour le pavillon des arts appliqués, Michele de Lucchi pour celui de l'archéologie et de l'histoire de Groningue et, plus surprenant encore, le groupe autrichien Coop Himmelblau, pour les arts visuels de 1600 à 1950. C'est un don de 25 millions de florins de la société de gaz Nederlandse Gasunie à la ville qui a permis cette réalisation. La générosité de cette société, inhabituelle dans un pays où 1% seulement des revenus des musées proviennent des entreprises, s'explique par la découverte de vastes réserves de gaz dans la région en 1961. Le musée, sorte de version contemporaine du temple de Philae, est situé sur une île au milieu du Verbindingskanaal. Il est traversé par un pont qui relie le centre-ville à la gare. Près de deux millions de personnes parcourront ainsi chaque année ce nouvel ensemble, chiffre qui prend tout son intérêt au regard des options radicales de Mendini et du directeur du musée, Frans Haks. Comme l'écrit Mendini: «Je pense que, de nos jours, un musée joue un rôle similaire à celui de l'église au cours des siècles passés. C'est un lieu de détente, mais qui rend hommage au passage du temps. Ceci coïncide avec l'intention de libérer enfin les musées de la rhétorique et du paternalisme élitiste de l'art.» Haks et Mendini pensent tous deux qu'il ne faut pas différencier autant qu'on le fait les arts plastiques, le design et l'architecture, et ils ont voulu prouver ici la viabilité de cette symbiose. Très joyeux dans sa débauche de formes et de couleurs, le Groninger Museum ne s'en intègre pas moins résolument à la ville

Page 20/21: The Groninger Museum, Groningen. The central tower or "treasure house" designed by Alessandro Mendini. The historical and decorative arts pavilion on the left (right hand page) is by Michele de Lucchi for the lower part, and Philippe Starck for the upper section. On the right, the Coop Himmelblau pavilion.

Seite 20/21: Groninger Museum, Groningen. Für den Mittelturm, die »Schatzkammer«, zeichnete Alessandro Mendini verantwortlich. Auf der linken Seite (der rechten Abbildung) liegt im unteren Teil der Pavillon für Archäologie und Geschichte von Michele de Lucchi; im oberen Abschnitt befindet sich die Abteilung für Kunsthandwerk von Philippe Starck. Rechts: Der Pavillon von Coop Himmelblau.

Page 20/21: Le Groninger Museum, à Groningue. La tour centrale, le «trésor», a été dessinée par Alessandro Mendini. Le pavillon de l'histoire de l'art et des arts décoratifs (à gauche, page de droite) est de Michele de Lucchi pour la partie inférieure, et Philippe Starck pour la partie supérieure. A droite, le pavillon de Coop Himmelblau.

A view past the Philippe Starck/Michele de Lucchi designed section of the Groninger Museum, Groningen.

Ein Blick auf den von Philippe Starck und Michele de Lucchi entworfenen Teil des Groninger Museums.

Une vue de la section du Groninger Museum dessinée par Philippe Starck et Michele de Lucchi.

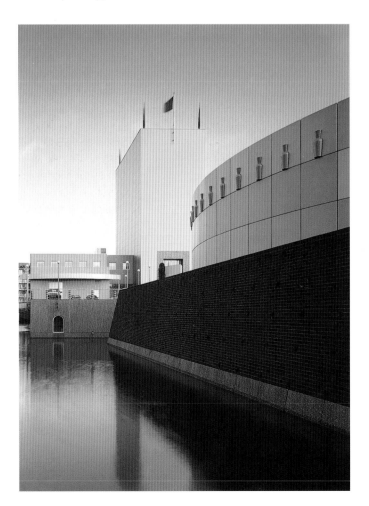

highlighted the significant holdings of the institution in Memphis-type furniture but did little to allay the suspicion that there were more "smoke and mirrors" here than great art. Architecture and design seem to be at the center of this effort, which is not in itself a negative observation. The Groninger Museum had already played a central role in the "What a Wonderful World" exhibition organized in the city in 1990 which brought together the deconstructivist architectural talents of Zaha Hadid, Peter Eisenman, Rem Koolhaas, Bernard Tschumi and Coop Himmelblau in the rather unexpected service of music videos. With the new structure, Groningen asserts itself as an obligatory stop for anyone who wants to understand the ways in which contemporary European architecture has continued to evolve toward a more significant public role.

Continuing influence of the Grands Travaux
The Grands Travaux launched by French President François Mitterrand in the early 1980s are now winding down, but they have had a continuing impact on cultural projects both in Paris, and in the provinces. In fact two of the largest of these undertakings are only now nearing completion. The first, the Cité de la Musique, was already considered by Valéry Giscard d'Estaing at the end of his term, but the idea was enacted as a "Beaubourg for music" by Mitterrand and his Minister of Culture Jack Lang in July 1983. The young Parisian architect Christian de Portzamparc was chosen for the design after a competition in January 1985. The Cité was in fact intended from the outset as an integral part of a new, larger cultural complex at the outer periphery of Paris in the Villette area. Here, the massive Cité des Sciences (Adrien Fainsilber), together with a rock concert hall (the Zénith) and the Grande Halle de la Villette which houses temporary exhibitions are woven together by a series of gardens and bright red "follies" designed by Bernard Tschumi. Carried out with a limited budget (6 500 francs per square meter), Portzamparc's Cité is divided into two separate areas. The western side, the first part of the complex to be completed, houses the National Musical Conservatory with its teaching and concert facilities. On the east, inaugurated on

einem anderen Architekten anvertraut: Den zentralen, 30 Meter hohen, mit goldgelbem Laminat versehenen Turm entwarf Mendini, der Pavillon für den Bereich Kunsthandwerk stammt von dem französischen Designer Philippe Starck, und den Pavillon für Archäologie und Geschichte Groningens konzipierte Michele De Lucchi. Aber die wohl größte Überraschung bereitete der von der österreichischen Architektengruppe Coop Himmelblau errichtete Pavillon für die Sammlung visueller Kunst (1600 bis 1950). Das Museumsprojekt wurde erst durch ein Geschenk der Nederlandse Gasunie (Niederländische Gasunion) ermöglicht, die der Stadt Groningen anläßlich ihres 25jährigen Firmenjubileums im Jahre 1987 eine Summe von 25 Millionen Gulden spendete. Groningen, im Norden der Niederlande gelegen, ist die Hauptstadt der gleichnamigen Provinz und hat etwa 160 000 Einwohner. Die für die Niederlande ungewöhnliche Großzügigkeit der Gasunie (im allgemeinen werden dort nur etwa 1 Prozent der Bau- und Unterhaltskosten eines Museums aus Firmenspenden bestritten) beruhte zweifelsohne darauf, daß hier 1961 ein gewaltiges Erdgasvorkommen entdeckt wurde. Das Groninger Museum liegt – wie eine moderne Version der ägyptischen Tempelanlagen auf der Nilinsel Philae – in der Mitte des Verbindingskanaal. Die durch das Museum hindurchführende Brücke verbindet den Hauptbahnhof mit der Innenstadt. Dies garantiert, daß schätzungsweise zwei Millionen Passanten jährlich am Haupteingang dieses neuen Gebäudes vorbeigehen werden; es spricht aber auch für die radikale Haltung Mendinis und des Museumsdirektors Frans Haks. Mendini formulierte es so: »Ich bin der Überzeugung, daß ein Museum heute die gleiche Rolle besitzt wie die Kirche in vergangenen Zeiten. In bezug auf den schnellen Wandel der Zeit ist es ein Ort der Entspannung – und dies deckt sich mit der Intention, die Museen zumindest von der rhetorischen und elitären Bevormundung der Kunst zu befreien.« Haks und Mendini vertreten beide die Ansicht, daß zwischen Kunst, Architektur und Design kein Unterschied gemacht werden sollte, und sie versuchen beständig die Möglichkeit einer vollständigen Symbiose zu beweisen. Obwohl das Groninger Museum ausgelassen in Farben und Formen schwelgt, ist es den-

et à l'histoire de l'architecture, du plus lointain passé (l'Egypte) au modernisme éclaté illustré par le pavillon de Coop Himmelblau. Ceci en dépit de l'effort proclamé par Mendini de créer des espaces intérieurs qui «aliènent» le visiteur, et des proximités avec des styles qui connurent leur heure de gloire au cours des années 80, et même avant. Il faut souligner que la flamboyante architecture de Mendini et de ses complices n'abrite pas des collections artistiques d'une grande importance. L'exposition inaugurale, consacrée à l'architecte lui-même, mit en valeur les importantes acquisitions de l'institution en mobilier de style Memphis, mais ne contribua guère à effacer l'impression que l'on était plus en présence d'un rideau de fumée que de grand art. L'architecture et le design semblent malgré tout se réconcilier dans cette réalisation, ce qui n'est pas en soi négatif. Le Groninger Museum avait déjà joué un rôle central dans l'exposition «What a Wonderful World» organisée dans la même ville en 1990, et qui avait réuni les talents déconstructivistes de Zaha Hadid, Peter Eisenman, Rem Koolhaas, Bernard Tschumi et Coop Himmelblau, dans des kiosques vidéo assez inattendus. Avec ces nouveaux édifices, Groningue s'affirme comme une halte obligatoire pour quiconque voudra comprendre la diversité des voies empruntées par l'architecture européenne contemporaine pour affirmer un rôle public encore plus significatif.

La permanence de l'influence des Grands Travaux

Si les Grands Travaux, lancés par le président François Mitterrand au début des années 80, touchent actuellement à leur fin, ils auront exercé un impact durable sur les projets culturels français, que ce soit à Paris ou en province. Deux des plus importantes de ces opérations sont en cours d'achèvement. La première, la Cité de la Musique, avait déjà été envisagée par Valéry Giscard d'Estaing à la fin de son mandat. L'idée en fut reprise par Mitterrand et son ministre de la Culture, Jack Lang, en juillet 1983, et le jeune architecte parisien Christian de Portzamparc fut choisi par concours en janvier 1985. La Cité fut conçue au départ pour faire partie de l'énorme complexe culturel édifié aux limites de la capitale, la Villette. Là, dans une suc-

Page 24/25: The western section of the Cité de la Musique by Christian de Portzamparc in Paris contains a large concert hall, a museum of musical instruments, and office space.

Seite 24/25: Der westliche Teil der Cité de la Musique von Christian de Portzamparc in Paris umfaßt einen großen Konzertsaal, ein Museum für Musikinstrumente sowie verschiedene Büros.

Page 24/25: Due à Christian de Portzamparc, la partie Ouest de la Cité de la Musique à Paris, contient un grand auditorium, un musée des instruments de musique, et des bureaux.

January 12, 1995, a large, flexible oval concert hall for Pierre Boulez's Ensemble Intercontemporain and other, less experimental types of music, is flanked by a museum of musical instruments whose interior design was handed over to Franck Hammoutène. Despite being dragged out over a ten year period for budgetary reasons, the completed Cité de la Musique does not appear to be dated. Although "fragmented" into numerous sub-structures, its design has little to do with the "deconstructivism" whose popularity seems to have come and gone so rapidly. Rather, in its lyrical complexity, it is very much in the personal style of 50 year old Portzamparc, and the Cité de la Musique is certainly one of the major reasons he was given the 1994 Pritzker Prize awarded to the most outstanding current architects.

Fundamentally different in its nature, but also covered by the Grands Travaux budgets, the Galerie de l'Evolution opened in 1994 in Paris. This science museum has a prestigious history because it evolved from the "Jardin royal des plantes médicinales et du Cabinet des drogues" created in 1635. The current building, designed by Jules André in 1877, one of the most impressive pieces of 19th century iron and glass architecture in Paris, had been closed to the public since 1965 for security reasons. The French architects Chemetov/Huidobro won the 1986 competition for refurbishment of the building and, with a budget of 400 million francs for a total area of 16 000 square meters, they managed, together with the exhibition designer René Allio, to create an attractive display which outlines the theory of evolution for a very large audience.

The final and most imposing of Mitterrand's Grands Travaux is the massive Bibliothèque de France, with its four towers, sitting on the Left Bank of the Seine, opposite the Bercy area. Scheduled to be opened in early 1997, it was designed by Dominique Perrault, a young and virtually unknown architect. The brutal modernism of this complex is relieved only by a large internal garden which boasts 40 year old trees brought in by crane. Although it is still too early to judge the architectural merits of the Bibliothèque de France it does not promise a very successful end to 15 years of massive French investment in culture.

noch deutlich mit der Stadt einerseits und der Architekturgeschichte andererseits verbunden, die bis zur ägyptischen Zeit zurückreicht und mit dem überraschend dekon-
struktivistischen Pavillon von Coop Himmelblau frohgemut
in die Zukunft schaut – und dies trotz Mendinis öffentlich
verkündetem Anspruch, Innenräume zu schaffen, die den
Besucher »befremden« sollen, und auch ungeachtet der
offensichtlichen Verbindung des Museumsgebäudes zu
diversen Designrichtungen, die ihren Zenith bereits in den
80er Jahren überschritten hatten. Es sollte an dieser Stelle
darauf hingewiesen werden, daß die überschwengliche
Architektur Mendinis et alii zu dieser bedeutenden Kunstsammlung nicht so recht passen will. Die ausschließlich
Mendini selbst gewidmete Eröffnungsfeier betonte den
bedeutenden Bestand dieser Institution durch Memphis-
artige Möbel, aber trug nur wenig zur Beseitigung des Ver-
dachtes bei, daß es sich hierbei eher um »Schall und
Rauch« denn um wirkliche Kunst handele. Architektur und
Design scheinen im Mittelpunkt dieses Bemühens zu
stehen, was nicht negativ gemeint ist. Das Groninger
Museum spielte bereits bei der Ausstellung »What a Wonderful World« eine zentrale Rolle, die 1990 in dieser Stadt
stattfand und das dekonstruktivistische architektonische
Potential von Zaha Hadid, Peter Eisenman, Rem Koolhaas,
Bernard Tschumi und Coop Himmelblau auf eher uner-
wartete Weise – in Form von Musikvideos – zusammen-
brachte. Dank des neuen Bauwerks zählt Groningen zum
Pflichtprogramm all derjenigen, die die Entwicklung der
zeitgenössischen europäischen Architektur und ihre zuneh-
mende Bedeutung in der Öffentlichkeit verstehen wollen.

Der anhaltende Einfluß der Grands Travaux
Die von dem französischen Präsidenten François Mitterrand Anfang der 80er Jahre in die Wege geleiteten
»Grands Travaux« sind nun fast alle abgewickelt, üben
aber nach wie vor ihren Einfluß auf kulturelle Projekte
sowohl in Paris als auch im gesamten Land aus. Zwei der
größten Bauprojekte aus dieser Reihe nähern sich zur
Zeit ihrer Vollendung. Bei dem ersten Projekt handelt es
sich um die Cité de la Musique, die von Valéry Giscard
d'Estaing gegen Ende seiner Amtszeit bereits geplant, von

cession de jardins et de «folies» au rouge éclatant, imagi-
nées par Bernard Tschumi, s'élèvent la massive Cité des
Sciences d'Adrien Fainsilber, une salle de concert rock
(Le Zénith), et la Grande Halle de la Villette qui accueile
des expositions temporaires. Réalisée dans le cadre d'un
budget limité (6 500 F le m²), la Cité de Portzamparc est
divisée en deux espaces distincts. Le côté ouest, premier
à être achevé, a reçu le Conservatoire national de musique
et ses installations d'enseignement et de concert. A l'est,
inauguré le 12 janvier 1995, la vaste salle de concert ovale
et modulaire destinée à l'Ensemble Intercontemporain
de Pierre Boulez et d'autres styles de musiques moins
expérimentales est flanquée d'un musée des instruments
de musique dont l'aménagement intérieur a été confié
à Franck Hammoutène. Même si le projet, victime de
difficultés budgétaires, s'est étalé sur dix ans, la Cité de la
Musique n'en apparaît pas pour autant datée. Bien que
fragmentée en de nombreuses sous-structures, sa
conception n'a rien à voir avec un déconstructivisme dont
la popularité ne semble pas avoir survécu à ses premiers
feux. Dans sa complexité lyrique, elle exprime le style personnel d'un brillant architecte de 50 ans. La Cité est certainement l'une des principales raisons qui lui ont valu, en
1994, le Prix Pritzker qui récompense les plus remarquables architectes du moment.

De nature fondamentalement différente, mais émar-
geant de même au budget des Grands Travaux, la Galerie
de l'Evolution a ouvert ses portes à Paris, en 1994. Le
Muséum auquel elle appartient peut se flatter d'une presti-
gieuse histoire, puisqu'il est l'héritier du Jardin royal des
herbes médicinales et du Cabinet des drogues, créé en
1635. Le bâtiment actuel, dessiné par Jules André en
1877, et l'une des plus imposantes structures de fer et de
verre du XIXe siècle parisien, était fermé au public depuis
1965 pour des raisons de sécurité. Les architectes français
Chemetov et Huidobro remportèrent le concours pour la
rénovation de l'édifice en 1986, et, grâce à un budget de
400 millions de francs pour 16 000 m², ils ont réussi, avec
l'assistance du concepteur d'exposition René Allio, à créer
une présentation séduisante, qui fait comprendre la théorie de l'évolution au grand public.

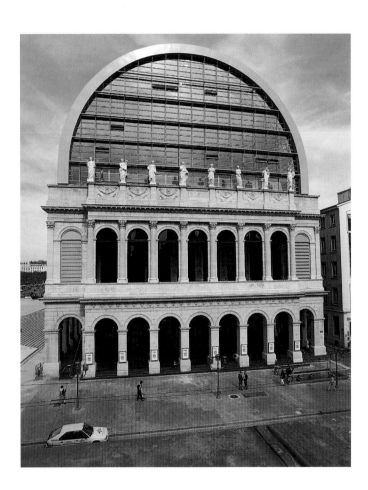

The Opéra de Lyon as it was redesigned by Jean Nouvel, with a large, barrel-shaped volume added to the existing structure.

Die von Jean Nouvel umgebaute Opéra de Lyon mit dem neuen, halbzylindrischen Aufsatz auf den bestehenden Mauern.

L'Opéra de Lyon rénové par Jean Nouvel, et sa vaste structure en tonneau posée sur les murs existants.

The desire to choose a French architect over the numerous excellent foreign participants in the original competition seems to have been a considerable mistake in the light of the behemoth now taking form on the banks of the Seine.

A new tune in the French provinces

It seems likely however that large state projects devoted essentially to culture and designed by good architects have had a lasting impact on the attitude of French provincial politicians and some private sector clients. The city of Lyon, whose Palais Saint Pierre art museum is undergoing a complete overhaul which began with Grands Travaux credits, has undertaken several other interesting projects, the most visible of which was the new Opéra designed by Jean Nouvel. Situated opposite the town hall and one block from the art museum and the Terreaux Square recently redesigned by the artist Daniel Buren, the opera was originally built by Chenavard and Pollet in 1831. Nouvel, who won the 1986 competition, managed to triple the volume of the structure without touching its existing outer walls. This feat was accomplished by digging below the building, and adding a 20 meter high drum to the roof. The result is altogether surprising, with the semi-cylindrical roof now forming a visible cultural landmark in the city. Critics have been less charitable about the claustrophobic black entrance hall of the Opéra, but Jean Nouvel's taste for clair-obscur is well known.

Certainly, with Portzamparc the best known of currently active French architects, Nouvel took a very different approach in designing the new Fondation Cartier building on the Boulevard Raspail in Paris. Here, his trade mark black has been abandoned in favor of the total transparency of a glass building. At a time when corporate sponsorship of the arts has been flagging as much in France as elsewhere, Cartier's president Alain-Dominique Perrin, who had already funded his company's domain in Jouy-en-Josas, took the risk of calling on a very high profile architect for a visible site. One can only conclude that he reckons good design makes good business sense.

Although he recently lost the competition for the new

The four towers of the new Bibliothèque
Nationale de France, designed by Dominique
Perrault, situated on the banks of the Seine in
the 13th arrondissement of Paris.

Die vier Türme der neuen Bibliothèque Nationale de France von Dominique Perrault. Das
Bauwerk befindet sich am linken Ufer der Seine
im 13. Arrondissement von Paris.

Les quatre tours de la Bibliothèque Nationale de
France, de Dominique Perrault, s'élèvent au
bord de la Seine, dans le XIIIe arrondissement
de Paris.

Mitterrand und seinem Kulturminister Jack Lang aber im
Juli 1983 als »Beaubourg der Musik« in Auftrag gegeben
wurde. Nach einem Architekturwettbewerb im Januar
1985 betraute die Jury den jungen Pariser Architekten
Christian de Portzamparc mit dem Entwurf. Die Cité war
von Beginn an als Teil eines neuen, größeren Kulturkom-
plexes am Rande von Paris in La Villette konzipiert, wo
bereits die Cité des Sciences (Adrien Fainsilber), eine
Rockkonzerthalle (Le Zénith) und die Grande Halle de la
Villette mit ihren Wechselausstellungen durch eine von
Bernard Tschumi entworfene Gartenanlage (Parc de la Villette) mit leuchtend roten, als »Folies« bezeichnete Pavillons miteinander verbunden sind. Portzamparcs Cité, für
die nur ein begrenztes Budget zur Verfügung stand (6 500
Francs pro Quadratmeter), ist in zwei getrennte Bereiche
unterteilt. Die westliche Seite, die zuerst fertiggestellt
werden sollte, beherbergt das Nationalkonservatorium für
Musik mit Unterrichts- und Veranstaltungsräumen. Der im
Osten gelegene, große ovale Mehrzweck-Konzertsaal (am
12. Januar 1995 eröffnet) für Pierre Boulez' »Ensemble
Intercontemporain« und andere, weniger experimentelle
Musik wird von einem Musikinstrumenten-Museum flan-
kiert, mit dessen Innenausstattung man Franck Hammoutène betraute. Trotz der zehnjährigen Bauphase (aus
Budgetgründen) wirkt die nun fertiggestellte Cité de la
Musique keineswegs veraltet. Obwohl sie in zahllose Teile
»fragmentiert« ist, hat ihr Design nur wenig gemeinsam
mit dem »Dekonstruktivismus«, dessen Popularität so
schnell wieder verschwand, wie sie gekommen war. Statt
dessen ist die lyrische Komplexität der Cité Ausdruck
des sehr persönlichen Stils ihres 50jährigen Architekten
Portzamparc – und sicherlich trug dieses Projekt nicht
unerheblich zur Verleihung des Pritzker-Preises 1994 (für
den herausragendsten zeitgenössischen Architekten) an
Portzamparc bei.

Vollkommen anderer Natur, aber ebenfalls durch das
Budget der Grands Travaux gedeckt, konnte die Pariser
Galerie de l'Évolution 1994 ihre Pforten öffnen. Dieses
Wissenschaftsmuseum besitzt eine prestigeträchtige
Geschichte, da es aus dem 1635 erbauten Jardin royal des
plantes médicinales et du Cabinet des drogues entstand.

Le dernier et le plus imposant des Grands Travaux est la
massive Bibliothèque de France dont les quatre tours
dominent la Seine, face au quartier de Bercy. Prévue pour
1997, elle a été dessinée par Dominique Perrault, un jeune
architecte pratiquement inconnu lors de sa sélection. Le
modernisme brutal de cet ensemble n'est sauvé que par
un vaste jardin intérieur où repousseront des arbres de 40
ans d'âge, amenés par grue. Bien qu'il soit encore trop tôt
pour juger des mérites architecturaux de cette bibliothèque, elle ne semble pas constituer l'aboutissement
triomphal de 15 années d'investissements culturels mas-
sifs que l'on pouvait espérer. Le souhait de choisir un Français, face aux nombreux participants étrangers de talent
au concours de cette bibliothèque, semble avoir été une
erreur considérable, si l'on en juge par le monstre qui se
dresse maintenant sur les rives de la Seine.

Un air nouveau souffle sur les régions françaises
Les grands projets étatiques, essentiellement consacrés à
la culture et confiés à de grands architectes, ont exercé un
fort impact sur les responsables politiques régionaux et
certains donneurs d'ordre privés. La ville de Lyon, dont le
musée des Beaux-Arts du Palais Saint-Pierre est en cours
de rénovation complète amorcée grâce aux crédits des
Grands Travaux, s'est lancée dans d'autres projets de
poids, dont le plus remarqué est la reconstruction de
l'Opéra, par Jean Nouvel. Situé en face de l'hôtel de ville,
et non loin du musée et de la place des Terreaux récemment réaménagée par l'artiste Daniel Buren, l'opéra fut
construit en 1831 par Chenavard et Pollet. Nouvel, qui remporta le concours en 1986, a réussi a tripler la surface
utile, sans toucher aux murs extérieurs. Cet exploit a été
accompli en creusant sous le bâtiment et en remplaçant la
toiture par un surprenant demi tambour de 20 mètres de
haut, «toit» semi-cylindrique qui se détache désormais sur
le paisible panorama du centre-ville. Les critiques ont été
moins charitables pour le hall d'entrée noir et claustropho-
bique, même si le goût de l'architecte pour le clair-obscur
est bien connu.

Nouvel, qui, avec Portzamparc, est certainement le plus
célèbre des architectes français, a suivi une approche

stadium being built close to Paris for the 1998 World Cup in very controversial circumstances, Nouvel has left his mark in numerous French provincial cities. In Tours for example, his new Centre des Congrès flares out its modern facade just opposite the train station. In this very traditional small city, his structure is, to say the least, a surprising presence, but its impeccable finishing (generally not a characteristic of Nouvel's buildings) and its practical design have made it quite popular. If even the more conservative French can be brought to accept contemporary architecture, a change in attitudes, but also a change in the architecture itself has certainly been brought about.

Nouvel has also played a role in the broadest French provincial effort to place architecture and design at the center of city planning. His Nemausus public housing buildings in Nîmes have been widely published despite their essentially prison-like aspect. More appealing is Sir Norman Foster's Carré d'Art, situated just opposite the famous Maison Carrée. Built between 10 B.C. and 5 A.D., this temple dominated the forum of the Roman colony of Nemausus, built on land which was probably offered by the Emperor Augustus to his troops after their victory over the fleet of Anthony and Cleopatra at Actium in 31 B.C. It had already attracted the attention of French rulers in 1535 when François I ordered that the temple be better cared for, and a century later, when Louis XIV had liked the building so much that he had wanted Colbert to transfer it stone by stone to Versailles or Paris. The Maison Carrée owes its survival on its present location to the fact that it was purchased by Augustine monks in 1670.

Norman Foster was chosen to build a new "media-thèque" opposite the Maison Carrée at the instigation of mayor Jean Bousquet in 1984. His Carré d'Art, is a "calm and classical building" which houses both a museum for contemporary art and a public library. As Norman Foster says, "The project suggests ways in which the new can relate to the old, can be respectful of the past but can also speak of its own age with integrity and without pastiche. The Carré d'Art also demonstrates that quality is more about attitude of mind and less about budget." Once again, excellent design has been deemed useful in the

Page 28/29: The Carré d'Art in Nîmes, southern France, was designed by Sir Norman Foster, and is located directly opposite the well-known Roman monument, the Maison Carrée.

Seite 28/29: Das Carré d'Art in Nîmes, Südfrankreich, wurde von Sir Norman Foster entworfen und liegt direkt gegenüber einem römischen Tempel, dem berühmten Maison Carrée.

Page 28/29: Le Carré d'Art à Nîmes, de Sir Norman Foster, est situé juste en face du monument le plus célèbre de la ville, la Maison Carrée.

Das gegenwärtige Gebäude, das Jules André 1877 entworfen hatte und das zu den aufsehenerregendsten architektonischen Beispielen Pariser Stahl- und Glasbauten des 19. Jahrhunderts zählt, mußte 1965 aus sicherheitstechnischen Gründen geschlossen werden. Die französischen Architekten Chemetov/Huidobro gewannen 1986 die Ausschreibung für die umfassenden Renovierungsarbeiten. Mit einem Budget von 400 Millionen Francs für eine Gesamtfläche von 16 000 m² gelang ihnen in Zusammenarbeit mit dem Ausstellungsdesigner René Allio die Realisierung eines attraktiven Museums, das die Evolutionstheorie einem großen Publikum vermittelt.

Das letzte von Mitterrands Grands Travaux ist die gewaltige, viertürmige Bibliothèque de France am linken Ufer der Seine, gegenüber von Bercy. Dieses Bauwerk, das im Frühjahr 1997 eröffnet werden soll, wurde von Dominique Perrault entworfen, einem jungen, praktisch unbekannten Architekten. Perraults roher Modernismus ist nur durch den großen, innerhalb des Komplexes gelegenen Garten gemildert, dessen zahlreiche, über 40 Jahre alte Bäume man mit Hilfe eines Krans auf das Gelände transportierte. Obwohl es natürlich noch sehr früh ist, die architektonischen Verdienste der Bibliothèque de France zu beurteilen, verspricht dieses Gebäude keinen krönenden Abschluß dieser 15 Jahre dauernden, massiven Investitionsperiode in die Kultur Frankreichs. Der Wunsch nach einem französischen Architekten – trotz zahlloser exzellenter ausländischer Teilnehmer an diesem Architekturwettbewerb – scheint angesichts des zur Zeit Form annehmenden Kolosses am Ufer der Seine ein großer Fehler gewesen zu sein.

Neue Töne in der französischen Provinz

Dennoch scheinen die großen staatlichen, der Kultur gewidmeten und von guten Architekten ausgeführten, Projekte einen dauerhaften Einfluß auf Politiker in der französischen Provinz und einige Klienten aus dem privaten Sektor auszuüben. Die Stadt Lyon, deren Kunstmuseum Palais Saint Pierre zur Zeit einer vollständigen Renovierung unterzogen wird, die teilweise mit Krediten aus dem Topf der Grands Travaux finanziert ist, realisierte weitere inter-

radicalement différente pour le nouveau bâtiment de la Fondation Cartier, boulevard Raspail, à Paris. Il a abandonné le noir pour la transparence totale d'un immeuble de verre. Au moment où le mécénat artistique connaît autant de difficultés en France qu'ailleurs, le président de Cartier, Alain-Dominique Perrin, qui avait déjà eu l'initiative d'installer la Fondation Cartier au château de Jouy-en-Josas, a pris le risque de faire appel à un architecte très attendu sur un site aussi sensible. Dans son esprit, le design de qualité est à l'évidence synonyme de bonnes affaires.

Bien qu'il ait récemment perdu, dans des circonstances très controversées, le concours du nouveau stade de Saint-Denis pour la Coupe du monde de football 1998, Nouvel a par ailleurs laissé sa marque dans plusieurs grandes villes régionales. A Tours, par exemple, son nouveau Centre des Congrès dresse sa moderne façade face à la gare du TGV. Dans cette ville moyenne très traditionnelle, ce bâtiment est pour le moins surprenant, mais sa finition irréprochable (ce qui n'est pas toujours la caractéristique première des œuvres de Nouvel) et ses aspects fonctionnels l'ont fait apprécier de la population. Si même les Français les plus conservateurs acceptent l'architecture contemporaine, des changements d'attitudes, mais également de l'architecture elle-même, peuvent enfin être espérés.

Nouvel a également participé à l'un des plus importants efforts jamais réalisés par une ville pour intégrer l'architecture et le design à l'urbanisme. Ses deux immeubles de logements sociaux de Nîmes, Nemausus, sont connus dans le monde entier, en dépit de leur aspect carcéral. Plus séduisant est le Carré d'Art de Norman Foster, face à la fameuse Maison Carrée. Construit entre 10 Av. J.–C. et 5 , ce temple dominait le forum de la colonie romaine de Nemausus, construit sur un terrain probablement offert par l'empereur Auguste à ses troupes après leur victoire sur les flottes d'Antoine et de Cléopâtre à Actium en 31 Av. J.–C. Il avait déjà attiré l'attention d'un souverain français en 1535, puisque François 1er avait alors ordonné qu'il soit mieux entretenu. Un siècle plus tard, il séduisit Louis XIV qui demanda même à Colbert de le transférer

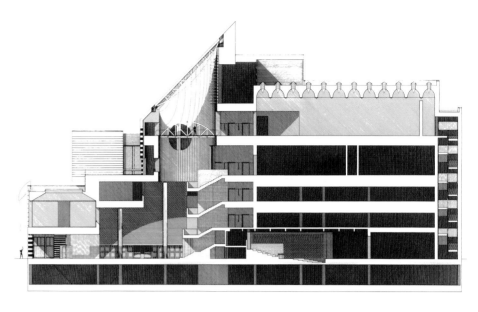

context of a relatively coherent program of urban redevelopment.

Although its design options are very different, the new San Francisco Museum of Modern Art by Swiss architect Mario Botta makes references to ideas which seem distinctly similar to those expressed by Mendini in the Groninger Museum. Botta declares that "In today's city, the museum plays a role analogous to that of the cathedral of yesterday. A place of common encounter and confrontation. A place we require in order to challenge the hopes and contradictions of our time... In fact, it might be possible to interpret the museum as a space dedicated to witnessing and searching for a new religiosity, which promotes and enriches those spiritual values that we so strongly need." Inscribed in the Yerba Buena urban redevelopment program which also includes an arts center designed by the Japanese architect Fumihiko Maki, and a theater by the New York architect James Stewart Polshek, Botta's SFMoMA building imposes itself through its vast and largely blank brick veneer façades. Its single cyclopean opening brings light into much of the massive 18 500 square meter structure, and yet many visitors have concluded that this architecture is related less to the cathedral than to the tombs of antiquity. Its entrance area is positively funerary, which seems curious for an institution so justifiably proud of its collections of modern art. Botta's $60 million museum is testimony to the continuing emphasis placed on the relationship between culture and quality architecture throughout the industrialized world. However, the lack of collaboration which presided over the conception of practically contiguous structures by three of the most famous architects hardly augurs well for true urban renewal spearheaded by quality design, unless such exceptional personalities as Alessandro Mendini or, in a different style, Rem Koolhaas are involved.

The challenge of public facilities
The decision announced on June 21, 1991 that Berlin would succeed Bonn as the capital of a reunited Germany will undoubtedly continue to have a deep influence on the architecture of public facilities for decades to come. For

essante Projekte, von denen die neue Opéra (von Jean Nouvel) die meiste Aufmerksamkeit erregte. Das gegenüber dem Rathaus und einen Häuserblock vom Kunstmuseum und dem Place des Terraux entfernt gelegene Opernhaus wurde ursprünglich 1831 von Chenavard und Pollet errichtet. Es gelang Nouvel, der die Ausschreibung im Jahre 1986 gewann, den Innenraum des Gebäudes zu verdreifachen, ohne die bestehenden Außenwände anzutasten. Dies erreichte er durch die Ausschachtung des Bodens unterhalb der Oper und durch einen 20 Meter hohen, halbzylindrischen Aufsatz. Das außergewöhnliche Dach des Gebäudes bildet nun einen weithin sichtbaren, kulturellen Orientierungspunkt in der städtischen Skyline. Die Klaustrophobie erzeugende, schwarze Eingangshalle der Oper stieß bei den Kritikern zwar nicht gerade auf Begeisterung, aber Jean Nouvels Vorliebe für clair-obscur ist schließlich bekannt.

Da Portzamparc als der bekannteste zeitgenössische Architekt Frankreichs gilt, wählte Nouvel bei der Gestaltung des neuen Gebäudes für die Fondation Cartier am Boulevard Raspail in Paris einen völlig anderen Ansatz. Hier verzichtete er zugunsten der völligen Transparenz eines Glasgebäudes auf sein Markenzeichen – die Farbe Schwarz. Zu einer Zeit, als das Interesse an der Förderung der Kunst seitens der Wirtschaft überall in Frankreich gleichermaßen erlahmte, ging der Präsident der Firma Cartier, Alain-Dominique Perrin (der bereits das Firmengelände in Jouy-en-Josas zur Verfügung gestellt hatte), das Risiko ein, einen Architekten mit stark ausgeprägter Persönlichkeit für ein weithin sichtbares Gelände zu engagieren. Daraus läßt sich folgern, daß er gutes Design mit einer guten Geschäftsentwicklung gleichsetzt.

Obwohl Nouvel vor kurzem den Wettbewerb für ein großes Stadion in der Nähe von Paris verlor, in dem die Fußballweltmeisterschaft 1998 ausgetragen werden soll, prägte er die Architektur zahlreicher französischer Städte. In Tours beispielsweise präsentiert Nouvels Centre des Congrès seine moderne Fassade genau gegenüber dem Hauptbahnhof. In dieser sehr traditionsverhafteten, kleinen Stadt bildet sein Gebäude einen – gelinde gesagt – überraschenden Anblick, aber dank seiner untadeligen Aus-

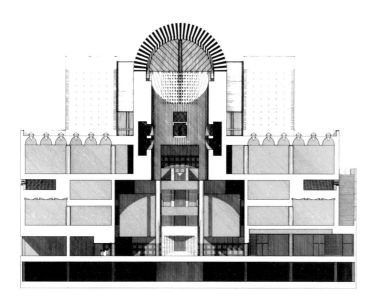

pierre par pierre à Versailles ou à Paris. La Maison Carrée ne dut sa survie in situ qu'à son achat par les moines augustins, en 1670.

En 1984, à l'instigation du maire Jean Bousquet, Norman Foster fut choisi pour construire la nouvelle médiathèque de la ville, juste en face de la Maison Carrée. Son «Carré d'Art» est un «bâtiment calme et classique» qui regroupe un musée d'art contemporain et une bibliothèque publique. Comme le dit Foster: «Le projet suggère comment le nouveau peut se rapprocher de l'ancien, mais respecter le passé tout en témoignant de sa propre époque, avec intégrité et sans pastiche. Le Carré d'Art prouve par ailleurs que la qualité est plus une attitude qu'une question de budget.» Là encore, on a jugé qu'il fallait une conception de haut niveau dans le contexte d'un programme de rénovation urbaine relativement cohérent.

Bien que très différent de celui de Groningue (Mendini), le nouveau San Francisco Museum of Modern Art, de l'architecte suisse Mario Botta, part d'idées assez similaires à celles du créateur italien. Par exemple, Botta a déclaré: «Dans la cité d'aujourd'hui, le musée joue un rôle analogue à celui de la cathédrale d'hier. Un lieu de rencontre et de confrontation. Un lieu dont nous avons besoin pour répondre au défi des espoirs et des contradictions de notre époque… En fait, il est possible d'interpréter le musée comme un espace consacré au témoignage et à la recherche d'une nouvelle religiosité, qui promeut et enrichit ces valeurs spirituelles dont nous avons tellement besoin.» Inclus dans le programme de rénovation urbaine de Yerba Buena, qui comprend également le centre artistique de l'architecte japonais Fumihiko Maki, et le théâtre du New-yorkais James Stewart Polshek, le SFMoMA de Botta s'impose par ses immenses façades de brique en grande partie aveugles. Une unique ouverture, cyclopéenne, éclaire cette massive construction de 18 500 m². De nombreux visiteurs pensent qu'elle fait cependant moins penser à une cathédrale qu'aux mausolées de l'Antiquité. Son hall d'entrée, par exemple, est franchement funéraire, ce qui peut sembler curieux pour une institution fière à juste titre de ses collections d'art moderne. Ce musée de 60 millions de dollars confirme

Two sections of the San Francisco Museum of Modern Art, by the Swiss architect Mario Botta. The cylindrical form at the center brings daylight into the entrance and the lower areas of the museum. Below, a view of the gallery space.

Zwei Schnitte des San Francisco Museum of Modern Art, vom Schweizer Architekten Mario Botta entworfen. Der zentrale Zylinder versorgt den Eingangsbereich und die unteren Geschosse des Museums mit Licht. Unten: Ein Blick auf den Ausstellungsteil.

Deux sections du San Francisco Museum of Modern Art, de l'architecte suisse Mario Botta. Le vaste cylindre, au centre, éclaire l'entrée et les parties inférieures du musée. En-dessous: Vue de la galerie d'exposition.

A drawing by Axel Schultes for his winning competition entry for the Berlin Spree-bogen project.

Eine Zeichnung aus Axel Schultes preis-gekröntem Wettbewerbsbeitrag für die Ausschreibung zum Spreebogen-Projekt in Berlin.

Un dessin d'Axel Schultes pour le projet lauréat du concours du Spreebogen, à Berlin.

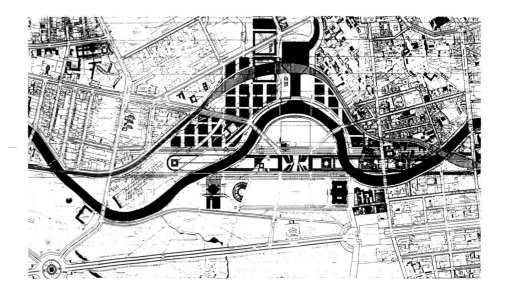

the time being, this influence is essentially limited to the architectural competitions for the renovation of the Reichs-tag and the design of the Spreebogen district. This area had already been the object of official attention on numer-ous occasions since the 19th century, most memorably when, in 1936, Adolf Hitler commissioned Albert Speer to design a monumental boulevard leading to a square in the area of the Königsplatz. The axis of the Spreebogen would have been dominated by a "Great Hall" with a square large enough to receive one million people. That design was, of course, never to be carried out, and when Hans Scharoun became the Urban Development Director of the Berlin Magistrate in May 1945, he declared that "What remained after air raids and 'final struggle' had reduced the density of development and ripped apart the urban fab-ric," offering material to "create a new urban landscape and giving order to the fragmentary and the unpropor-tioned in the same way that forest, meadow, mountain, and lake work together in a beautiful landscape." Before this vision could be brought to fruition, the Spreebogen, together with the portentous volume of the Reichstag, were relegated to the periphery of West Berlin by the con-struction of the Wall in 1961, putting an end to all major development plans until the joint competition whose results were announced on February 18, 1993. No fewer than 1900 architects requested the program for the Spree-bogen competitions, and 835 architects from 44 countries submitted entries, a testimony to the historical and politi-cal significance of the site. The winner, a 50 year old archi-tect educated in Berlin, Axel Schultes proposed a simple east-west bar, extending the boundaries of the competi-tion to include sites that were once in opposite parts of the divided city. His own comment is significant of the nature of the challenge which he has taken up: "According to Aldo Rossi the capacity for synthesis in our time is destroyed ... the most we can offer is fragments; frag-ments of life, historical fragments, fragments of buildings – political fragments? Fragments of Berlin resolutions? A firm, spatial event, a Spreebogen convention, can provide the synthesis of some of these fragments."

Although it is continuous with the Spreebogen site,

führung (die im allgemeinen nicht zu den charakteristischen Eigenschaften von Nouvels Gebäuden gehört) und aufgrund seines praktischen Designs erfreut es sich großer Beliebtheit. Wenn selbst konservativere Franzosen dazu veranlaßt werden konnten, zeitgenössische Architektur zu akzeptieren, dann muß ein Wandel in der Geisteshaltung, aber auch in der Architektur stattgefunden haben.

Nouvel spielte ebenfalls eine wichtige Rolle bei den Bemühungen zahlreicher französischer Départements, Architektur und Design in den Mittelpunkt der Stadtplanung zu stellen. Seine »Nemausus« -Wohnanlage in Nîmes wurde trotz ihres eher gefängnisartigen Erscheinungsbildes viel besprochen. Dagegen wirkt Sir Norman Fosters Carré d'Art, das gegenüber dem berühmten Maison Carrée liegt, doch ansprechender. Dieser römische Tempel aus der Zeit zwischen 10 v. Chr. und 5 n. Chr. beherrschte das Forum der römischen Kolonie Nemausus und war auf einem Stück Land errichtet worden, das angeblich Kaiser Augustus seinen Legionären nach ihrem Sieg bei Actium über Antonius' und Cleopatras Flotte im Jahre 31 v. Chr. geschenkt hatte. Bereits 1535 zog dieses Gelände die Aufmerksamkeit der französischen Herrscher auf sich, als Francois I. verfügte, daß der Tempel besser gepflegt werden müsse; ein Jahrhundert später war Louis XVI. so angetan von diesem Bauwerk, daß er von Colbert den Transfer jedes einzelnen Steins nach Versailles oder Paris verlangte. Nur dem Erwerb durch die Augustinermönche im Jahre 1670 verdankt das Maison Carrée den Verbleib an seinem angestammten Standort.

Auf Veranlassung des Bürgermeisters von Nîmes, Jean Bousquet, betraute man Norman Foster 1984 mit der Errichtung einer neuen »Médiathèque« genau gegenüber dem Maison Carrée. Fosters Carré d'Art ist ein »ruhiges und klassisches Gebäude«, das ein Museum für zeitgenössische Kunst und eine öffentliche Bibliothek beherbergt. Foster beschrieb es so: »Das Projekt deutet verschiedene Wege an, wie Neues an Altes anknüpfen, seinen Respekt vor der Vergangenheit erweisen, aber auch für sich selbst stehen und ohne Anleihen bei anderen Stilen für sein eigenes Zeitalter sprechen kann. Darüber hinaus demonstriert das Carré d'Art, daß Qualität keine Frage des Budgets,

l'intérêt constant porté dans les pays développés aux relations entre la culture et l'architecture de qualité. Le manque de collaboration qui a présidé à la conception de bâtiments pratiquement contigus par trois des plus célèbres architectes du monde, laisse cependant mal augurer des perspectives d'une rénovation urbaine authentique au seul nom de la qualité architecturale, à moins que des personnalités aussi exceptionnelles que Alessandro Mendini, ou, dans un style différent, Rem Koolhaas, ne soient impliquées.

Le défi des services publics

La décision du 21 juin 1991 de faire de Berlin la capitale de l'Allemagne réunifiée, exercera sans aucun doute pour longtemps une profonde influence sur l'architecture publique de ce pays. Pour l'instant, son impact se limite essentiellement aux concours d'architecture pour la restauration du Reichstag, et la rénovation du quartier du Spreebogen. Cette dernière zone a été l'objet de multiples attentions officielles depuis le XIXe siècle, en particulier en 1936, lorsque Hitler demanda à Albert Speer de dessiner une avenue monumentale. Le méandre de la Spree (Spreebogen) aurait été dominé par un «Grand Dôme» élevé au bord d'une place assez vaste pour contenir un million de personnes. Ce projet ne fut jamais exécuté, et lorsque Hans Scharoun devint directeur de l'urbanisme de Berlin en mai 1945, il déclara: «Les raids aériens et le combat final avaient diminué la densité urbaine et détruit le tissu urbain», ouvrant la voie «à la création d'un nouveau paysage urbain et permettant de réordonner le fragmentaire et le disproportionné, de la même façon qu'une forêt, des champs, des montagnes et des lacs peuvent concourir à la naissance d'un magnifique paysage.» Mais avant que cette vision ne puisse se matérialiser, le Spreebogen et l'imposant volume du Reichstag se trouvèrent relégués à la bordure de la ville par la construction du Mur, en 1961. Les plans prévus furent abandonnés et il fallut attendre jusqu'au 18 février 1993, date de la proclamation des résultats des concours internationaux. Pas moins de 1 900 architectes demandèrent le dossier des concours du Spreebogen, et 835 praticiens de 44 pays y participèrent,

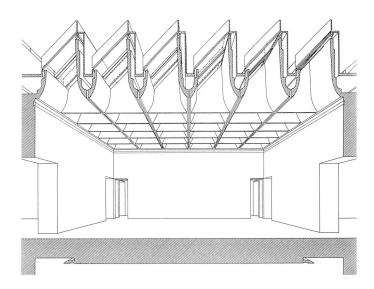

A drawing of the gallery space (top of page 34) shows how natural light is admitted. Below, a floor plan demonstrates how the architect generates square and rectangular spaces from the overall square design.

Eine Zeichnung der Ausstellungsräume (Seite 34 oben) zeigt, wie natürliches Licht in den Raum gelangt. Der Grundriß unten zeigt, wie der Architekt es geschafft hat, quadratische und rechteckige Räume in die quadratische Gebäudeform einzufügen.

En haut, un dessin montre la façon dont la lumière naturelle éclaire l'espace du musée. En dessous, un plan de masse montre la manière dont l'architecte aménage des espaces carrés et rectangulaires à partir d'une structure générale carrée.

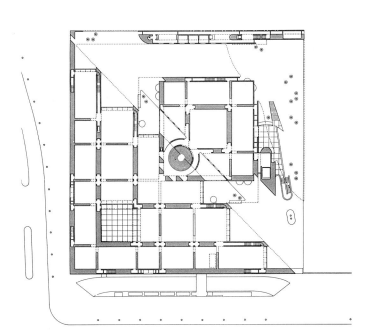

the Reichstag competition announced on June 26, 1992 (following the decision taken on October 31, 1991 that it should be renovated as the seat of the Bundestag) did not require a clear connection to the adjacent site. As a result, two of the selected candidates, Norman Foster and the Dutch architect De Bruijn, did not take the Schultes design into account. It should be recalled that the Reichstag, whose construction was decided on March 28, 1871 at the eastern end of the Königsplatz, had more than once caused architectural problems in the past. The original 1871 competition winner, Friedrich Bohnstedt, was set aside in favor of Paul Wallot a decade later. Wallot himself abandoned the project in 1899, some 17 years before the motto he proposed, "Dem deutschen Volke" was finally engraved on the building. The agony of the Reichstag, from the 1933 fire to the arrival of the Soviets is well known. Sir Norman Foster won the Reichstag competition over De Bruijn and the Spaniard Santiago Calatrava, but his original scheme was abandoned in favor of a dome outwardly much like Calatrava's. This revised design was approved by the Bundestag on June 29, 1994.

Although conceived before the fall of the Wall, in 1986, the new Kunstmuseum Bonn by Axel Schultes has also played a role in the Bonn/Berlin rivalry. This composition made up of triangles and squares shares a 100 by 300 meter site in a formerly undeveloped no-man's land between Bonn and Bad Godesberg with the Bundeskunsthalle which was originally to have been part of a homogeneously structured whole. Here, culture serves the political ambitions of Bonn, eager to prove that in this area it can be the rival of larger cities.

In two other German public projects, very different styles show the variety of idioms available to contemporary architects. The first of these is the work of an Australian, Peter Wilson and his partner Julia Bolles Wilson, who first came to international attention as participants in the 1990 Garden and Greenery Exposition in Osaka. There, a number of architects with experience teaching at the Architectural Association in London such as Zaha Hadid, Coop Himmelblau, Morphosis, Daniel Libeskind and the Spaniards Lapeña and Torres were asked by Arata Isozaki

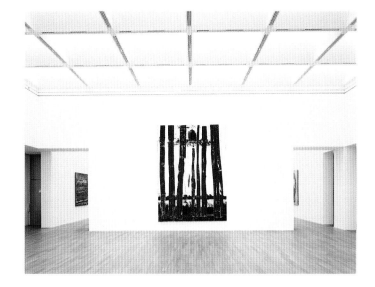

sondern eine Frage der Einstellung ist.« Auch hier wurde
gutes Design als nützliche Komponente in einem relativ
einheitlichen Stadtsanierungsprogramm betrachtet.

Obwohl sich das neue San Francisco Museum of
Modern Art des Schweizer Architekten Mario Botta in
seinem Design erheblich von Mendinis Groninger Museum
unterscheidet, scheint sein Architekt auf verschiedene
Ideen Bezug genommen zu haben, die denen Mendinis
nicht unähnlich sind. Botta erklärte, daß »in der heutigen
Stadt ein Museum die gleiche Rolle besitzt wie die Kirche
in den vergangenen Jahrhunderten. Es ist ein Ort der
Begegnung und der Konfrontation. Ein Ort, den wir benöti-
gen, um die Hoffnungen und Widersprüche unserer Zeit zu
hinterfragen … Tatsächlich könnte man das Museum als
einen Raum interpretieren, der der Suche nach einer
neuen Religiösität gewidmet ist, welche die spirituellen
Werte, derer wir so dringend bedürfen, fördert.«

Bottas Gebäude des San Francisco Museum of Modern
Art ist Teil eines städtischen Sanierungsprogramms im
Yerba Buena-Distrikt, das auch ein von dem japanischen
Architekten Fumihiko Maki entworfenes Kunstzentrum
sowie ein Theater des New Yorker Architekten Stewart
Polshek umfaßt.

Das Gebäude beeindruckt durch seine gewaltigen, fast
fensterlosen Ziegelsteinfassaden. Aber obwohl sein zentraler, gigantischer Okulus ausreichend Licht in große Teile
des massiven, 18 500 m² umfassenden Baus einfallen läßt,
stellten viele Besucher übereinstimmend fest, daß diese
Architektur nicht an eine Kathedrale, sondern eher an
Grabstätten der Antike erinnert. Zweifellos erweckt der
Eingangsbereich Assoziationen an ein Begräbnis – erstaun-
lich für eine Institution, die sich zu Recht ihrer umfang-
reichen Sammlung moderner Kunst rühmt.

Bottas 60 Millionen Dollar teures Museum ist ein
Beweis dafür, welchen Wert die Industriestaaten nach wie
vor auf eine Verknüpfung von Kultur und hochwertiger
Architektur legen. Allerdings spricht die mangelnde Koope-
ration, die die Konzeption dreier, praktisch aneinandergren-
zender Bauten (von drei der bekanntesten Architekten der
Welt) überschattete, nicht gerade für die glanzvolle
Zukunft einer von Qualitätsdesign bestimmten Stadtsanie-

preuve de l'intérêt historique et politique du site. Le
vainqueur, un architecte de 50 ans formé à Berlin, Axel
Schultes, proposa un simple axe est-ouest, repoussant les
limites de la zone du concours jusqu'à englober des sites
qui se trouvaient naguère de part et d'autre du Mur. Ses
commentaires expriment la nature du défi qu'il a cherché
à relever: «Selon Aldo Rossi, la capacité de synthèse est
aujourd'hui détruite … le mieux que nous puissions offrir,
ce sont des fragments; fragments de vie, fragments historiques, fragments de bâtiments – fragments politiques?
Fragments des souhaits de la ville de Berlin? Un projet
volontariste, spatial même, pour le Spreebogen peut offrir
la synthèse de certains de ces fragments.» Bien que le
Reichstag soit au bord du méandre de la Spree, le
concours du 26 juin 1992 pour sa rénovation et sa conversion en siège du Bundestag, qui avaient été décidées le 31
octobre 1991 n'imposait pas d'intégration claire dans le
site. C'est ainsi que deux des candidats retenus, Norman
Foster et l'architecte néerlandais De Bruijn, ne tinrent
aucun compte des orientations de Schultes. Il faut rappeler que le Reichstag dont la construction à l'extrémité est
de la Königsplatz fut ordonnée le 28 mars 1871, avait sou-
levé à plusieurs reprises des controverses. Le vainqueur
du concours de 1871, Friedrich Bohnstedt, fut écarté dix
ans plus tard en faveur de Paul Wallot, qui abandonna le
projet en 1899, 17 ans avant que l'inscription «Dem deutschen Volk» ne soit finalement gravée au fronton de l'édifice. L'agonie du Reichstag, de l'incendie de 1933, jusqu'à
l'arrivée des Soviétiques est, par ailleurs, bien connue.
Norman Foster remporta le concours face à De Bruijn et à
l'Espagnol Santiago Calatrava, mais son premier projet fut
abandonné pour revenir à un dôme, assez proche de celui
de Calatrava. Ce projet révisé fut approuvé par le Bundestag le 29 juin 1994.

Bien qu'il ait eut conçu en 1986, avant la chute du Mur,
le nouveau Kunstmuseum construit à Bonn par Axel
Schultes a également joué un rôle dans la rivalité
Bonn/Berlin. Cette composition de triangles et de carrés
se dresse dans un no-man's land entre Bonn et Bad
Godesberg. Elle partage un terrain de 100 x 300 m avec la
Bundeskunsthalle avec laquelle, à l'origine, elle devait

to build "follies." By that time Bolles and Wilson had won their competition for the new Münster public library. Situated in the "historic" center of the city, the library was planned as the main monument to be built for the 1200th anniversary of the founding of the city and the monastery created there by Charlemagne in 793. In the case of Münster, the word historic is placed in quotation marks when referring to the city center because 95 % of the area was destroyed by an air raid on October 10, 1943.

With some diligence, numerous monuments, including the Church and the Town Hall, were rebuilt in their "original" form. But as Bolles and Wilson have pointed out, the reconstruction brought some fundamental changes in the architecture of the city, such as the displacement of the entrance of the Cathedral. That history and much more is inscribed in the Münster public library, which is divided into two sections, forming a perspective toward the Church of St Lambert. On one side there is a traditional library, and on the other, a "supermarket of information." A glazed bridge linking the two areas is compared to the Bridge of Sighs in Venice, the unique entrance to the building to the "primitive and mysterious heads on Easter Island," and so forth. Despite these references, which seem to owe more to the reflection of the architects than to the casual observation of the uninformed visitor, the Münster public library is a very contemporary building. No longer a splendidly isolated modernist monument, nor a post-modern pastiche, the library is on the contrary a clear indication of the maturation of current architecture. Historical reference, both in absolute terms, and in terms of the shifting patterns of the city is evident. Strong modern forms blend here with an undeniable respect for the urban environment and the comfort of users and passers-by.

While the new Ulm University Engineering Sciences buildings represent a fundamentally different approach to architecture than that of the Münster building, it should be borne in mind that this is not a densely built urban site, but a peripheral, almost rural setting. The architect Otto Steidle says that he "mistrusts all buildings which only have one possible function," and in Ulm his efforts have been directed toward creating not "a world for specialists,

rung – außer man beteiligt solche außergewöhnlichen Architekturpersönlichkeiten wie Alessandro Mendini oder Rem Koolhaas.

Öffentliche Einrichtungen als Herausforderung

Die am 21. Juni 1991 verkündete Ernennung Berlins zur Hauptstadt des wiedervereinigten Deutschlands wird in den kommenden Jahrzehnten zweifellos einen nachhaltigen Einfluß auf die Architektur öffentlicher Bauten ausüben. In der Zwischenzeit ist dieser Einfluß im wesentlichen auf die Wettbewerbe beschränkt, die für die Renovierung des Reichstags und für die Gestaltung des Spreebogens ausgeschrieben wurden. Dieses Gebiet stand seit dem 19. Jahrhundert bereits bei vielen Gelegenheiten im Mittelpunkt öffentlichen Interesses, so auch 1936, als Adolf Hitler Albert Speer mit dem Entwurf einer monumentalen Prachtstraße beauftragte, die zu einem Platz im Bereich des heutigen Königsplatzes führen sollte. Die Achse des Spreebogens wäre dann von einer »Großen Halle« mit einem Platz beherrscht gewesen, der eine Million Menschen hätte aufnehmen können. Dieser Entwurf wurde natürlich nicht ausgeführt. Als man Hans Scharoun im Mai 1945 zum Direktor für Stadtentwicklung des Berliner Magistrats ernannte, erklärte er: »Was nach den Luftangriffen und dem »totalen Krieg« übrigblieb, hatte die Entwicklungsdichte reduziert und das städtische Gewebe auseinandergerissen«. Laut Scharoun bot dieses Gebiet aber die Möglichkeit »zur Schaffung einer neuen urbanen Landschaft, die dem Fragmentarischen und dem Unproportionierten auf die gleiche Weise eine neue Ordnung gibt, wie Wälder, Wiesen, Gebirge und Seen in einer wunderschönen Landschaft zusammenarbeiten.« Bevor sich diese Vision verwirklichen ließ, wurde der Spreebogen zusammen mit dem gewaltige Ausmaße besitzenden Reichstag durch den Bau der Mauer im Jahre 1961 an den Rand West-Berlins verbannt, was alle großen städtebaulichen Planungen zum Erliegen brachte – bis zur gemeinschaftlichen Ausschreibung, deren Ergebnisse am 18. Februar 1993 verkündet werden konnten. Nicht weniger als 1 900 Architekten baten um die Wettbewerbsbedingungen für die Spreebogen-Ausschreibung, und 835 Teilneh-

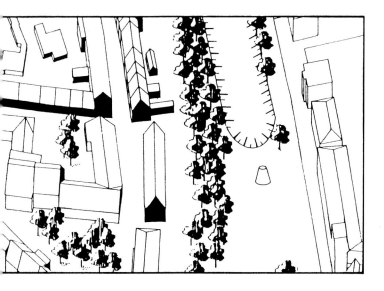

constituer un ensemble homogène. Ici, comme ailleurs,
la culture a été mise au service des ambitions politiques
de Bonn, qui tenait à prouver qu'elle pouvait rivaliser dans
ce domaine avec des villes plus importantes.

Dans deux autres cités allemandes, des projets publics
de styles très différents illustrent la variété de vocabulaire
des architectes contemporains. Le premier est l'œuvre
d'un Australien, Peter Wilson, et de son associée Julia
Bolles-Wilson, qui se firent remarquer sur la scène internationale pour la première fois à l'occasion de l'exposition de
jardins et d'espaces verts d'Osaka, en 1990. Un certain
nombre d'architectes, qui avaient pour point commun
l'expérience de l'enseignement de l'Architectural Association de Londres, comme Zaha Hadid, Coop Himmelblau,
Morphosis, Daniel Libeskind et les Espagnols Lapeña et
Torres, avaient été invités par Arata Isozaki à construire
des «folies». Bolles et Wilson avaient déjà à ce moment-là
remporté le concours pour la nouvelle bibliothèque
publique de Münster. Principal monument édifié à l'occasion du 1 200 ème anniversaire de la création de la cité
et du monastère fondé par Charlemagne en 793, cette
bibliothèque s'élève en plein centre historique. Le mot
«historique» doit être ici placé entre guillemets car, le
10 octobre 1943, 95% du centre de la cité furent détruits
par des bombardements. De nombreux monuments, dont
l'église et l'hôtel de ville, furent rapidement reconstruits
dans leur style original. Mais, comme le font remarquer
Bolles et Wilson, la reconstruction a entraîné d'importantes modifications dans l'architecture de la ville, comme
le déplacement de l'entrée de la cathédrale. Cette longue
histoire se lit, entre autres, dans la bibliothèque de Münster dont les deux parties sont séparées par un passage,
dans la perspective de l'église Lamberti. D'un côté se
trouve la bibliothèque traditionnelle, et de l'autre, «un
supermarché de l'information». Les architectes ont comparé la passerelle vitrée qui relie les deux sections, au
Pont des Soupirs de Venise, et l'entrée unique du bâtiment «aux mystérieuses têtes primitives de l'île de
Pâques». Malgré ces références, plus utiles sans doute à
la réflexion des créateurs qu'évidentes pour un visiteur
non informé, la bibliothèque est un édifice résolument

View of the exterior of Münster Public Library
by Peter Wilson and Julia Bolles Wilson and a
site plan (above).

Außenansicht der Stadtbücherei Münster und
ein Lageplan (oben) von Peter Wilson und Julia
Bolles Wilson.

Vue extérieure de la bibliothèque municipale de
Münster, et un plan (en haut) de Peter Wilson et
Julia Bolles Wilson.

but more an indicator of the links between and the closeness of art and science." This theoretical input is of course interesting, but the final result is more than a little surprising, with its heavy reliance on inexpensive materials such as plywood (for budgetary reasons again), and its complex, colorful façades. The color scheme is visually based on a rhythmic diagram of Bach's Fugue in C Minor, which does not prevent the whole from having a slightly prison-like appearance, perhaps due to the towers erected at the nodal points of the complex. Seeking, as he was asked to do by local officials, not to upset the Obere Eselsberg site in its function as an important climatic factor for Ulm, Otto Steidle has created numerous passageways between the forest side and the opposite direction, corresponding to Richard Meier's nearby Research Center for Daimler-Benz. The whole university complex is built with an environmental respect symbolized by a rainwater collection and distribution system. Together with the substantial use of wood in the upper sections, these design elements undoubtedly qualify the Ulm University as an ecologically sound structure. Perhaps more fundamentally significant in architectural terms, the flexibility of the design, or in some sense its intellectual modesty in the positive sense of the term, signal a very different approach to that which might have been taken a few years ago when strict modernism, or worse, post-modernism were in vogue.

Rem Koolhaas thinks big

The Euralille complex, already mentioned above in the context of transportation and communication also provides an interesting example of current public architecture. The Grand Palais designed by Rem Koolhaas is meant to form an integral part of the very urban complex of which he is in charge, and yet this enormous center for congresses, exhibitions and concerts stands aloof from the group of buildings around the Lille-Europe train station. His own description of a future use of the building gives an idea of its scale, "There is an event planned for 1996: all the Mazda dealers of Europe are in the Zénith; the doors are closed. A new model is driven through the Grand Palais;

Page 38/39: View of the lecture hall of the Ulm University Engineering Sciences buildings by Otto Steidle. To the right, an overall plan of the complex. The cylindrical volume at the top is the lecture hall.

Seite 38/39: Ansicht des Vorlesungssaals der Universität Ulm West (Entwurf Otto Steidle). Rechts: Gesamtansicht des Komplexes. Die zylindrische Form (oben) beherbergt den Vorlesungssaal.

Page 38/39: La salle de lecture du bâtiment de l'Université des sciences de l'ingénierie d'Ulm, dessiné par Otto Steidle. A droite, une vue générale du complexe. Le volume cylindrique, en haut, est la salle de lecture.

mer aus 44 Ländern reichten ihren Beitrag ein – ein Zeugnis für die historische und politische Bedeutung dieses Geländes. Der Gewinner Axel Schultes, ein in Berlin aufgewachsener 50jähriger Architekt, schlug eine einfache Ost-West-Traverse vor, um dadurch die Ausschreibung um Gebiete zu erweitern, die früher auf der gegenüberliegenden Seite der geteilten Stadt gelegen hatten. Schultes eigener Kommentar spricht für den Charakter dieser Herausforderung: »Laut Aldo Rossi ist in unserer Zeit die Fähigkeit zur Synthese zerstört ... das Beste, was wir bieten können, sind Fragmente; Lebensfragmente, historische Fragmente, Gebäudefragmente – politische Fragmente? Fragmente der Berlin – Deklaration? Ein festes, räumliches Gleichgewicht, eine Spreebogen-Konferenz kann die Synthese für einige dieser Fragmente liefern.« Obwohl der Reichstag, dessen Renovierung und Ernennung zum Sitz des Bundestages man am 23. Oktober 1991 beschlossen hatte, direkt an das Gebiet des Spreebogens angrenzt, verlangte der am 26. Juni 1992 ausgeschriebene Architekturwettbewerb keine direkte Verbindung zum Nachbargelände. Dies führte dazu, daß zwei der nominierten Teilnehmer, Norman Foster und der niederländische Architekt De Bruijn, Schultes Entwurf nicht mit in ihre Konzeption einbezogen. Der Reichstag, dessen Bau am östlichen Ende des Königsplatzes 1871 beschlossen worden war, hatte in der Vergangenheit schon mehrfach architektonische Probleme aufgeworfen. Der Entwurf des ursprünglichen Gewinners der Ausschreibung von 1871, Friedrich Bohnstedt, wurde ein Jahrzehnt später zugunsten Paul Wallots Konstruktionszeichnungen beiseite geschoben. Wallot wiederum gab das Projekt 1899 auf – 17 Jahre, bevor seine Inschrift »Dem deutschen Volke« am Gebäude angebracht wurde. Das weitere Schicksal des Reichstags – vom Brand im Jahre 1933 bis zur Ankunft der sowjetischen Armee – ist hinlänglich bekannt. Die nächste Ausschreibung im Jahre 1992 gewann Sir Norman Foster (vor De Bruijn und dem Spanier Santiago Calatrava), der seinen ursprünglichen Entwurf aber zugunsten einer Kuppel abwandeln mußte, die äußerlich sehr stark an Calatravas Konzept erinnert. Dieser überarbeitete Entwurf wurde am 29. Juni 1994 vom Bundestag verabschiedet.

contemporain. Loin d'être un monument moderniste isolé dans sa splendeur, ou un pastiche post-moderne, elle est au contraire le signe manifeste de la maturité de l'architecture d'aujourd'hui. La référence historique, que ce soit en termes absolus ou dans ceux du visage changeant de la cité, est fortement présente. Ses formes puissantes et actuelles se marient à un indéniable respect pour l'environnement urbain, pour l'agrément des utilisateurs et celui des passants.

Le nouveau bâtiment des sciences de l'ingénierie de l'université d'Ulm illustre, quant à lui, une approche très dissemblable. Le site sur lequel il s'élève est d'ailleurs très différent et beaucoup moins construit, puisqu'il se trouve en périphérie urbaine, dans une zone semi-rurale. Son architecte, Otto Steidle, a déclaré à son sujet qu'il se «défiait des bâtiments qui n'offrent qu'une fonction», que ses efforts avaient consisté non à «créer un monde clos pour spécialistes, mais bien plutôt un indicateur des liens de proximité entre l'art et la science». Cette position théorique est bien entendu intéressante, mais le résultat final ne manque pas de surprendre, par son recours massif à des matériaux économiques comme le contre-plaqué (pour des raisons budgétaires), et à des façades aussi complexes que colorées. Cette coloration s'inspire d'un diagramme rythmique de la fugue de Bach en ut mineur, ce qui n'empêche pas l'ensemble d'offrir une apparence légèrement carcérale, sans doute provoquée par la présence de tours aux points nodaux. Cherchant, ainsi qu'il le lui avait été demandé, à ne pas porter atteinte au site boisé de l'Oberer Eselsberg, Otto Steidle a créé de nombreux passages entre la forêt et la zone toute proche, sur laquelle Richard Meier a édifié le Centre de recherches Daimler-Benz. L'ensemble universitaire est construit dans un parti-pris de respect de l'environnement, qu'illustre le système de collecte et de distribution des eaux de pluie. Si l'on y ajoute l'utilisation importante du bois dans les parties supérieures, on peut penser à une construction écologique. Plus fondamentalement important en termes d'architecture, la souplesse de la conception ou, en un certain sens, sa modestie, au sens positif du mot, signale une approche très différente de celle qui aurait pu être choisie

Page 40/41: Three views of the Grand Palais in Lille, France, part of the Euralille complex designed by the Dutch architect Rem Koolhaas.

Seite 40/41: Drei Ansichten des Grand Palais in Lille, das zum Euralille-Komplex des nieder-ländischen Architekten Rem Koolhaas gehört.

Page 40/41: Trois vues du Grand Palais de Lille, qui fait partie du complexe Euralille conçu par l'architecte néerlandais Rem Koolhaas.

the doors open and it comes into the auditorium. The doors close; the dealers descend to the arena and throng around the car. In the meantime, the entire space of the Grand Palais is filled with 5000 new Mazdas. The doors open; the dealers are guided to their own new Mazdas and drive out of the building. That event will take place in the space of 30 minutes."

An 18000 square meter exhibition hall is adjoined to a 5500 seat rock concert hall called the Zénith. A grand total of 50000 square meters also includes three amphitheaters with seating capacities of 1500, 500 and 350 places, a parking lot with 1200 places – the whole inscribed in a 300 meter long oval. What makes this structure all the more remarkable is that as functional as it is, its construction cost (about 5500 francs per usuable square meter) is very low. Using exposed concrete surfaces and a great deal of plywood and plastic, Koolhaas has nonethe-less made his Grand Palais a unique esthetic experience. But once outside, especially on foot, the visitor is greeted by a maze of roads, and already sordid underpasses are the best way to escape a very unpleasant environment. How does this fit in with Koolhaas's sophisticated theories of urbanism? "The Grand Palais," he answers, "is a piece of equipment that with minimal dissociation from the generic urban plane, minimum means of intensification, accommodates the urban condition – but inside rather than outside." In other words, urbanism is fine on paper, but when it comes right down to building, Koolhaas has allowed himself to do what any other self-respecting archi-tect might do, which is to say build the best building he can.

Frank O. Gehry's thoughts about Koolhaas include more than a little irony, and some envy as well. As he says, "I love Rem. He has the big picture. He thinks urban. He thinks social. He thinks human. He thinks people. He thinks. He's doing what I would give my eyeteeth to do... He's creating a city." Although it is easy to criticize the urbanistic stance of the Grand Palais in Lille, it should be pointed out that Koolhaas' theories on the subject are rather unexpected. In the monumental 1300 page book he was to have published for his 1994 retrospective at the

Obwohl Axel Schultes das Kunstmuseum Bonn 1986 – also vor dem Fall der Berliner Mauer – entworfen hatte, spielte dieses Bauwerk ebenfalls eine wichtige Rolle im alten Konkurrenzkampf zwischen Bonn und Berlin. Die aus Dreiecken und Quadraten bestehende Konstruktion war ursprünglich als homogenes Ganzes mit der Bundeskunsthalle geplant, die ebenfalls auf diesem 100 Meter breiten und 300 Meter langen ehemaligen Brachland zwischen Bonn und Bad Godesberg liegt. Hier diente ein Kulturprojekt den politischen Ambitionen der Stadt Bonn, die auf diesem Gebiet durchaus mit den größeren Städten konkurrieren wollte.

Zwei weitere deutsche öffentliche Bauten demonstrieren aufgrund ihrer unterschiedlichen Stilrichtungen die Vielfalt der zeitgenössischen Architektur. Bei dem ersten Projekt handelt es sich um die Arbeit des Australiers Peter Wilson und seiner Partnerin Julia Bolles Wilson, die bei der Garden and Greenery Expo '90 in Osaka erstmalig international auf sich aufmerksam machten. Dort arbeiteten sie zusammen mit anderen Architekten, die ebenfalls Lehrerfahrung an der Architectural Association in London besaßen – wie etwa Zaha Hadid, Coop Himmelblau, Morphosis, Daniel Libeskind oder die Spanier Lapeña und Torres – im Auftrag von Arata Isozaki an der Gestaltung der »Garden follies«. Zu diesem Zeitpunkt hatten Bolles und Wilson bereits die Ausschreibung für die neue Stadtbücherei Münster gewonnen. Die im »historischen« Stadtzentrum gelegene Bibliothek entstand als wichtigstes Monument im Rahmen der 1200-Jahrfeier der Stadt Münster, die im Jahre 793 von Karl dem Großen als Kloster gegründet worden war. Das Wort »historisch« ist deswegen in Anführungsstriche gesetzt, weil 95 Prozent der Innenstadt Münsters bei einem Luftangriff am 10. Oktober 1943 zerstört wurden. Zahlreiche Gebäude, darunter auch die Lambertikirche und das Rathaus, wurden in »Originalform« wiederaufgebaut. Aber diese Rekonstruktion bewirkte – laut Bolles und Wilson – einige fundamentale Veränderungen der Architektur der Stadt, wie etwa die Verlagerung des Domportals. Viele dieser historischen Fakten befinden sich in der Stadtbücherei Münster, die in zwei Bereiche unterteilt ist und eine Achse zur Lamberti-

quelques années auparavant, lorsque régnait un strict modernisme, ou pire, le post-modernisme.

Rem Koolhaas voit grand

Le complexe Euralille, déjà présenté plus haut, offre un intéressant panorama des tendances actuelles de l'architecture. Si le Grand Palais conçu par Koolhaas est censé faire partie de cet ensemble dont l'architecte a été chargé, cet énorme centre de congrès, d'expositions et de concerts n'en est pas moins isolé du groupe de bâtiments réunis autour de la gare Lille-Europe. La propre description par l'architecte de la fonction future de l'édifice donne une idée de son échelle: «Voici, par exemple, un événement prévu pour 1996: tous les concessionnaires Mazda d'Europe sont réunis au Zénith, portes fermées. Un nouveau modèle est amené dans le Grand Palais; les portes s'ouvrent et il fait son entrée dans la grande salle. Les portes se referment. Les invités descendent vers la scène et s'agglutinent autour de la voiture. Pendant ce temps, le Grand Palais se remplit de 5 000 nouvelles Mazda. Les portes rouvrent, les concessionnaires sont guidés vers la voiture qui leur est réservée et quittent le bâtiment à son volant. Tout ceci se déroulera en 30 minutes.» Le hall d'exposition de 18 000 m² est relié à une salle de concert rock de 5 500 places, le Zénith. Les 50 000 m² de surface comprennent en plus trois amphithéâtres de 1 500, 500 et 300 places, un parking pour 1 200 voitures, le tout inscrit dans un ovale de 300 m de long. Le résultat est d'autant plus remarquable que tout ceci a été réalisé pour le prix très peu élevé de 5 500 francs le mètre carré. A grand renfort de béton brut, de contre-plaqué et de plastique, Koolhaas n'en a pas moins fait de ce Grand Palais une expérience esthétique exceptionnelle. De l'extérieur, cependant, surtout s'il arrive à pied, le visiteur est accueilli par un labyrinthe de routes et de passages souterrains déjà sordides qu'il doit emprunter pour échapper à un environnement éprouvant. Comment ceci se marie-t-il aux théories sophistiquées de Koolhaas sur l'urbanisme? «Le Grand Palais, répond-il, est un équipement qui grâce à une dissociation minimale du plan urbain général, et à des moyens réduits d'intensification, prend en compte les

Museum of Modern Art in New York, *S,M,L,XL* Koolhaas used the example of the city of Atlanta to demonstrate the contemporary disintegration of the urban idea. "If the center no longer exists, it follows that there is no longer a periphery either. The death of the first implies the evaporation of the second. Now all is city, a new pervasiveness that includes landscape, park, industry, rust belt, parking lot, housing trace, single-family house, desert, airport, beach, river, skislope, even downtown." In a memorable formula, he has summed up his urban philosophy as follows: "What if we simply declare there is not a crisis – redefine our relationship with the city not as its makers but as its mere subjects, as its supporters?" Rather than trying to rationalize a process which is fundamentally irrational, Koolhaas proposes collaborating with or even emulating the uncontrolable forces behind urban development. He is for what he calls "urban congestion" rather than any doomed attempt to make a pretty landscape in a city.

It goes almost without saying that an ordered plan like the Schultes Spreebogen scheme would be anathema to Rem Koolhaas, but both approaches are indicative of the current upheaval in European architecture which aims at addressing the increasingly evident problems of the urban environment. Much of the chaotic incoherence of cities can be traced back to the fact that, for many years, architects did not accept any responsibility toward the environments they built in. This was due to such simplistic modernist dictums as "Form follows function." Today's motto might be "Form follows function, and history and environment," and not necessarily in that order. Forces such as the growth in communications or the importance of culture may dictate the type of buildings which are being built the most, but shifts in attitude have brought about a concentration of architectural thought. Although economic circumstances are most probably a determining factor, architects have finally accepted that the search for original and powerful forms does not necessarily require enormous budgets. The brief post-modern vogue liberated many architects in the sense that it allowed them to look to the past for inspiration. Significantly, this inspiration can come just as easily from the high Baroque as it can from the Villa

kirche bildet. Auf der einen Seite dieser Achse liegt die traditionelle Bücherei und auf der anderen ein »Supermarkt der Informationen«. Die Brücke, die die beiden Hauptbereiche der Bücherei miteinander verbindet, wurde mit der Seufzerbrücke in Vendig verglichen, und der einzigartige Eingangsbereich mit den »primitiven und geheimnisvollen Köpfen auf der Osterinsel«. Ungeachtet dieser Bezüge, die eher in der Vorstellung der Architekten verhaftet und für den unbedarften Besucher nicht notwendigerweise sofort ersichtlich sind, ist die Stadtbücherei Münster ein sehr zeitgenössisches Bauwerk. Dabei stellt sie weder ein bewußt isoliertes Monument der Moderne dar, noch ein postmodernes Sammelsurium, sondern erweist sich als klarer und lebendiger Indikator für das Heranreifen der aktuellen Architektur. Hier finden sich geschichtliche Bezüge, sowohl im historischen Sinne als auch bezüglich sich verändernder Stadtanlagen. Bei diesem Gebäude gingen ausdrucksstarke moderne Formen mit dem unbestreitbaren Respekt für die urbane Umgebung und dem Komfort von Besuchern und Passanten eine enge Verbindung ein.

Dagegen stellt die neue Universität Ulm West für Elektrotechnik und Hochfrequenztechnik einen grundverschiedenen Architekturansatz dar. Es muß aber darauf hingewiesen werden, daß es sich bei diesem Gelände nicht – wie im Falle der Stadtbücherei Münster – um ein dichtbebautes Stadtgebiet handelte, sondern um eine am Rand der Stadt gelegene, fast ländliche Umgebung. Der Architekt Otto Steidle sagt, daß er »allen Bauwerken mißtraue, die nur eine mögliche Funktion aufweisen«, und in Ulm richteten sich seine Bemühungen nicht auf die Schaffung »einer Spezialistenwelt«. Vielmehr handelt es sich hierbei um einen »Hinweis auf die Zusammenhänge und Nähe zwischen Kunst und Wissenschaft«. Dieser theoretische Unterbau klingt bereits sehr interessant, aber das Ergebnis ist noch überraschender – eine fast ausschließliche Verwendung von preiswerten Materialien wie Spanplatten (aus budgetbedingten Gründen) und komplexen, farbenfrohen Fassaden. Das Farbschema dieser Flächen beruht auf einem visuell umgesetzten rhythmischen Diagramm von Bachs Fuge in c-moll. Dennoch erinnert es an ein Gefängnis – möglicherweise aufgrund der an den Knoten-

One of the first relatively large buildings built by Rem Koolhaas, the Rotterdam Kunsthal.

Eines der ersten großen Bauwerke von Rem Koolhaas, die Rotterdam Kunsthal.

L'une des premières grandes realisations de Rem Koolhaas: le Rotterdam Kunsthal.

conditions urbanistiques, mais de l'intérieur plutôt qu'à l'extérieur.» En d'autres termes, l'urbanisme est parfait sur le papier, mais lorsqu'il s'agit de construire, Koolhaas s'autorise ce que tout autre bon architecte aurait fait, c'est-à-dire réaliser le meilleur bâtiment possible.

Ce que Frank O. Gehry pense de Koolhaas n'est pas dénué d'une certaine ironie, voire d'une pointe de jalousie: «J'aime Rem. Il voit tout en grand. Il pense ville. Il pense social. Il pense humain. Il pense aux gens. Il pense. Il fait ce pourquoi je donnerais la prunelle de mes yeux… Il crée une ville.» Bien qu'il soit aisé de critiquer la position urbanistique de ce Grand Palais lillois, il faut se souvenir que les théories de Koolhaas sur le sujet sont assez inattendues. Dans l'ouvrage monumental de 1 300 pages qu'il voulait publier à la suite de sa rétrospective au Musée d'Art Moderne de New York «S, M, L, XL» (1994), il s'est ainsi servi de l'exemple de la ville d'Atlanta pour prouver la désintégration actuelle de l'idée urbaine. «Si le centre n'existe plus, il n'y a plus de périphérie. La mort du premier implique l'évaporation du second. Maintenant, tout est ville, une nouvelle tendance à se répandre inclut le paysage, les parcs, l'industrie, les friches industrielles, les parkings, les restes d'habitat, les maisons individuelles, le désert, l'aéroport, la plage, la rivière, les pistes de ski, et même le centre.» Dans une formule mémorable, il résume ainsi sa philosophie urbaine: «Que va-t-il se passer si nous nous contentons de déclarer qu'il n'y a pas de crise – allons-nous redéfinir notre relation avec la ville non comme ceux qui la font, mais tout au plus comme ses sujets, comme ses supporteurs?» Plutôt que d'essayer de rationaliser un processus fondamentalement irrationnel, Koolhaas propose de collaborer avec les forces incontrôlables qui se cachent derrière le développement urbain ou même de les favoriser. Il est partisan de ce qu'il appelle «la congestion urbaine», plutôt que de toute tentative nécessairement vouée à l'échec de faire d'une ville un paysage agréable.

Il va presque sans dire qu'un plan aussi ordonné que celui de Schultes pour le Spreebogen est une provocation pour un Rem Koolhaas, mais les deux approches n'en sont pas moins indicatives de la résurgence actuelle de l'archi-

Savoye. This augurs well for the future, but also fits in with Europe's rich history much better than the minimalist or *tabula rasa* approach which can be linked, at least at its origin, to the Bauhaus school of thinking. Whereas the political and economic integration of Europe still seems to face many stumbling blocks, architecture has taken a step forward in a period of recession. Where architects with an international reputation are concerned, European borders have come to matter less and less. This trend does not correspond to any homogenization of style, far from it. Rather, there are as many styles as there are creative architects, or as many styles as there are historically rich environments to build in. The definition of the word "quality" may have changed, but good design, encouraged by such massive initiatives as the Grands Travaux or the Eurostar project has made considerable headway in Europe.

punkten des Komplexes errichteten Türme. Da die Stadt Ulm Otto Steidle gebeten hatte, die Funktion des »Oberen Eselsberg« als wichtiger klimatischer Faktor für die Innenstadt nicht zu beeinträchtigen, schuf der Architekt zahlreiche Schneisen zwischen dem Waldgebiet und der entgegengesetzten Richtung – gemäß Richard Meiers nahegelegenem Forschungszentrum für Daimler-Benz. Der gesamte Universitäts-Komplex entstand mit dem gebührenden Respekt vor der Umwelt, wie die offene Sammlung und Retardierung des Regenwassers dokumentieren. In Kombination mit der fast ausschließlichen Verwendung von Holz als Baumaterial für die oberen Geschosse weisen diese Designelemente die Universität Ulm als ökologisch durchdachtes, umweltverträgliches Bauwerk aus. In bezug auf die Architektur kennzeichnet die Flexibilität des Designs oder seine intellektuelle Bescheidenheit (im positiven Sinne des Wortes) eine neue Richtung und unterscheidet sich damit erheblich von den Ansätzen, die vor wenigen Jahren noch gegolten hätten, als die strenge Moderne oder – schlimmer noch – die Postmoderne sich großer Beliebtheit erfreuten.

Rem Koolhaas will hoch hinaus

Der bereits im Zusammenhang mit Transport und Kommunikation erwähnte Euralille-Komplex dient auch als reizvolles Beispiel für die heutige Architektur öffentlicher Bauten. Das von Rem Koolhaas entworfene Grand Palais soll integraler Bestandteil eines urbanen Komplexes werden, für dessen Bebauungspläne Koolhaas verantwortlich zeichnet, und doch liegt dieses riesige Zentrum mit Kongreßsälen, Ausstellungsräumlichkeiten und einer Rockkonzerthalle (Zénith) abseits von den Gebäuden, die sich um den Bahnhof Lille-Europe gruppieren. Koolhaas Beschreibung des zukünftigen Verwendungszweckes seines Bauwerks vermittelt eine Vorstellung von den Dimensionen dieses Zentrums: »Für 1996 ist folgende Veranstaltung geplant: Alle Mazda-Händler Europas kommen im Zénith zusammen; die Türen sind geschlossen. Ein neues Automodell wird durch das Grand Palais gefahren; die Türen öffnen sich, und der Wagen fährt in das Auditorium. Die Türen schließen sich; die Händler begeben sich hinab in

tecture européenne, qui a bien l'intention de prendre en main les problèmes croissants de plus en plus évidents de l'environnement urbain. L'incohérence chaotique des villes s'explique surtout par le fait que les architectes ont longtemps considéré qu'ils h'avaient aucune responsabilité envers l'environnement. Ce rejet est né de dogmes modernistes simplistes comme «La forme suit la fonction». Celui du jour pourrait bien être «La forme suit la fonction, et l'histoire, et l'environnement», et pas nécessairement dans cet ordre. Des mouvements comme la montée en puissance des communications, ou l'importance de la culture, peuvent influer sur le type de bâtiments que l'on construit le plus souvent aujourd'hui, mais des évolutions d'attitudes ont amené un approfondissement de la pensée architecturale. Bien que les circonstances économiques soient très certainement un facteur déterminant, les architectes ont finalement accepté que la recherche de formes originales et fortes ne dépende pas forcément de la dimension budgétaire. La brève vague post-moderne a libéré de nombreux architectes, dans le sens où elle les a déculpabilisés de se tourner vers le passé pour trouver leur inspiration. Celle-ci peut maintenant aussi bien venir du Baroque que de la Villa Savoye. Tout ceci laisse bien augurer de l'avenir, et correspond également parfaitement à la richesse de l'histoire de l'Europe, en tous cas mieux qu'une approche minimaliste – ou de table rase – qui remonte à l'école de pensée du Bauhaus. Alors que l'intégration politique et économique de l'Europe doit encore affronter de nombreux blocages, l'architecture a su avancer, malgré la période de récession actuelle. Pour les architectes de réputation internationale, les frontières européennes comptent de moins en moins. Cette tendance ne correspond pas, loin de là, à une homogénéisation du style. On pourrait penser, au contraire, qu'il existe autant de styles que d'architectes créatifs, ou autant de styles que d'environnements historiques dans le cadre desquels il faut construire. La définition du mot «qualité» peut avoir changé, mais le bon design, encouragé par des initiatives de poids, comme les Grands Travaux, ou la liaison Eurostar, ouvre de nouvelles frontières en Europe.

die Arena und drängen sich um den Wagen. In der Zwischenzeit wird der gesamte Raum des Grand Palais' mit 5 000 neuen Mazda gefüllt. Die Türen gehen auf; die Händler werden zu ihrem eigenen neuen Mazda geführt und fahren den Wagen aus dem Gebäude heraus. Die gesamte Veranstaltung wird sich innerhalb von 30 Minuten abspielen.« Bei diesem Bau grenzt eine 18 000 m² große Ausstellungshalle direkt an die »Zénith« genannte Rockkonzerthalle mit 5 500 Plätzen, wobei die Nettonutzfläche von 50 000 m² drei weitere Amphitheater mit jeweils 1 500, 500 bzw. 350 Plätzen sowie Parkplätze für 1 200 Wagen umfaßt – und das alles in einer 300 Meter langen ovalen Konstruktion. Bemerkenswert ist auch, daß die Baukosten (mit etwa 5 500 Francs pro Quadratmeter Nutzfläche) ungeachtet der offensichtlichen Funktionalität sehr niedrig ausfielen. Nichtsdestotrotz verlieh Koolhaas seinem Grand Palais mit Hilfe von Sichtbeton, Sperrholz und Kunststoff ein einzigartiges ästhetisches Erscheinungsbild. Sobald der Besucher das Gebäude aber einmal verlassen hat, wird er von einem unüberschaubaren Straßengewirr empfangen – eine äußerst unangehme Umgebung, der er nur mit Hilfe unansehnlicher Unterführungen entfliehen kann. Wie paßt dies zu Koolhaas' anspruchsvoller Theorie des Urbanismus? »Das Grand Palais«, antwortete er, »ist ein Bauwerk, das durch ein minimales Abrücken von der allgemeinen urbanen Fläche und minimalen Mitteln der Intensivierung den urbanen Bedingungen Raum bietet – aber in seinem Inneren, anstatt an der Außenfassade.« Mit anderen Worten: Die Theorie des Urbanismus ist auf dem Papier hervorragend, aber sobald es um ein konkretes Gebäude geht, erlaubt sich Koolhaas, das zu tun, was jeder andere Architekt mit ein wenig Selbstachtung wahrscheinlich auch tun würde – das beste Gebäude zu errichten, zu dem er fähig ist.

Frank O. Gehrys Ansichten über Koolhaas zeichnen sich nicht nur durch Ironie, sondern auch durch eine gewisse Eifersucht aus: »Ich liebe Rem. Er hat den großen Durchblick. Er denkt urban. Er denkt sozial. Er denkt menschlich. Er denkt Menschen. Er denkt. Er tut das, wofür ich meine rechte Hand geben würde ... er erschafft eine Stadt.« Obwohl es natürlich leicht ist, die urbanistische Stellung

des Grand Palais in Lille zu kritisieren, sollte an dieser Stelle vermerkt werden, daß Koolhaas' Theorien zu diesem Thema als eher ungewöhnlich bezeichnet werden können. In seinem monumentalen, 1 300 Seiten starken Buch »S, M, L, XL«, das er anläßlich seiner Retrospektive '94 im Museum of Modern Art in New York veröffentlichen wollte, bediente er sich der Stadt Atlanta als Beispiel, um den heutigen Zerfall der urbanen Idee zu demonstrieren. »Wenn es kein Zentrum mehr gibt, dann folgt daraus, daß es auch keinen Stadtrand mehr gibt. Der Tod des ersteren impliziert die Auflösung des letzteren. Nun ist alles Stadt, eine neue Durchdringung, die Landschaften, Parkanlagen, Industrie, den Rust Belt, Parkflächen, Wohnsiedlungen, Einfamilienhäuser, Wüsten, Flughäfen, Strände, Flüsse, Skihänge und sogar die Stadtmitte einschließt.« Seine Stadtphilosophie hat er in der folgenden, einprägsamen Formel zusammengefaßt: »Was wäre, wenn wir einfach sagen, daß es keine Krise gibt – und unser Verhältnis zur Stadt neu definieren, nicht als deren Erbauer, sondern als reine Subjekte, als ihre Anhänger?« Statt einen im Grunde irrationalen Prozeß rational erklären zu wollen, schlägt Koolhaas vor, daß man mit den unkontrollierbaren Kräften hinter der städtischen Entwicklung zusammenarbeiten oder ihnen sogar nacheifern solle. Er plädiert für eine »urbane Agglomeration« anstatt zum Scheitern verurteilte Versuche zu unterstützen, die die Stadt in eine hübsche Landschaft verwandeln wollen.

Es versteht sich fast von selbst, daß ein geordneter Bauplan wie Schultes Spreebogen-Konzept Rem Koolhaas ein Greuel wäre, aber beide Ansätze deuten auf die momentanen Umwälzungen in der europäischen Architektur hin, die darauf abzielt, sich den zunehmend offensichtlichen Problemen der städtischen Umgebung zu stellen. Ein Großteil der chaotischen Zusammenhangslosigkeit der Städte beruht auf der seit langem kultivierten Weigerung der Architekten, die Verantwortung für die Umgebung zu übernehmen, in die sie ihre Bauwerke setzen. Diese Weigerung entstand aus solch stark vereinfachenden modernistischen Maximen wie »Form follows function (Die Form folgt der Funktion)«. Das heutige Motto könnte dagegen lauten: »Die Form folgt der Funktion – und der

Geschichte und der Umgebung« – und das nicht einmal notwendigerweise in dieser Reihenfolge. Zwar bestimmen Einflüsse wie das Wachstum im Bereich Kommunikation oder die gestiegene Bedeutung der Kultur, welcher Gebäudetypus zur Zeit am häufigsten errichtet wird, aber erst eine Veränderung der Geisteshaltung hat zu einer Verdichtung architektonischer Theorien geführt. Obwohl die finanziellen Umstände höchstwahrscheinlich einen entscheidenden Faktor bilden, haben die Architekten endlich akzeptiert, daß die Suche nach originellen und aussagekräftigen Formen nicht zwangsläufig ein üppiges Budget erfordert. Die kurze postmoderne Modewelle stellte für viele Architekten insofern eine Befreiung dar, als daß sie ihnen das Gefühl vermittelte, sich durchaus der Vergangenheit als Inspirationsquelle bedienen zu dürfen. Bezeichnenderweise kann diese Inspiration mit der gleichen Leichtigkeit dem Hochbarock wie auch der Villa Savoye entspringen. Diese Haltung ist nicht nur ein gutes Omen für die Zukunft, sie paßt auch erheblich besser zu Europas reicher Vergangenheit als der minimalistische oder tabula rasa-Ansatz, der – zumindest in seinem Ursprung – eng mit dem Bauhaus-Gedanken verbunden ist. Während die politische und wirtschaftliche Integration Europas noch immer manchen Hemmschuh zu überwinden hat, konnte die Architektur in einer Zeit der Rezession einen Schritt nach vorne machen. Die Grenzen innerhalb Europas spielen eine immer geringere Rolle – zumindest für Architekten von internationalem Ruf. Aber dieser Trend bedeutet keineswegs eine Homogenisierung der Stile; vielmehr gibt es in Europa so viele Stilrichtungen wie kreative Architekten – oder so viele Stile, wie es historisch bedeutende Umgebungen gibt, die bebaut werden können. Die Definition des Wortes »Qualität« mag sich verändert haben, aber gutes Design, das von solch umfassenden Initiativen wie den Grands Travaux oder dem Eurostar-Projekt gefördert wird, hat in Europa beachtliche Fortschritte gemacht.

Bolles+Wilson

Peter Wilson, born in Melbourne, Australia in 1950 and Julia Bolles Wilson, born in 1948 in Münster, bring an unusual international experience to their partnership. Both have spent time at the Architectural Association in London where Julia Bolles did postgraduate studies (1978–79) and Wilson was Unit Master (1978–88). Selected by Arata Isozaki to build a "garden folly" at the International Garden and Greenery Expo '90 in Osaka, with nine other individuals and A.A. teams of architects with experience teaching at the A.A., such as Zaha Hadid, Peter Cook, Coop Himmelblau, Morphosis or Daniel Libeskind, Peter Wilson formed his vision of the contemporary city in the apparent chaos of Tokyo, where Bolles+Wilson recently built the Suzuki House (1993). Architekturbüro Bolles+Wilson was formed in 1987 in London and moved in 1988 to Münster. Other current projects of the office include the WLV Office Building in Münster, and Quay Rotterdam, a waterfront design for the harbor.

Peter Wilson (1950 in Melbourne, Australien geboren) und Julia Bolles Wilson (1948 in Münster geboren) vereinigen in ihrer Partnerschaft eine Reihe außergewöhnlicher internationaler Erfahrungen. Beide gehörten der Architectural Association in London an, wo Julia Bolles ein postgraduiertes Studium absolvierte (1978–79) und Wilson als Dozent tätig war (1978–88). Zusammen mit neun weiteren Architekten bzw. Architektenteams, die ebenfalls Lehrerfahrung an der A.A. besaßen – wie Zaha Hadid, Peter Cook, Coop Himmelblau, Morphosis und Daniel Libeskind – arbeitete Wilson im Auftrag von Arata Isozaki an der Gestaltung einer »garden folly« für die International Garden and Greenery Expo '90 in Osaka. Wilson entwickelte seine Vision einer modernen Stadt mitten im offensichtlichen Chaos Tokios, wo Bolles+Wilson 1993 das Suzuki House errichtete. Das Architekturbüro Bolles+Wilson wurde 1987 in London gegründet und 1988 nach Münster verlegt. Zu den weiteren aktuellen Projekten dieses Architekturbüros zählen das Verwaltungsgebäude der WLV in Münster und die Kaianlagen im Rotterdamer Hafen.

L'association de Peter Wilson, né à Melbourne (Australie), en 1950, et de Julia Bolles Wilson, née en 1948 à Münster (Allemagne) bénéficie d'une expérience internationale assez unique. Tous deux passent par l'Architectural Association de Londres, où Julia Bolles poursuit ses études (1978–79), et Wilson est responsable d'unité (1978–88). En 1990, ils sont retenus par Arata Isozaki pour construire une «folie» pour l'exposition internationale de jardins et de serres de 1990, à Osaka, avec neuf autres architectes ou équipes également sortis de l'A.A., comme Zaha Hadid, Peter Cook, Coop Himmelblau, Morphosis ou Daniel Libeskind. Peter Wilson tire sa vision de la ville contemporaine de l'apparent chaos de Tokyo, où Bolles+Wilson a récemment construit la Suzuki House (1993). Architekturbüro Bolles+Wilson se constitue en 1987, à Londres, et s'installe à Münster en 1988. Parmi leurs récents projets: un immeuble de bureaux pour WLV, à Münster, et «Quai Rotterdam», une proposition pour le front de mer du grand port.

Interior of Münster Public Library.

Innenansicht der Stadtbücherei Münster.

Vue intérieure de la Bibliothèque municipale de Münster.

Public Library, Münster
1987–1993

This 9751 m² library is located in the city center. Its collection of 200000 books and media items is stored in a structure which is divided into a traditional library and a "supermarket of information." The passageway dividing the two sections, which leads from the Mauritzstrasse to the Alter Steinweg forms an axis leading to the historic Church of St Lambert, one of the sites of the Anabaptist revolution of 1535, Chosen in a competition held in 1985 Julia Bolles and Peter Wilson, respectively of German and Australian origin, both spent time at the Architectural Association in London, a distinction they share with Zaha Hadid and Daniel Libeskind. Their first large-scale project, this library was intended as the main monument to be built for the 1200th anniversary of Münster, whose ancient monastery was founded by Charlemagne in 793. Prominent design features are the use of copper cladding on two large exterior surfaces and the small glazed bridge linking the two main sections of the library, which the architects have compared to the Bridge of Sighs in Venice.

Diese 9751 m² große Bibliothek liegt in der Stadtmitte und beherbergt eine Sammlung von 200000 Büchern und anderen Medien. Das Gebäude ist in zwei Bereiche unterteilt, in eine traditionelle Bücherei und einen »Supermarkt der Informationen«. Beide Bereiche werden durch eine Passage von einander getrennt, die eine Achse zur spätgotischen Lambertikirche bildet, auf deren Gelände 1535 die Wiedertäufer dem bischöflichen Heer unterlagen. Die aus Deutschland bzw. Australien stammenden Architekten Julia Bolles und Peter Wilson gewannen 1985 den für die Bücherei ausgeschriebenen Wettbewerb. Sie gehörten wie Zaha Hadid und Daniel Libeskind der Londoner Architectural Association an. Das Bibliotheksgebäude war ihr erster großer Bauauftrag; es entstand als wichtigstes Monument im Rahmen der 1200-Jahrfeier der Stadt Münster, die im Jahre 793 von Karl dem Großen als Kloster gegründet worden war. Zu den herausragendsten Kennzeichen der Stadtbücherei zählen zwei mächtige, geneigte Kupferschürzen an den Fassaden zur Passage sowie eine Brücke, die von ihren Architekten mit der Seufzerbrücke in Venedig verglichen wird und die beiden Hauptbereiche der Bibliothek miteinander verbindet.

Cette bibliothèque de 9751 m² est située en plein centre-ville. Elle abrite une collection de 200000 livres, disques, vidéos, films, dorénavant conservée dans un ensemble réparti en une bibliothèque traditionnelle et un «supermarché de l'information». Les deux sections sont séparées par un passage piétonnier qui relie la Mauritzstrasse à l'Alter Steinweg, dans l'axe de l'église Lamberti, l'un des hauts lieux de la révolution anabaptiste de 1535. Retenus à l'issue d'un concours organisé en 1985, Julia Bolles et Peter Wilson, respectivement d'origine allemande et australienne, sont tous deux passés par l'Architectural Association de Londres, distinction qu'ils partagent avec Zaha Hadid ou Daniel Libeskind. Première de leurs grandes réalisations, cette bibliothèque est le plus important des chantiers lancés à l'occasion de la célébration des 1200 ans de Münster, monastère fondé par Charlemagne en 793. Particulièrement remarquables: le placage en cuivre de la grande avancée extérieure, et la passerelle vitrée qui relie les deux sections de la bibliothèque, et que les architectes ont comparée au Pont des Soupirs de Venise.

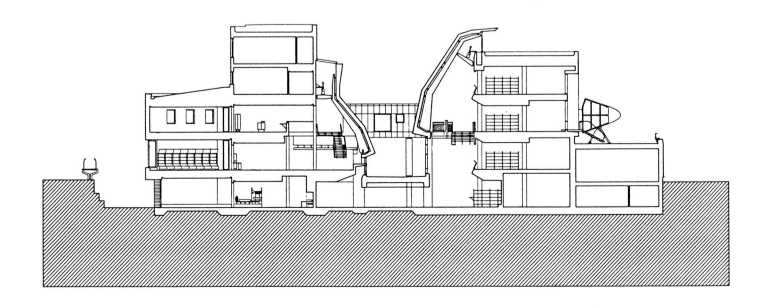

Page 50/51: To the left a cross section of the library, showing the division of the building into two sections and the connecting bridge. The photo above frames the spire of the Church of St Lambert. A distinctive copper cladding is a notable design feature (left).

Seite 50/51: Links: Querschnitt der Bücherei, der die Unterteilung des Gebäudes in zwei Bereiche mit Verbindungsbrücke darstellt. Die Abbildung oben zeigt die Spitze der Lamberti-kirche. Die bezeichnende Kupferverkleidung (links) ist ein hervorstechendes Merkmal.

Page 50/51: A gauche, coupe de la bibliothèque, montrant la division du bâtiment en deux parties et la passerelle les réunissant. La photo au-dessus est cadrée sur la flèche de l'église Lamberti. Un original revêtement de cuivre constitue l'une des caractéristiques les plus remarquables de ce projet.

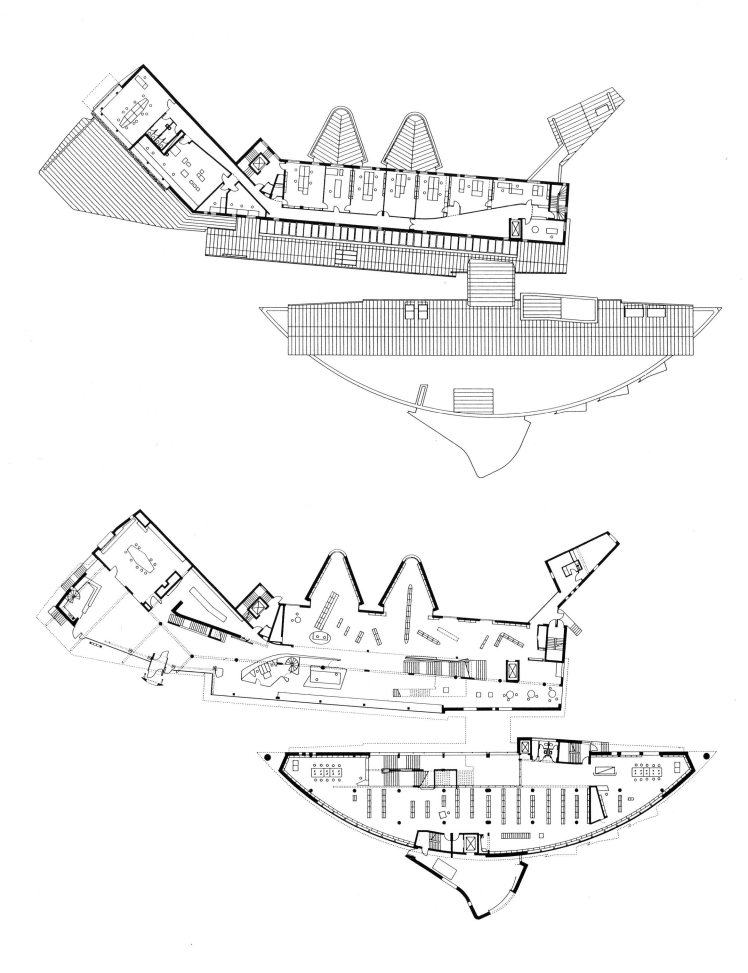

Page 52: Above left, the third floor plan, below the ground floor. Page 53: An interior view, and above, an image of the Library as seen from Alter Steinweg. The book building is to the right.

Seite 52: Grundriß des dritten Obergeschosses, darunter das Erdgeschoß. Seite 53: Innenansicht. Oben: Ansicht der Stadtbücherei vom Alten Steinweg aus. Die Bibliothek liegt auf der rechten Seite.

Page 52: Ci-dessus, à gauche, plan du troisième niveau de sous-sol. Page 53: Vue intérieure, et au-dessus, vue de la bibliothèque prise de l'Alter Steinweg. Le bâtiment réservé aux livres est à droite.

Mario **Botta**

Bridge at the upper level of San Francisco Museum of Modern Art.

Brücke im obersten Geschoß des San Francisco Museum of Modern Art.

Pont dans le niveau supérieur du San Francisco Museum of Modern Art.

Born in 1943 in Mendrisio, Switzerland, near the Italian border, Mario Botta designed his first house at the age of 16. Brief contact with Le Corbusier in Paris in 1965, and with Louis Kahn in Venice in 1968 seem to have influenced him, but by the 1970's, he had developed a strong personal style most clearly expressed in the private houses built in Cadenazzo (1970–71), Riva San Vitale (1971–73) and Ligornetto (1975–76). In the 1980's, Botta continued to create powerful geometric designs for houses, often built of brick, but he also began larger scale work, such as his Médiathèque in Villeurbanne (1984–88) or his cultural center in Chambéry (1982–87). With work in Tokyo, San Francisco and Evry near Paris, where his new cathedral was completed in 1995, Mario Botta has now joined the elite group of international architects who determine predominant styles. Though modern in its geometry, Botta's architecture retains a kind of primordial strength which sets it apart from any movement.

Der 1943 in Mendrisio (Schweiz) geborene Mario Botta entwarf sein erstes Haus im Alter von 16 Jahren. Die kurze Zusammenarbeit mit Le Corbusier in Paris (1965) und Louis Kahn in Venedig (1968) schien ihn zunächst stark zu beeinflussen, aber bereits in den 70er Jahren hatte er einen ausgeprägten persönlichen Stil entwickelt, der in den Privathäusern in Cadenazzo (1970–71), Riva San Vitale (1971–73) und Ligornetto (1975–76) besonders zum Ausdruck kommt. In den 80er Jahren entwarf Botta weiterhin expressive, geometrische, häufig aus Ziegelsteinen errichtete Häuser, aber er widmete sich auch größeren Projekten wie etwa der Médiathèque in Villeurbanne (1984–88) oder dem Kulturzentrum in Chambéry (1982–87). Dank seiner Bauwerke in Tokio, San Francisco und Evry bei Paris (wo seine neue Kathedrale 1995 fertiggestellt wurde) zählt Botta inzwischen zu der kleinen Gruppe internationaler Architekten, die die dominierenden Baustile bestimmen. Obwohl Bottas Architektur aufgrund ihrer Geometrie als modern gilt, hat sie sich eine ursprüngliche Kraft bewahrt, die seine Entwürfe von allen Architekturströmungen deutlich abhebt.

Né en 1943, à Mendrisio, en Suisse, près de la frontière italienne, Mario Botta conçoit sa première maison à l'âge de 16 ans. Un bref contact avec Le Corbusier à Paris, en 1965, et Louis Kahn, à Venise, en 1968, semblent l'avoir influencé, mais dès les années 70, il met au point un style personnel et puissant, qui s'exprime particulièrement dans des villas de Cadenazzo (1970–71), Riva San Vitale (1971–73), ou Ligornetto (1975–76). Au cours des années 80, Botta dessine des plans d'une forte géométrie pour des maisons, souvent en brique, mais intervient également sur des chantiers plus importants, comme la médiathèque de Villeurbanne (1984–88), ou la Maison de la culture de Chambéry (1982–87). Ses interventions à Tokyo, San Francisco, et Evry, près de Paris, où sa cathédrale sera achevée en 1995, lui valent maintenant de faire partie de cette élite de grands architectes internationaux qui détermine les styles dominants. Bien que moderne dans sa géométrie, l'architecture de Botta conserve une sorte de force primale, qui la place résolument à part.

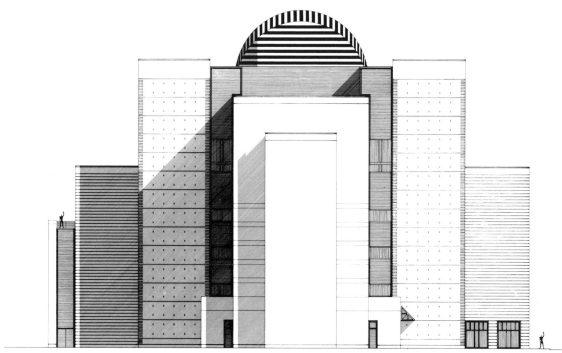

San Francisco Museum of Modern Art, San Francisco 1990–1994

There was no competition as such to choose the architect of this centrally located 18,500 m² museum. Rather, the Trustees of the Museum, which was created in 1935, interviewed five architects: Mario Botta, Frank O. Gehry, Thomas Beeby, Tadao Ando, and Charles Moore. Located on Third Street, near the Moscone Convention Center, the museum, which opened on January 18, 1995 is part of an urban redevelopment program covering an area of more than 40 hectares, first envisaged by the city of San Francisco in 1954. It is located across the street from Fumihiko Maki's new Yerba Buena Center, whose light, ship-like style seems at odds with Botta's brick veneer cladding, and massive, almost windowless design. A central oculus, which appears on the exterior of the building in the form of a truncated cylinder, brings light to the five stories of the building, and particularly to the generous, seven meter high top-lit galleries on the upper floor. Built on city land put at the disposition of SFMoMA by the redevelopment agency responsible for the Yerba Buena district, the new structure was built at a cost of $60 million, provided almost entirely by private donations.

To the left, a photo of the entrance façade of the museum. No visible windows interrupt the brick façade, as is also visible in the elevation of the rear of the building on the left, but light enters the whole of the structure through the central, sliced cylinder. To the right, a ground floor plan.

Links: Der Eingangsbereich des Museums. Obwohl die Ziegelverblendung von keinem Fenster durchbrochen wird, was auch auf dem Außriß (links) der Gebäuderückseite deutlich wird, fällt durch den zentralen Zylinder genügend Licht in das Gebäude. Rechts: Grundriß des Erdgeschosses.

A gauche, façade d'entrée du musée. Aucune fenêtre apparente n'interrompt la façade principale en brique, comme on le voit également sur la façade arrière, à gauche. Mais la lumière pénètre néanmoins la totalité du bâtiment dans la construction par le cylindre central coupé en biseau. A droite, plan du rez-de-chaussée.

Die Wahl des Architekten für dieses zentral gelegene, etwa 18 500 m² umfassende Museum fand ohne offizielle Ausschreibung statt; das Kuratorium des 1935 gegründeten Museums führte statt dessen mit fünf Architekten – Mario Botta, Frank O. Gehry, Thomas Beeby, Tadao Ando und Charles Moore – intensive Gespräche. Das an der Third Street, in der Nähe des Moscone Convention Center gelegene Museum wurde am 18. Januar 1995 eröffnet. Es ist Teil eines Sanierungsprogramms, das von der Stadt San Francisco 1954 geplant wurde und heute eine Fläche von über 40 Hektar umfaßt. Das Museum befindet sich gegenüber von Fumihiko Makis Yerba Buena Center, dessen leichter, schiffsähnlicher Stil in krassem Widerspruch zu Bottas Ziegelverblendung und dem massiven und fast fensterlosen Design seines Museums steht. Ein zentraler Oculus, der von außen als abgeflachter Zylinder sichtbar ist, versorgt die fünf Stockwerke des Gebäudes und insbesondere die Galerien im obersten Stockwerk mit Licht. Das Bauwerk entstand auf städtischem Gelände, das die für den Yerba Buena-Distrikt zuständige Sanierungsbehörde dem SFMoMA zur Verfügung stellte; die Baukosten beliefen sich auf 60 Millionen Dollar, die fast ausschließlich von privaten Spendern aufgebracht wurden.

Ce musée de 18 500 m², construit au centre de la ville, n'a pas fait l'objet d'un véritable concours. Les administrateurs de cette institution, créée en 1935, ont interrogé cinq architectes, Mario Botta, Frank O. Gehry, Thomas Beeby, Tadao Ando et Charles Moore. Edifié sur Third Street, non loin du Centre de congrès Moscone, ce bâtiment inauguré le 18 janvier 1995, fait partie d'un programme de rénovation urbaine de plus de 40 ha, projeté par la ville dès 1954. Il est situé en face du nouveau Yerba Buena Center de Fumihiko Maki, dont le style léger et le côté nautique ne font guère bon ménage avec les murailles de brique et le dessin massif, presque sans ouverture, de Botta. Un oculus central, cylindre tronqué ressortant de la façade, éclaire les cinq niveaux intérieurs, et en particulier les vastes galeries de sept mètres de haut de l'étage supérieur. Construit sur un terrain municipal mis à la disposition du SFMoMA par l'agence de rénovation urbaine responsable du quartier de Yerba Buena, le nouvel édifice a coûté 60 millions de dollars, d'origine presque entièrement privée.

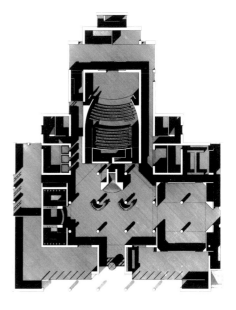

Above, a view of the museum showing the
skyscrapers of the nearby downtown area.
A cross section shows the top-lit upper floor,
and explains how light is brought down into the
monumental lobby (right-hand page).

Oben: Ansicht des Museums mit den Wolken-
kratzern der nahegelegenen Innenstadt. Ein
Querschnitt zeigt das von oben beleuchtete,
oberste Geschoß und veranschaulicht, wie das
Licht bis in das monumentale Foyer fällt (rechte
Seite).

En haut, le musée et les tours du centre-ville
tout proche. La coupe montre les niveaux
supérieurs éclairés zénithalement, et explique la
façon dont la lumière est dirigée vers le hall
d'entrée monumental (page de droite).

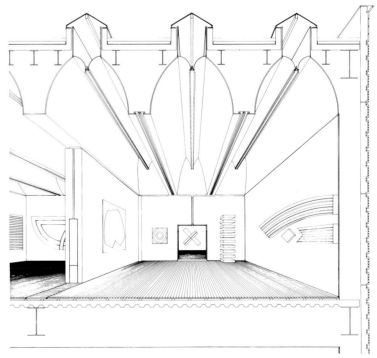

Santiago **Calatrava**

Born in Valencia in 1951, Santiago Calatrava studied art and architecture in his native city (1968–73) before entering the ETH where he obtained a doctorate in Technical Science in 1981, and opened his own architecture and civil engineering office the same year. Though strongly influenced by biological forms such as bird wings, Calatrava has already gone beyond the anthropomorphic work of predecessors such as the Italian Pier Luigi Nervi to create an exciting new style which blends art, architecture and engineering. His presence was certainly noticed at Expo '92 in Seville, where he designed the Kuwait Pavillion and the Alamillo Bridge. A 250 meter high telecommunications tower built for the 1992 Olympic Games in Barcelona, his Gallery and Heritage Square project for BCE Place in Toronto (1987–92), together with the new Lyon-Satolas TGV station have made Calatrava a well-known figure in the world of international architects.

Santiago Calatrava wurde 1951 in Valencia geboren, wo er von 1968 bis 1973 Kunst und Architektur studierte, bevor er zur ETH nach Zürich wechselte und dort 1981 in Technischer Wissenschaft promovierte. Im gleichen Jahr gründete er dort auch sein eigenes Architektur- und Bauingenieurbüro. Obwohl Calatravas Werk von biologischen Formen wie Vogelschwingen deutlich beeinflußt ist, hat er die anthropomorphen Arbeiten seiner Vorgänger wie etwa des Italieners Pier Luigi Nervi bereits weit hinter sich gelassen und einen faszinierenden neuen Stil geschaffen, der Kunst, Architektur und Technik miteinander verschmilzt. Auf der Expo '92 in Sevilla gestaltete er den Pavillon Kuwaits sowie die Alamillo-Brücke, die beide viel Aufmerksamkeit erregten. Sein 250 Meter hoher Fernmeldeturm, den er für die Olympiade 1992 in Barcelona errichtete, sowie der Gallery and Heritage Square, BCE Place in Toronto (1987–92) und der neue TGV-Bahnhof Lyon-Satolas haben Calatrava zu einer der bekanntesten Persönlichkeiten der internationalen Architekturwelt gemacht.

Né à Valence en 1951, Santiago Calatrava étudie l'art et l'architecture dans sa ville natale (1968–73), avant de rejoindre l'ETH de Zurich, où il obtient un doctorat en Sciences des Techniques en 1981, avant d'ouvrir, la même année, sa propre agence d'architecture et d'ingénierie. Fortement influencé par des formes biologiques, comme les ailes d'oiseau, il a déjà dépassé les recherches zoomorphiques de prédécesseurs tels l'Italien Pier Luigi Nervi, pour créer un style neuf qui associe l'art, l'architecture et l'ingénierie. Sa participation à Expo 92, à Séville – le pavillon du Koweit et le pont Alamillo – est très remarquée. Une tour de télécommunications de 250 m de haut pour les Jeux Olympiques de Barcelone de 1992, son projet de Gallery and Heritage Square pour BCE Place à Toronto (1987–92), et la nouvelle gare du TGV à Lyon-Satolas, en ont fait l'un des architectes internationaux les plus réputés.

The Lyon-Satolas TGV terminal.

TGV-Bahnhof Lyon-Satolas.

La gare TGV de Lyon-Satolas.

Lyon-Satolas Railway Station, Lyon-Satolas 1990–1994

This 5600 m² station located at the Lyon-Satolas airport is one of a new generation of rail facilities designed to serve France's growing network of high-speed trains (TGV). The juxtaposition of rail, air and local transport facilities at a single location makes for a particularly efficient system. 120 meters long, 100 meters wide, and 40 meters high, the passenger terminal, which opened on July 7, 1994, is based on a central steel element weighing 1300 tons. Calatrava's station evidently echoes Eero Saarinen's TWA Terminal at Kennedy Airport (1957–62) in its suggestion of a bird in flight, but it is more exuberant than its American ancestor. The plan of the complex, with its link to the airport, also resembles a manta ray. These references to the animal world are typical of the work of Calatrava. A total of six train lines run below the main building and stop at a 500 meter long covered platform also designed by Calatrava. The middle tracks, intended for through trains moving at over 300 kilometers per hour, are enclosed in a concrete shell, a system which required careful calculation of the TGV "shock waves". Shared by the French national rail company (SNCF), the Rhône-Alpes region and the Rhône Department, the total cost of this facility exceeded 600 million francs.

Dieser 5600 m² große Bahnhof am Flughafen Lyon-Satolas gehört zu einer neuen Generation von Bahnhöfen, die für Frankreichs wachsendes Netz von Hochgeschwindigkeitszügen (TGV) konzipiert wurden. Durch die Kombination von Bahn, Flugzeug und öffentlichem Nahverkehr entstand ein besonders effizientes Transportsystem. Der am 7. Juli 1994 eröffnete, 120 Meter lange, 100 Meter breite und 40 Meter hohe Passagierterminal ruht auf einem zentralen, 1 300 Tonnen schweren Stahlgerüst. Der Bahnhof in Form eines zum Flug ansetzenden Vogels erinnert an Eero Saarinens TWA Terminal am Kennedy International Airport (1956–62), wirkt jedoch expressiver als sein amerikanischer Vorläufer. Der Grundriß des Komplexes mit seiner Verbindung zum Flughafen ähnelt einem Manta. Diese Bezüge zur Tierwelt sind typisch für Calatravas Arbeiten. Unterhalb des Hauptgebäudes verlaufen sechs Gleise, deren Züge an 500 Meter langen, überdachten Bahnsteigen halten, ebenfalls ein Entwurf von Calatrava. Die beiden mittleren Gleise für Hochgeschwindigkeitszüge mit ihren Spitzengeschwindigkeiten von über 300 km/h sind von einer Betonhülle umgeben, deren Konstruktion eine sorgfältige Berechnung der »Druckwelle« erforderte, die den TGV umgibt. Die Gesamtkosten von über 600 Millionen Francs teilten sich die Französische Staatsbahn (SNCF), die Regionalverwaltung Rhône-Alpes und das Rhône-Département.

Située sur l'aéroport de Lyon-Satolas, cette gare de 5600 m² fait partie d'une nouvelle génération d'équipements que la SNCF met en place tout au long de son réseau TGV. La conjonction en un seul point du rail, de l'air et des transports locaux contribue à l'efficacité du système. Avec ses 120 m de long, 100 de large et 40 de haut, cette gare de voyageurs, ouverte le 7 juillet 1994, s'organise autour d'une structure centrale qui a nécessité 1 300 tonnes d'acier. L'œuvre de Calatrava n'est pas sans rappeler le terminal TWA d'Eero Saarinen pour l'aéroport Kennedy (1957–62), mais en plus exubérant encore. Le plan de masse et la liaison avec l'aéroport peuvent aussi évoquer une raie manta. Ces références zoomorphiques sont caractéristiques des recherches de Calatrava. La verrière principale couvre six voies et les quais sous auvents de 500 m de long ont également été dessinés par l'architecte. Les voies centrales, sur lesquelles les trains peuvent rouler à 300 km/h, sont protégées dans une coquille de béton qui absorbe l'onde de choc provoquée par le passage du TGV, système qui a exigé des calculs approfondis. Le financement (plus de 600 millions de francs) a été assuré par la SNCF, la région Rhône-Alpes et le département du Rhône.

Page 65: To the right, above, a view over the passageway leading from the airline terminal to the rear of the station. Below right, the sweep of the wings of the structure adds to the dramatic effect, and is used to admit daylight into the interior.

Seite 65: Oben rechts: Blick über die Passage vom Terminal zur Rückseite der Station. Unten rechts: die geschwungene Bogenform verstärkt den dramatischen Effekt und ist gleichzeitig geeignet, um Tageslicht in den Innenraum zu lassen.

Page 65: A droite et en haut, le passage conduisant de l'aéroport à l'arrière de la nouvelle gare. En dessous, à droite, la courbure des ailes du bâtiment crée un effet spectaculaire, et contribue à éclairer l'intérieur.

Page 66/67: An Interior view of the passenger hall of the station showing the spectacular vaulted space.

Seite 66/67: Eine Innenansicht der Passagierhalle zeigt den beeindruckend gewölbten Raum.

Page 66/67: Vue intérieure du hall des voyageurs, révélant le caractère spectaculaire de la voûte.

Page 62/63: A frontal view emphasizes the image of a prehistoric bird.

Seite 62/63: Eine Frontansicht, die den Eindruck eines prähistorischen Vogels im Flug bestärkt.

Page 62/63: La vue de face confirme l'évocation «d'oiseau préhistorique» de la construction.

Paul **Chemetov/** Borja **Huidobro**

Whale skeleton in the Galerie de l'Evolution, Paris, France.

Walskelett in der Galerie de l'Evolution, Paris, Frankreich.

Squelette de baleine, dans la Galerie de l'Evolution, Paris, France.

Paul Chemetov was born in Paris in 1928, and graduated from the Ecole des Beaux-Arts in 1959. His early work was concentrated in low-cost housing, or in sports facilities built on the outskirts of Paris, particularly in Saint-Ouen. Since his association in 1983 with Borja Huidobro, who was born in Santiago, Chile in 1936, he has become a much more visible figure in French architecture, completing the French embassy in New Delhi, the underground galleries in the Halles district of Paris, and, most notably, the 900 meter long Ministry of Finance building at the eastern limit of Paris at Bercy, extending from the rail lines of the Gare de Lyon to the banks of the Seine. The construction of this massive new block, called "Stalinist" by critics of the design, became necessary when François Mitterrand decided to move the services of the ministry out of the Louvre, to make way for the expansion of the museum. With the Galerie de l'Evolution, Chemetov thus has the privilege of having been the only architect to carry out two of Mitterand's Grands Travaux.

Paul Chemetov wurde 1928 in Paris geboren und studierte bis 1959 an der Ecole des Beaux-Arts. Seine ersten Arbeiten konzentrierten sich auf den sozialen Wohnungsbau und Sporteinrichtungen in den Vorstädten von Paris, insbesondere in Saint-Ouen. Seit seinem Zusammenschluß 1983 mit Borja Huidobro (geb. 1936 in Santiago, Chile) avancierte Chemetov zu einer Persönlichkeit in der französischen Architekturwelt. Herausragende Bauwerke dieses Architekturbüros sind die Fertigstellung der französischen Botschaft in Neu Delhi, die unterirdischen Passagen in Les Halles (Paris) sowie das 900 Meter lange Gebäude des Finanzministeriums im Osten von Paris bei Bercy. Dieser massive neue Gebäude-block, den Kritiker als »stalinistisch« bezeichneten, wurde notwendig, als François Mitterrand beschloß, die Verwaltung des Finanzministeriums aus dem Louvre auszulagern, um den Ausbau des dortigen Museums zu ermöglichen. Mit der ebenfalls von ihm errichteten Galerie de l'Evolution gebührt Chemetov also die Ehre des einzigen Architekten, der zwei der sogenannten »Grands Travaux« Mitterrands ausführen durfte.

Paul Chemetov est né en 1928 à Paris. Il est diplômé de l'Ecole des Beaux-Arts en 1959. Ses premiers travaux portent sur des H.L.M. et des installations sportives, construites dans la banlieue de Paris, en particulier à Saint-Ouen. Depuis son association, en 1983, avec Borja Huidobro, né à Santiago-du-Chili en 1936, il est devenu une des grandes figures de l'architecture française, réalisant l'ambassade de France à New Delhi, le centre commercial souterrain des Halles, à Paris, et surtout, le ministère des Finances, bâtiment de 900 m de long dans le quartier de Bercy, à Paris, entre les voies de la gare de Lyon et la Seine. La construction de cet ensemble massif, qualifié de «stalinien» par certains, répondait à la décision de F. Mitterrand de déménager les services du ministère jusque-là implantés au Louvre, pour permette l'agrandissement du musée. Avec la Galerie de l'Evolution, Chemetov peut se targuer du privilège d'avoir été le seul architecte chargé de deux des «Grands Travaux» du président français.

Galerie de l'Evolution, Paris
1990–1994

The eleventh of President François Mitterrand's Grand Travaux, the Galerie de l'Evolution had an overall budget of 400 million francs for a total area of 16 000 m². Chosen for the project in 1989, Paul Chemetov and Borja Huidobro took on the task of the massive renovation of the building designed by Jules André in 1877. Closed since 1965 for reasons of security, the Galerie de l'Evolution is one of the most spectacular examples of iron and glass architecture in Paris, on a par with the Musée d'Orsay or the Grand Palais. The completed gallery is intended to explain the diversity of species to a very large audience, often consisting of school groups, since this museum is under the control of the French Ministry of Education. Chemetov and Huidobro created a new entrance on the side of the building and dug down ten meters to provide extra exhibition space below grade. Together with the scenographer René Allio, they managed to created a well designed layout within the existing architectural shell, although low light levels intended to better preserve the specimens are not appreciated by all visitors.

Das elfte Bauvorhaben von François Mitterrands »Grands Travaux«, die Galerie de l'Evolution, verfügte über ein Gesamtbudget von 400 Millionen Francs für eine Fläche von 16 000 m². Die während der Ausschreibung 1989 ausgewählten Architekten Paul Chemetov und Borja Huidobro übernahmen die umfassenden Renovierungsarbeiten dieses Gebäudes, das 1877 von Jules André entworfen wurde und seit 1965 aus sicherheitstechnischen Gründen geschlossen war. Die Galerie de l'Evolution zählt zu den aufsehenerregendsten architektonischen Beispielen Pariser Stahl- und Glasbauten und befindet sich auf einer Ebene mit dem Musée d'Orsay und dem Grand Palais. Aufgabe der Galerie ist es, die Mannigfaltigkeit aller Spezies einem möglichst breitgefächerten Publikum zu vermitteln, das sich häufig aus Schulklassen zusammensetzt (da dieses Museum dem französischen Erziehungsministerium untersteht). Chemetov und Huidobro entwarfen einen neuen Eingangsbereich an der Seite des Gebäudes und ließen den Grund bis in zehn Meter Tiefe ausschachten, um so weitere Ausstellungsflächen unterhalb des Geländeniveaus zu schaffen. Zusammen mit dem Szenographen René Allio gelang ihnen ein stimmiger Entwurf innerhalb der bestehenden architektonischen Vorgaben. Allerdings sind die zum Schutz der Exponate unterirdisch gelegenen und somit weniger gut beleuchteten Geschosse nicht bei allen Besuchern gleichermaßen beliebt.

Onzième des Grands Travaux décidés par le président Mitterrand, la Galerie de l'Evolution représente un investissement de 400 millions de francs, pour une surface totale de 16 000 m². Sélectionnés en 1989, Paul Chemetov et Borja Huidobro ont pris en charge la rénovation intégrale de ce bâtiment conçu par Jules André en 1877. Fermée en 1965 pour raisons de sécurité, la Galerie de l'Evolution est l'un des exemples les plus spectaculaires de l'architecture de fer et de verre de la capitale, du même niveau d'intérêt que la Musée d'Orsay ou le Grand Palais. Elle a pour fonction d'expliquer la diversité des espèces à un très vaste public – souvent des groupes d'écoliers, puisque le musée dépend du ministère de l'Education nationale. Chemetov et Huidobro ont créé une nouvelle entrée, latérale, et creusé le sol de dix mètres pour récupérer de nouveaux espaces d'exposition. Avec le scénographe René Allio, ils ont réussi à faire naître dans le cadre de l'architecture existante un espace très séduisant, bien que le niveau d'éclairage assez faible (pour préserver les spécimens exposés) ne soit pas apprécié de tous les visiteurs.

This parade of animals is one of the most spectacular items on display in this newly refurbished museum, located in the Jardin des Plantes, in Paris. The entrance is no longer in the main façade (top of page 70) but on the side of the building.

Diese Tierparade zählt zu den spektakulärsten Ausstellungsstücken des frisch renovierten Museums im Jardin des Plantes, Paris.
Der Eingang befindet sich nicht mehr auf der Vorderseite (Seite 70 oben), sondern an einer Seite des Gebäudes.

Cette parade d'animaux est l'un des éléments les plus spectaculaires de la présentation des collections du Muséum national d'histoire naturelle, à Paris, récemment rénové. L'entrée a été déplacée de la façade principale (page 70, en haut) sur le côté du bâtiment.

Jo **Coenen**

Born in 1949 in Heerlen, The Netherlands, Jo Coenen graduated from the Eindhoven University of Technology in 1979. Between 1976 and 1979, he lectured both in Eindhoven and in Maastricht, and worked with Luigi Snozzi, James Stirling and Aldo van Eyck. He opened his own office in 1979, and built his first project, a library and exhibition gallery in Heerlen in 1983. His Chamber of Commerce in Maastricht, situated next to the River Maas (1988) combines a modernist simplicity and the use of pilotis with large brick surfaces leading to the old city and nearby factory complex. Water is again an element in the composition of his structures for the Haans Company in Tillburg (1989), a complex sharing numerous stylistic similarities with the NAI buildings in Rotterdam. Though inevitably contested by other architects because of its highly symbolic presence for the profession, the Netherlands Architecture Institute confirms Jo Coenen as a competent and inventive designer.

Der 1949 in Heerlen (Niederlande) geborene Jo Coenen beendete 1979 sein Architekturstudium an der Technischen Hochschule in Eindhoven. Von 1976 bis 1979 war er in Eindhoven und Maastricht als Dozent tätig und arbeitete mit Luigi Snozzi, James Stirling und Aldo van Eyck. 1979 gründete er sein eigenes Architekturbüro. 1983 errichtete er sein erstes Bauprojekt, eine Bibliothek und Kunstgalerie in Heerlen. Bei der von ihm erbauten, direkt an der Maas gelegenen Handelskammer in Maastricht (1988) kombinierte Coenen modernistische Schlichtheit mit Pilotis, deren große Ziegelsteinverkleidungen einen Übergang zur Altstadt und dem nahegelegenen Fabrikkomplex darstellen. Auch bei seinem Entwurf für die Handelsgesellschaft Haans in Tilburg (1989) bildete Wasser eine wichtige Komponente. Dieser Gebäudekomplex trägt zahlreiche stilistische Übereinstimmungen mit dem Niederländischen Architekturinstitut in Rotterdam. Gerade das NAI, das aufgrund seiner starken symbolischen Bedeutung für diesen Berufsstand von anderen Architekten kontrovers diskutiert wurde, bekräftigte Jo Coenens Ruf als kompetenter und innovativer Designer.

Né en 1949 à Heerlen (Pays-Bas), Jo Coenen passe son diplôme de l'Université de Technologie d'Eindhoven en 1979. De 1976 à 1979, il enseigne déjà à Eindhoven et à Maastricht, et travaille avec Luigi Snozzi, James Stirling et Aldo van Eyck. Il ouvre sa propre agence en 1979, et réalise son premier projet, une bibliothèque et une galerie d'exposition à Heerlen, en 1983. Sa Chambre de commerce, à Maastricht, au bord de la Meuse (1988) mêle simplicité moderniste, pilotis et larges parois de brique, qui rappellent la vieille cité et le complexe industriel tout proche. L'eau participe aussi à la composition de son ensemble pour la société Haans, à Tilburg (1989), complexe qui présente de nombreuses similitudes avec le NAI de Rotterdam. Bien qu'inévitablement contesté par d'autres architectes, du fait de son importance pour la profession, l'Institut néerlandais d'architecture confirme le talent et l'inventivité de Jo Coenen.

Interior of the Netherlands Architecture Institute (NAI), with the tower of the Boymans-van Beuningen Museum visible outside.

Innenansicht des Niederländischen Architekturinstitutes (NAI), mit dem Turm des Museums Boymans-van Beuningen im Hintergrund.

Intérieur de l'Institut Néerlandais d'Architecture (NAI) avec, non loin, la tour du Boymans-van Beuningen Museum.

Netherlands Architecture Institute, Rotterdam 1988–1993

The Netherlands Architecture Institute (NAI) was formed in 1988, the same year that Jo Coenen was chosen as the designer for this building, which opened on October 23, 1993. Six architects had been invited for the competition, including Rem Koolhaas, who designed the nearby Museum park (with the French landscape architect Yves Brunier) as well as the new Kunsthal. Both of these are situated next to the Boymans-van Beuningen museum on the Hobokenplein, formerly a wasteland used for parking cars. Coenen's structure is clearly divided into several sections corresponding to the substantial reserves of the NAI (one million documents or models from 1825 to the present), the exhibition area, the library, and the entrance hall and foyer. As the architect says, "The use of material is sober. The concrete skeleton dominates the image, supplemented by steel, glass, wood and brickwork. The main building is of glass, and like the plinth building allows the concrete load-bearing structure behind it to be seen."
A steel tower the same height as the copper tower of the neighboring Boymans-van Beuningen Museum signals this strong architectural presence.

Das Niederländische Architekturinstitut (NAI) wurde 1988 gegründet. Im gleichen Jahr ernannte man Jo Coenen zum Architekten für das am 23. Oktober 1993 eröffnete Gebäude. Zur Ausschreibung waren sechs Architekten eingeladen, u. a. Rem Koolhaas, der (zusammen mit dem französischen Landschaftsarchitekten Yves Brunier) den nahegelegenen Museumspark sowie die neue Kunsthalle entworfen hatte. Beide befinden sich neben dem Museum Boymans-van Beuningen am Hobokenplein auf einem ehemaligen Brachgelände, das als Parkplatz diente. Coenens Entwurf ist deutlich in verschiedene Bereiche unterteilt – Depots und Archive des NAI (eine Million Dokumente und Modelle von 1825 bis zur Gegenwart), Ausstellungshallen, Bibliothek und Leseraum, Eingangshalle und Foyer. Coenen selbst über das Gebäude: »Der Materialgebrauch ist nüchtern: Die Betonskelettkonstruktion beherrscht das Bild – ergänzt von Stahl, Glas, Holz und Ziegelmauerwerk. Das Hauptgebäude besteht aus Glas und ermöglicht so einen Blick auf die tragende Betonkonstruktion und das Sockelgebäude.« Ein Stahlturm, dessen Höhe dem kupfernen Turm des benachbarten Boymans-van Beuningen Museum entspricht, zeugt von der ausdrucksstarken architektonischen Präsenz dieses Bauwerks.

L'Institut national néerlandais d'architecture (NAI) a été créé en 1988, et Joe Coenen a été choisi la même année pour construire ce bâtiment, qui a ouvert ses portes le 23 octobre 1993. Six architectes avaient été invités à concourir, dont Rem Koolhaas, qui concevait alors le Museum Park (avec l'architecte-paysagiste Yves Brunier) et le nouveau Kunsthal. Le NAI et le Kunsthal se dressent non loin du musée Boymans-van Beuningen, sur le Hobokenplein, parcelle de terrain longtemps abandonnée au stationnement des voitures. L'édifice de Coenen est nettement divisé en plusieurs sections, correspondant aux importantes collections de l'Institut (1 million de documents et maquettes, de 1825 à nos jours), à l'espace d'exposition, à la bibliothèque, au hall d'entrée et au foyer. Comme le déclare l'architecte: «L'utilisation des matériaux est sobre. Le squelette en béton domine, entouré d'acier, de verre, de bois et de brique. Le bâtiment principal est en verre, et comme pour le bâtiment bas, laisse entrevoir la structure porteuse en béton.» Une tour d'acier de la même hauteur que la tour voisine, parée de cuivre, du Boymans-van Beuningen Museum, signale cette forte présence architecturale.

Page 74/75: To the left, an aerial view shows the proximity of the NAI to the large buildings of downtown Rotterdam. To the right, above, the archive storage building; below, the exhibitions building, in the foreground. Page 76/77: The tallest element of the NAI contains an auditorium on the lowest level, offices and part of the library.

Seite 74/75: Links: Das Luftbild zeigt die Nähe des NAI zu den großen Bauwerken der Rotterdamer Innenstadt. Rechts oben: Das Archivgebäude. Unten: Das Gebäude mit den Ausstellungshallen im Vordergrund. Seite 76/77: Das höchste Gebäude des NAI umfaßt ein Auditorium im untersten Geschoß sowie Verwaltungsräume und Teile der Bibliothek.

Page 74/75: A gauche, vue aérienne du NAI à proximité des grands bâtiments du centre de Rotterdam. En haut et à droite, le bâtiment des archives, et en-dessous, au premier plan, les bâtiments des expositions. Page 76/77: La partie la plus haute du NAI contient un auditorium, des bureaux, et une section de la bibliothèque.

Sir Norman **Foster**

Detail of the Torre de Collserola,
Barcelona.

Detail des Torre de Collserola,
Barcelona.

Détail de la Torre de Collserola,
Barcelone.

Born in Manchester in 1935, Norman Foster studied at the University of Manchester and at Yale in 1963. After working briefly with Richard Buckminster Fuller, he founded "Team 4" with Richard Rogers, and created Foster Associates in 1967. Knighted in 1990, Sir Norman Foster is one most highly visible and successful architects in the world. Despite a slowdown in construction across large parts of the world, Foster's office had forty projects in different stages of development at the end of 1994, including the Commerzbank in Frankfurt, the tallest building in Europe, and Hong Kong's new airport. Recently completed projects include the widely published Hong Kong and Shanghai Bank tower in Hong Kong, and the terminal for Standsted Airport (1981–91), both of which carry Foster's penchant for technologically oriented architecture to new heights. Once labeled "high-tech" his style has however become less visibly machine-like, evolving toward a crisp modernity which is as easily accepted in Tokyo as in Saudi Arabia.

Norman Foster wurde 1935 in Manchester geboren und studierte bis 1963 an der University of Manchester und an der Yale University. Nach kurzer Zusammenarbeit mit Buckminster Fuller gründete Foster zusammen mit Richard Rogers das »Team 4« und 1967 »Foster Associates«. 1990 wurde er in den Adelsstand erhoben. Sir Norman Foster zählt zu den herausragendsten Architekten weltweit, und trotz einer spürbaren Rezession im Baugewerbe in vielen Teilen der Welt konnte sein Büro zum Jahresabschluß 1994 40 verschiedene Bauprojekte in unterschiedlichen Bauphasen vermelden, u. a. die Commerzbank in Frankfurt, das höchste Gebäude Europas, und Hongkongs neuen Flughafen. Zu den kürzlich fertiggestellten Bauten gehören das Gebäude der Hongkong and Shanghai Bank in Hongkong sowie der Terminal des Standsted Airport (1981–91). Beide Bauwerke trieben Fosters Begeisterung für technisch ausgerichtete Architektur zu neuen, ungeahnten Höhen. Dennoch wirkt sein einst als »High-Tech« beschriebener Stil heute weniger maschinenartig und tendiert eher zu einer lebendigen Moderne, die man in Tokio ebenso akzeptiert wie in Saudi Arabien.

Né à Manchester en 1935, Norman Foster étudie à l'Université de sa ville et à Yale, en 1963. Après avoir brièvement travaillé avec Richard Buckminster Fuller, il fonde «Team 4», avec Richard Rogers, puis Foster Associates, en 1967. Anobli en 1990, Sir Norman Foster est l'un des plus célèbres et des plus recherchés architectes du monde. Malgré un ralentissement général dans la construction, son agence travaillait sur 40 projets fin 1994, dont la Commerzbank de Francfort sur le Main, la plus haute tour d'Europe, et le nouvel aéroport de Hong Kong. Parmi ses dernières réalisations, on peut citer, la tour de la Hong Kong and Shanghai Bank, à Hong Kong, et le terminal de l'aéroport de Standsted (Londres, 1981–91), qui l'ont fait franchir de nouveaux sommets technologiques. Jadis étiqueté «High-Tech», son style est cependant devenu moins agressivement «machiniste», évoluant vers une modernité épurée, aussi bien accueillie à Tokyo qu'en Arabie Saoudite.

Carré d'Art, Nîmes
1985–1993

The mayor of Nîmes, Jean Bousquet, who is also the President of the Cacharel clothing company, instigated the 1984 competition which selected Sir Norman Foster to design a new "médiathèque" on a highly visible and historically sensitive site facing the temple known as the Maison Carrée, dating from between 10 and 5 B.C. Situated at the end of the Boulevard Victor Hugo which leads from the city's Roman arena (90–120 A.D.) to the Maison Carrée, Foster's Carré d'Art is a an example of how good contemporary architecture can fit into an historical site without any agressivity. A comparison to the classical designs of Ludwig Mies van der Rohe may be appropriate in this instance. Half of the nine story structure is located underground, and a five story internal courtyard brings light to lower levels. One criticism levelled at the Carré d'Art is that the very large atrium space drives the galleries and other public spaces into the edges of the building. It should also be noted that the coexistence of a library and a contemporary art museum in the same structure has not yet proved to enhance the function of either entity.

Jean Bousquet, Bürgermeister von Nîmes und Direktor der Bekleidungsfirma Cacharel – inizierte 1984 einen Architekturwettbewerb, den Sir Norman Foster gewann. Aufgabe war der Entwurf einer neuen »Médiathèque« auf einem weithin sichtbaren und historisch hochsensiblen Gelände gegenüber einem römischen Tempel aus der Zeit zwischen 10 und 5 v.Chr., dem Maison Carrée. Fosters Carré d'Art, das am Ende des Boulevard Victor Hugo liegt, der vom römischen Amphitheater (90–120 n.Chr.) zum Maison Carrée führt, ist ein hervorragendes Beispiel dafür, wie sich moderne Architektur in eine historische Umgebung einfügen läßt. Der Vergleich mit Mies van der Rohes klassischen Entwürfen drängt sich förmlich auf. Die Hälfte des neungeschossigen Gebäudes wurde unterirdisch angelegt, wobei ein fünf Stockwerke hoher Innenhof den unteren Geschossen genügend Licht bringt. Dieses sehr große Atrium zog die Kritik auf sich, da es die Galerien und die anderen dem Publikumsverkehr geöffneten Räume an den Rand des Bauwerkes drängt. Außerdem hat sich bisher nicht gezeigt, daß die Koexistenz einer Bibliothek und eines Museums mit zeitgenössischer Kunst im gleichen Gebäude vorteilhaft ist für die Funktionstüchtigkeit beider Einrichtungen.

C'est le maire de Nîmes, Jean Bousquet, par ailleurs président de l'entreprise de prêt-à-porter Cacharel, qui lança, en 1984, le concours qui chargea Sir Norman Foster de créer cette nouvelle médiathèque. L'emplacement prévu était hautement sensible puisque situé face au temple connu sous le nom de Maison Carrée, construit entre 10 et 5 av. J.-C. Erigé à l'extrémité du boulevard Victor-Hugo qui mène des arènes romaines (90–120) à la Maison Carrée, le Carré d'Art est exemplaire de la manière dont une bonne architecture contemporaine peut s'intégrer – sans agressivité aucune – dans un site historique. En l'espèce, la comparaison avec les projets classicisants de Ludwig Mies van der Rohe ne serait pas inappropriée. La moitié de cette construction de neuf niveaux est enterrée dans le sol, et une cour intérieure de cinq étages de haut éclaire les volumes inférieurs. Certains critiques ont fait remarquer que la taille de cet atrium repoussait les galeries d'exposition et les autres espaces publics dans les coins… On pourrait également faire remarquer que la coexistence d'une bibliothèque et d'un musée d'art contemporain dans le même bâtiment n'a pas encore prouvé son effet synergique.

To the left two interior views of the Carré d'Art, with its large, amply lit central atrium. To the right, the façade of the Roman Maison Carrée, as seen opposite the Carré d'Art, whose own classicism is meant to be a distant echo of the earlier structure.

Links: Zwei Innenansichten des Carré d'Art mit seinem großen, lichtdurchfluteten Atrium. Rechts: Die Fassade des römischen Maison Carrée, aus der Sicht des genau gegenüberliegenden Carré d'Art, dessen klassizistische Bauweise auf die viel ältere Konstruktion gegenüber anspielt.

A gauche, deux vues intérieures du Carré d'Art, à l'atrium central abondamment éclairé. A droite, la façade de la Maison Carrée, vue du Carré d'Art, dont le classicisme est un rappel discret de l'équilibre du bâtiment antique.

Reichstag Project
1993–

On June 29, 1994 the German Bundestag formally approved the final scheme of Sir Norman Foster to renovate the building designed by Paul Wallot at the end of the 19th century, and to add a dome close to the point where one had stood for much of the history of the structure. The announcement that Berlin would succeed Bonn as the new capital of a united Germany came on June 21, 1991 – and on October 31, 1991 the decision to renovate the Reichstag and make it the seat of the Bundestag was made. The international competition chose three winning designs at the same time as Axel Schultes was picked for the neighboring Spreebogen master plan. The Dutch architect Pi de Bruijn and Santiago Calatrava were then eliminated in favor of Foster, whose final design calls for a light dome intended to bring ample daylight into the parlia-

Am 29. Juni 1994 stimmte der Bundestag Sir Norman Fosters endgültigem Entwurf zur Renovierung des von Paul Wallot Ende des 19. Jahrhunderts entworfenen Reichstags zu. Das Gebäude sollte wieder eine Kuppel erhalten, möglichst an der Stelle, an der sich auch die ursprüngliche Kuppel befunden hatte. Am 21. Juni 1991 war Berlin zur neuen Hauptstadt des wiedervereinigten Deutschlands erklärt worden, und bereits am 31. Oktober fiel die Entscheidung, den Reichtstag renovieren zu lassen und zum Sitz des Bundestages zu ernennen. Im Rahmen der internationalen Ausschreibung erreichten auch die Entwürfe des niederländischen Architekten Pi de Bruijn und des Spaniers Santiago Calatrava die zweite Runde und wurden zusammen mit Norman Fosters Konzept als Sieger nominiert, schieden dann aber zugunsten Fosters aus. Gleichzeitig betraute

Le 29 juin 1994, le Bundestag a officiellement approuvé les plans de Sir Norman Foster pour la rénovation du bâtiment dessiné par Paul Wallot à la fin du XIXème siècle, et en particulier l'adjonction d'un dôme, pratiquement au même emplacement que l'ancien. La désignation de Berlin comme nouvelle capitale de l'Allemagne réunifiée, à la place de Bonn, avait été annoncée le 21 juin 1991, et c'est le 31 octobre 1991 que fut prise la décision de rénover le Reichstag pour en faire le nouveau siège du Bundestag. Le concours international retint trois projets, ainsi que le plan de masse d'Axel Schultes pour la zone du Spreebogen. L'architecte néerlandais Pi de Bruijn et Santiago Calatrava furent écartés en faveur de Foster, dont le projet final réintroduisait un dôme transparent destiné à éclairer l'amphithéâtre. Foster proposa également d'ouvrir ce bâtiment sévère, en

mentary chamber. He also makes a point of opening up the closed structure, for example allowing visitors to visit the roof of the building. Requested by German parliament itself, the idea of a dome replaced Foster's original, tent-like concept. The final scheme, which should be completed by the end of the century, calls for 12 000 m² of primary net usable area.

man Axel Schultes mit der Gestaltung des benachbarten Spreebogens. Fosters endgültiger Entwurf sieht eine Lichtkuppel vor, die ausreichend Tageslicht in den Plenarsaal läßt. Außerdem strebt Foster eine Öffnung des geschlossenen Bauwerks an, indem er z. B. die Dachkonstruktion für Besucher zugänglich macht. Sein ursprüngliches, zeltartiges Konzept wurde erst auf Bitte des Bundestages durch eine Kuppel ersetzt. Das Gebäude wird voraussichtlich gegen Endes des Jahrhunderts fertiggestellt und verfügt dann über eine Nettonutzfläche von 12 000 m².

permettant, par exemple, aux visiteurs de déambuler sur les toits. A la demande du parlement lui-même, un dôme a été substitué au concept de tente, initialement proposé par l'architecte britannique. La réalisation définitive, prévue pour la fin du siècle, offrira 12 000 m² d'espace utile.

Page 82/83. After numerous changes, and at the request of the German parliament, Sir Norman Foster designed a dome for the Reichstag. Model photos and the drawing to the right demonstrate how the structure will bring light into the building.

Seite 82/83: Nach zahlreichen Abänderungen und auf Bitte des Bundestages entwarf Sir Norman Foster eine Kuppel für den Reichstag. Die Modellfotografien und Zeichnungen (rechts) zeigen, wie diese Konstruktion das Gebäude mit Licht versorgt.

Page 82/83: Après de nombreuses modifications, et à la demande du parlement allemand, Sir Norman Foster a dessiné une coupole pour le Reichstag. Les photographies de la maquette et le dessin, à droite, expliquent la façon dont elle éclairera le bâtiment.

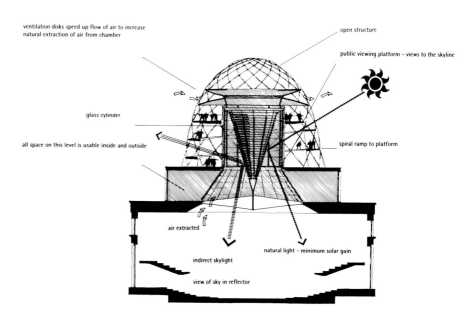

Torre de Collserola, Barcelona
1988–1992

Inaugurated on June 27, 1992, the Torre de Collserola is 288 meters tall, with a public viewing platform situated at 135 meters above ground. Held to the mountainside, 440 meters above sea-level by three pairs of guy wires made of pre-tensioned high strength steel, the tower is extremely stable, despite its extremely thin (4.5 meter diameter) shaft. As always, Norman Foster is fascinated by the technological aspects of his buildings, calling on the most sophisticated techniques and materials available. The project description made by Foster's office proudly points out for example that "the upper guys are made from Aramid fiber cable which does not conduct electricity so makes unrestricted transmission and reception of signals possible." Foster is also proud of the fact that a more conventional design for a tower of this height would have required a main shaft more than six times broader (25 meters in diameter). It was in May 1988 that the British architect won the competition for a "monumental technological element" as part of the city's renovation for the 1992 Summer Olympic Games.

Der am 27. Juni 1992 eingeweihte, 288 Meter hohe Torre de Collserola besitzt in 135 Metern Höhe eine dem Publikumsverkehr zugängliche Aussichtsplattform. Der Turm wird auf der dem Gebirge zugewandten Seite in 440 Metern Höhe über dem Meeresspiegel von drei doppelten Abspannseilen aus vorgespanntem hochfestem Stahl gehalten und ist – trotz des extrem geringen Durchmessers (4,5 Meter) des Säulenschaftes – außerordentlich standfest. Auch hier begeisterte sich Foster für die technologischen Aspekte seines Bauwerks, die den Einsatz hochentwickelter Techniken und Materialien erforderten. Sein Architekturbüro vermeldet in der Projektbeschreibung nicht ohne Stolz: »... die oberen Abspannseile wurden aus nicht leitender Aramidfaser gefertigt, so daß ein ungestörtes Senden und Empfangen von Funksignalen möglich wird.« Darüber hinaus ist Foster sehr stolz darauf, daß ein konventionellerer Entwurf eines Turms von dieser Größe einen sechsmal breiteren Säulenschaft mit einem Durchmesser von 25 Metern erfordert hätte. Mit diesem Konzept hatte der britische Architekt im Mai 1988 die Ausschreibung für ein »monumentales technologisches Element« gewonnen, die zu den Sanierungsplänen der Stadt für die Olympischen Sommerspiele 1992 gehörte.

Inaugurée le 27 juin 1992, la Torre de Collserola s'élève à une hauteur de 288 m, et comporte une plate-forme d'observation à 135 m. Accrochée au flanc d'une montagne, à 440 m au-dessus du niveau de la mer, par trois paires de haubans d'acier haute résistance pré-tensionnés, cette tour est extrêmement stable, malgré la finesse de son mât central (4,5 m de diamètre). Comme toujours, Foster est fasciné par les aspects technologiques de ses constructions et n'hésite pas à faire appel aux techniques et aux matériaux les plus sophistiqués du moment. Le descriptif du projet publié par le bureau de l'architecte relève ainsi que «les haubans supérieurs sont des câbles en fibre Aramid non conducteurs de l'électricité, qui rendent possible une réception et une transmission parfaite des signaux». Foster fait également remarquer, avec fierté, qu'une conception conventionnelle pour une tour de cette hauteur aurait exigé un mât principal six fois plus important (25 m de diamètre). C'est en mai 1988 que l'architecte britannique a remporté le concours pour ce «monument technologique», prévu par le plan de modernisation de la capitale catalane lancé à l'occasion des Jeux Olympiques d'Eté 1992.

Page 84/85: Few would deny that Sir Norman Foster is at his best when tackling the sort of technological challenges represented by this 288 meter high tower. A spectacular symbol, it remains extremely light and elegant.

Seite 84/85: Man wird wohl kaum bestreiten können, daß Sir Norman Foster angesichts der technischen Herausforderungen des 288 Meter hohen Turms zur Höchstform auflief. Dieser Turm bildet ein aufsehenerregendes und zugleich luftiges und elegantes Wahrzeichen Barcelonas.

Page 84/85: Sir Norman Foster se sent certainement à son aise lorsqu'il doit répondre à un défi technologique comme celui de cette tour de 288 m de haut. Symbole spectaculaire, elle reste néanmoins extrêmement légère et élégante.

The concept

- The only constant is change

- A new symbol

- not a conversion

- The new age – the future.

- max freedom here!

Page 86/87: A site plan and a panoramic view of Barcelona and the Torre de Collserola show how the structure dominates the city without marring its skyline.

Seite 86/87: Lageplan und Panoramaansicht von Barcelona und dem Torre de Collserola veranschaulichen, wie das Bauwerk das Bild der Stadt beherrscht, ohne die Stadtsilhouette zu beeinträchtigen.

Page 86/87: Plan du site et vue panoramique de Barcelone et de la Torre de Collserola, qui domine la ville sans porter atteinte au paysage.

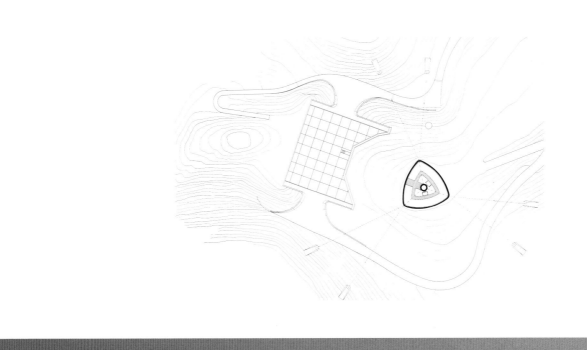

Nicholas **Grimshaw**

A 1965 graduate of the Architectural Association, Nicholas Grimshaw was born in 1939 in London. He created his present firm, Nicholas Grimshaw and Partners Ltd., in 1980. Known as a practitioner of the "high tech" style, Grimshaw has built numerous industrial structures, including factories for Herman Miller in Bath (1976), B.M.W. at Bracknell (1980), the furniture maker Vitra at Weil am Rhein, Germany (1981) or for *The Financial Times* in London in 1988. Despite highly visible projects such as the British Pavilion at the Expo '92 in Seville, Nicholas Grimshaw is not as well known internationally as Richard Rogers or Norman Foster, other members of the so-called London School. Like Foster though, Nicholas Grimshaw seems to have shifted the emphasis in his work from considerations of surface articulation to a more profound interest in light and space, as seen in the Waterloo terminal.

Der 1939 in London geborene Nicholas Grimshaw beendete 1965 sein Studium an der Architectural Association. Seine heutige Firma – Nicholas Grimshaw and Partners Ltd. – gründete er im Jahre 1980. Als Vertreter des »High Tech«-Stils errichtete Grimshaw zahlreiche Industriebauten, einschließlich der Fabrikanlagen für Herman Miller in Bath (1976), für BMW in Bracknell (1980), für den Möbelhersteller Vitra in Weil am Rhein (1981) oder für die *Financial Times* in London (1988). Trotz seiner vielbeachteten Projekte wie etwa dem Pavillon Großbritanniens für die Expo '92 in Sevilla ist Nicholas Grimshaw international weit weniger bekannt als Richard Rogers oder Norman Foster – andere Mitglieder der sogenannten London School. Dennoch scheint sich Nicholas Grimshaw (ebenso wie Foster) von seinen früheren Überlegungen zur Oberflächengestaltung zu entfernen und bei seinen heutigen Arbeiten mehr Wert auf Licht und Raum zu legen – wie der Terminal der Waterloo Station belegt.

Diplômé de l'Architectural Association en 1965, Nicholas Grimshaw est né en 1939 à Londres. Il a créé son agence actuelle, Nicholas Grimshaw and Partners Ltd., en 1980. Adepte reconnu du style «High Tech», il a construit de nombreux bâtiments industriels, dont des usines pour Herman Miller à Bath (1976), B.M.W. à Bracknell (1980), le fabricant de meubles Vitra, à Weil am Rhein, en Allemagne (1981), et pour le *Financial Times*, à Londres, en 1988. Même s'il a réalisé des projets très remarqués comme le pavillon britannique d'Expo 92 à Séville, Grimshaw n'est pas aussi internationalement connu que Foster ou Rogers, autres représentants de ce qu'il est convenu d'appeler l'Ecole de Londres. Comme Foster, cependant, il semble faire évoluer ses préoccupations d'articulation des surfaces vers un intérêt plus marqué pour la lumière et l'espace, comme le montre sa nouvelle gare Eurostar de Waterloo.

Looking down into the Waterloo Terminal, London.

Blick in den Londoner Bahnhof Waterloo Station.

Vue en plongée sur la nouvelle gare Eurostar de Waterloo, à Londres.

Waterloo Station, London
1990–1993

"Good detailing comes first and foremost, then making buildings understandable spatially and organizationally," says Nicholas Grimshaw who built this 400 meter long addition to London's Waterloo Station, intended as the five track arrival point for the French/British/Belgian Channel Tunnel Eurostar. The long, open sight lines and wide, asymmetrical spans ranging between 35 and 50 meters, arching over the tracks, do indeed make the entire structure readily understandable. Color is exceptionally part of the design in the form of the bright blue roof trusses, in a building which looks back to the heritage of such engineers or architects as Joseph Paxton, Gustave Eiffel, Pierre Chareau and Jean Prouvé. A curved form imposed by the turning radius of the trains and the nature of the site led Grimshaw to use a "loose fit" of overlapping glass panes which admit ample light to the track areas. "Fitting in," says Grimshaw, "has to do with things like scale and height, light and shade, the feeling that a building has at ground level, at people level... It's not to do with just matching the building next door."

»Gelungene Detailarbeit steht an erster Stelle, erst danach folgt die Verständlichkeit der räumlichen und organisatorischen Aspekte eines Gebäudes«, sagt Grimshaw, der die 400 Meter lange neue Bahnhofshalle für den Londoner Bahnhof Waterloo Station entwarf. Dieser Erweiterungsbau dient als Endstation für die französischen/britischen/belgischen Eurostarzüge durch den Kanaltunnel. Die asymmetrischen, zwischen 35 und 50 Meter breiten Satteldächer, die sich über die fünf Gleise spannen, und die große Transparenz des Baus lassen die gesamte Struktur tatsächlich leicht verständlich erscheinen. Bei diesem Gebäude, das auf das Erbe solch bedeutender Ingenieure und Architekten wie Joseph Paxton, Gustave Eiffel, Pierre Chareau und Jean Prouvé zurückzugreifen scheint, übernimmt die Farbe – in Gestalt eines leuchtendblauen Dachgerüstes – eine wichtige Rolle. Die geschwungene Form des Wendekreises der Züge und die Gegebenheiten des Geländes veranlaßten Grimshaw, eine Dachkonstruktion aus einander überlappenden Glaspanelen zu wählen, die ausreichend Licht auf den Gleisbereich fallen lassen. »Das Einfügen in die Umgebung«, sagt er, »hängt von solchen Aspekten wie Maßstab und Höhe, Licht und Schatten oder der Atmosphäre ab, die ein Gebäude auf ebenerdigem Niveau, auf Höhe der Menschen besitzt ... Es geht nicht darum, das Bauwerk einfach nur auf das benachbarte Gebäude abzustimmen.«

«C'est la qualité du détail qui prime, car elle rend les constructions compréhensibles, aussi bien dans l'espace que dans leur organisation», déclare Nicholas Grimshaw, qui vient de construire sur 400 m de long cette extension de Waterloo Station qui constitue le terminal à cinq voies du réseau franco-belgo-britannique, Eurostar. Les lignes allongées et transparentes, les longues portées asymétriques des arcs au-dessus des voies (de 35 à 50 m), rendent en effet la structure parfaitement lisible. La couleur (dont le bleu éclatant des poutrelles de la couverture) fait partie intégrante de la conception de cet édifice qui ne renie pas l'héritage d'ingénieurs ou d'architectes comme Joseph Paxton, Gustave Eiffel, Pierre Chareau ou Jean Prouvé. La forme courbe, imposée par le rayon de braquage des trains et la nature du site, a conduit Grimshaw à imaginer «l'ajustement libre» de panneaux de verre de recouvrement qui diffusent un abondant éclairage sur les voies. «L'intégration, dit par ailleurs Grimshaw, se juge à des éléments comme l'échelle et la hauteur, la lumière et l'ombre, l'impression que fait un bâtiment au niveau du sol, ou à celui du passant... et pas seulement à la façon dont il s'accorde au bâtiment d'à côté.»

Page 91: A section shows the asymmetrical alignment of the structure, over the five tracks and the parking facilities which are below grade. The gentle curve of the station relates to the large turning radius of the trains, and the complexities of the site.
Page 92/93: Like a glass snake, the long glass-covered shed which forms Waterloo Terminal is seen against the South Bank urban landscape.

Seite 91: Ein Schnitt zeigt die asymmetrische Ausrichtung der Konstruktion, die sich über die fünf Gleise und die Parkflächen erstreckt, welche sich unterhalb des Geländeniveaus befinden. Die geschwungene Form des Bahnhofs steht im Zusammenhang mit dem großen Wendekreis der Züge und den Gegebenheiten des Geländes.
Seite 92/93: Vor der urbanen Landschaft der South Bank erinnert die Dachkonstruktion des Bahnhofs Waterloo Station mit ihren einander überlappenden Glaspanelen an eine lange, gläserne Schlange.

Page 91: Coupe montrant l'alignement asymétrique de la construction, au-dessus des cinq voies et des parkings en sous-sol. La courbe douce de la gare épouse l'important diamètre de braquage des trains et les complexités du site.
Page 92/93: Telle un serpent de verre, la longue verrière du «Waterloo terminal» se déploie sur fond du paysage urbain de la rive Sud de la Tamise.

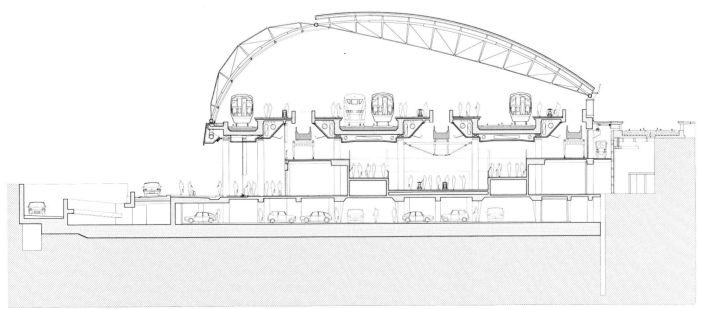

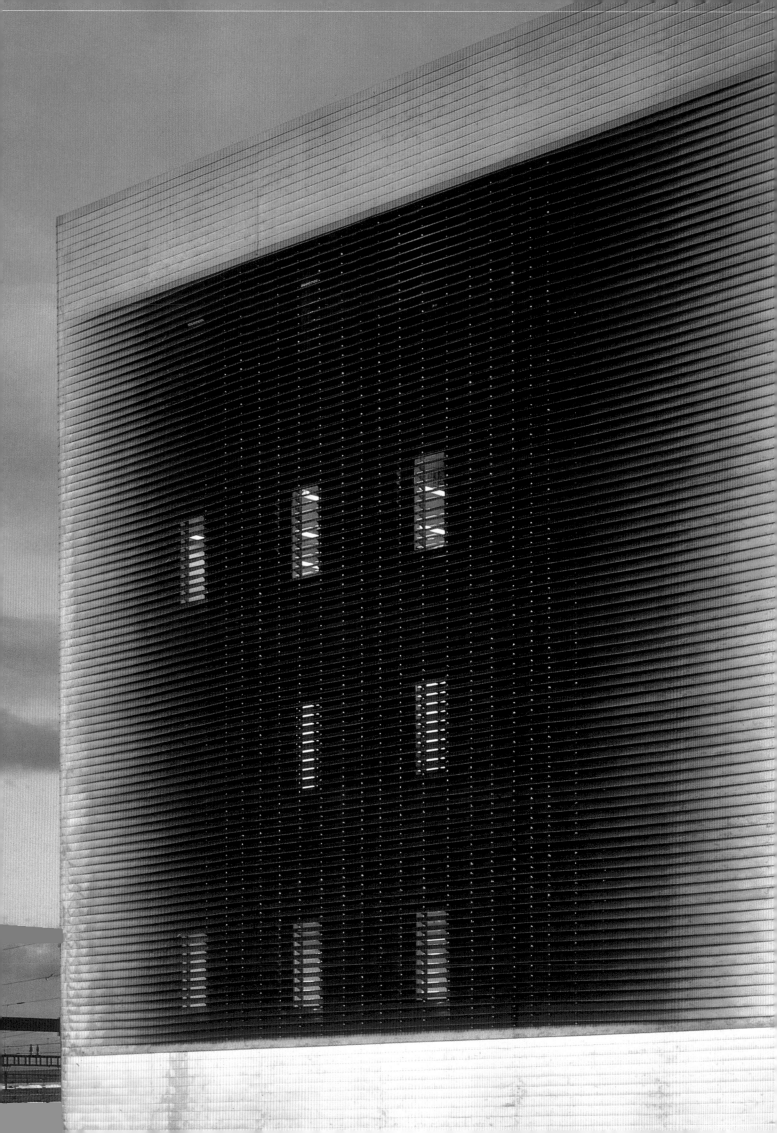

Herzog & de Meuron

Signal Box in the trainyards of Basel, Switzerland.

Stellwerk des Basler Bahnhofs, Schweiz.

Poste d'aiguillage de la gare de Bâle, en Suisse.

Jacques Herzog and Pierre de Meuron, both born in Basel in 1950 have become well-known figures beyond the architectural world since they won the competition for the Bankside Power Station in London, which the Tate Gallery hopes to make into a space for the exhibition of contemporary art by the end of the century. They won this competition in 1995 against the likes of Renzo Piano, Tadao Ando, Rafael Moneo and Rem Koolhaas. Both graduated in architecture at the ETH in Zurich in 1975, after studying with Aldo Rossi, and founded their firm Herzog & de Meuron Architecture Studio in Basel in 1978. Calling for an interaction of architecture with other forms of creativity such as painting or sculpture, they insist that construction materials should not be classified as noble or common, mixing them without concern for hierarchy. Their recent Ricola Europe Factory and Storage Building in Mulhouse (1993) or their gallery for a private collection of contemporary art in Munich (1991–92) have been widely published.

Jacques Herzog und Pierre de Meuron (beide 1950 in Basel geboren) wurden außerhalb der Architekturwelt bekannt, als sie 1995 den Wettbewerb für die Bankside Power Station in London gewannen, die die Tate Gallery bis zum Ende dieses Jahrhunderts in Ausstellungsräume für zeitgenössische Kunst verwandeln soll. Herzog und de Meuron setzten sich gegen Mitbewerber wie Renzo Piano, Tadao Ando, José Rafael Moneo und Rem Koolhaas durch. Nachdem die beiden Schüler von Aldo Rossi 1975 ihr Architekturstudium an der ETH in Zürich beendet hatten, gründeten sie 1978 das Architekturbüro Herzog & de Meuron in Basel. Auf der Suche nach Interaktion zwischen Architektur und anderen Formen von Kreativität wie Malerei oder Bildhauerkunst vertreten sie die Ansicht, daß Baumaterialien nicht in Kategorien wie edel oder preiswert unterteilt und ohne jeden Gedanken an eine hierarchische Klassifizierung miteinander kombiniert werden sollten. Ihr vor kurzem fertiggestelltes Fabrik- und Lagergebäude von Ricola Europe in Mulhouse (1993) sowie ihre Galerie für eine private Sammlung zeitgenössischer Kunst in München (1991–92) wurden in der Fachwelt ausführlich besprochen.

Jacques Herzog et Pierre de Meuron, tous deux nés à Bâle en 1950, se sont fait connaître auprès du grand public pour avoir remporté le concours de la Bankside Power Station, à Londres, centrale thermique que la Tate Gallery espère transformer en espace d'exposition pour la fin du siècle. Ils ont gagné cette compétition en 1995, contre Renzo Piano, Tadao Ando, Rafael Moneo et Rem Koolhaas. Diplômés en architecture à l'ETH de Zurich, en 1975, après avoir étudié avec Aldo Rossi comme professeur, ils fondent leur agence, Herzog & de Meuron Architecture Studio à Bâle en 1978. Faisant jouer l'interaction de l'architecture avec d'autres formes de créativité comme la peinture ou la sculpture, il se refusent à classer les matériaux en «nobles» ou «courants», les mélangeant sans se préoccuper d'une quelconque hiérarchie. Leur récente usine et entrepôt pour Ricola Europe, à Mulhouse (1993), ou leur galerie pour une collection privée d'art contemporain à Munich (1991–92), ont été abondamment publiées.

Signal Box, Basel
1992–1995

Built at a cost of 6.7 million Swiss francs, this structure houses the signal and switching equipment of the Basel train yards. Located near the old walls of the Wolf-Gottesacker cemetery, the six-story concrete building is clad with 20 centimeter wide copper strips, whose occasional twisted openings give some hint of interior activity without revealing the real nature of the inside. Acting as a Faraday Cage, which insulates the electronic equipment within from unwanted external interference, the copper wrapping of the Signal Box also dissimulates the number of floors, contrary to most technically oriented buildings, that seem anxious to display their prowess. Formerly students of Aldo Rossi, Herzog & de Meuron have written that "The reality of architecture is not built architecture. An architecture creates its own reality outside of the state of built or unbuilt and is comparable to the autonomous reality of a painting or a sculpture." What they call the "immaterial value" of their work, their skepticism about the validity of archetypes is evident in the Basel Signal Box.

Das 6,7 Millionen Schweizer Franken teure Bauwerk beherbergt die Signal- und Schaltanlagen des Basler Bahnhofs und liegt in der Nähe des alten Wolf-Gottesacker-Friedhofs. Das sechsgeschossige Betongebäude ist mit 20 Zentimeter breiten Kupferbändern verkleidet, die an einigen Stellen nach außen verdreht wurden und so einen Blick auf das Innere des Bauwerks freigeben. Die Kupferverkleidung des Stellwerks wirkt nicht nur wie ein Faradascher Käfig, der die Elektronik im Inneren des Bauwerks vor unerwarteten äußeren Einflüßen schützt, sondern verbirgt auch die Anzahl der Geschosse – im Gegensatz zu den meisten konventionellen Industriebauten, die ihre überragende Technologie begierig zu präsentieren scheinen. Die Architekten Herzog & de Meuron – ehemalige Schüler von Aldo Rossi – schrieben: »Die Wirklichkeit der Architektur ist nicht die gebaute Architektur. Eine Architektur bildet außerhalb dieser Zustandsform von gebaut/nicht gebaut eine eigene Wirklichkeit, vergleichbar der autonomen Wirklichkeit eines Bildes oder einer Skulptur.« Der »immaterielle Wert« ihrer Arbeit, wie die beiden Architekten ihre Skepsis gegenüber der Gültigkeit von Archetypen bezeichnen, tritt beim Basler Stellwerk deutlich zutage.

Construit pour 6,7 millions de francs suisses, ce bâtiment abrite les équipements d'aiguillage et de signalisation du trafic ferroviaire bâlois. Implanté près des anciens murs du cimetière Wolf-Gottesacker, ce bâtiment en béton à six niveaux est recouvert de bardeaux de cuivre de vingt centimètres de large. Soulevés par endroits, ils laissent passer la lumière et donnent une idée de l'activité qu'ils masquent sans rien révéler de l'intérieur. Jouant le rôle d'une cage de Faraday, qui isole les installations électroniques de toute interférence extérieure, cette couverture de cuivre dissimule également le nombre de niveaux, contrairement à de nombreux bâtiments techniques pressés d'exposer leurs entrailles. Anciens elèves d'Aldo Rossi, Herzog et de Meuron ont écrit que «la réalité de l'architecture n'est pas le construit. Une architecture crée sa propre réalité en dehors de l'état de construit ou de non-construit; elle est comparable à la réalité autonome d'une peinture ou d'une sculpture». Ce qu'ils appellent la «valeur immatérielle» de leur œuvre, leur scepticisme sur la validité des archétypes, transparaît à l'évidence dans ce poste d'aiguillage.

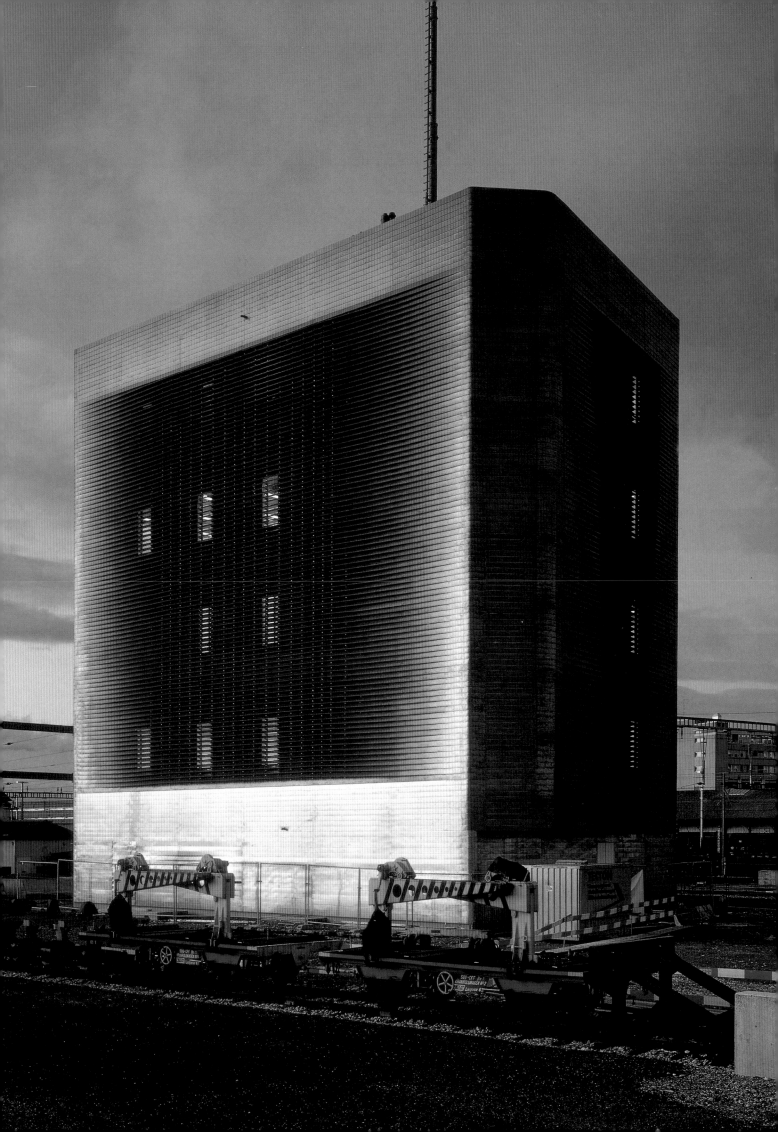

Rem **Koolhaas**

Rem Koolhaas was born in The Hague in 1944. Before studying at the Architectural Association in London, he tried his hand as a journalist for the *Haagse Post* and as a screenwriter. It is thus no surprise that he received public attention with the 1978 publication of his book *Delirious New York* where he argued that the glory of the city lies in the exceptional, the excessive, the extreme, in what he calls the "culture of congestion." In fact, the theories of Rem Koolhaas on contemporary urbanism only began to take built form when he was named head architect of the Euralille project in Lille in 1988. Given his considerable international reputation it may seem surprising that he has in fact built so little, but many reputations in contemporary architecture have been based more on theoretical work than on actual construction. But there is a harmony between his ideas and the recent buildings. As a critic at *The New York Times* has written, "Mr Koolhaas seeks a lyrical mythology for the city as it exists today."

Rem Koolhaas wurde 1944 in Den Haag geboren. Bevor er sein Studium an der Architectural Association in London aufnahm, versuchte er sein Glück als Journalist für die »Haagse Post« und als Drehbuchautor. Es überrascht denn auch nicht, daß er 1978 mit seinem Buch »Delirious New York« auf großes öffentliches Interesse stieß, in dem er argumentierte, daß der Glanz der Großstadt im Außergewöhnlichen, Exzessiven, Extremen liege – was er als »culture of congestion« (Kultur der Ballung) bezeichnet. Seine Theorien zur zeitgenössischen Urbanistik nahmen aber erst Formen an, als man ihn 1988 zum Chefarchitekten des Euralille-Projekts in Lille ernannte. In Anbetracht seines internationalen Rufes mag es verwundern, daß Koolhaas tatsächlich erst sehr wenig gebaut hat, aber in der modernen Architektur beruht so manche Reputation eher auf theoretischen Abhandlungen als auf wirklich ausgeführten Bauten. Zwischen seinen Ideen und seinen Bauwerken besteht jedoch durchaus eine harmonische Verbindung. Ein Kritiker der »New York Times« schrieb: »Rem Koolhaas strebt für die heutige Großstadt eine lyrische Mythologie an.«

Rem Koolhaas est né à La Haye en 1944. Avant d'étudier à l'Architectural Association de Londres, il s'essaye au journalisme pour le «Haagse Post», et aux scenarii de films. Ceci explique sans doute le succès qu'il rencontre avec la publication de son livre «Delirious New York» (1978), où il explique que la gloire de cette ville réside dans l'exceptionnel, l'excessif, et l'extrême dans ce qu'il appelle «une culture de la congestion». En fait, ses théories sur l'urbanisme contemporain ne commencent vraiment à prendre forme que lorsqu'il est nommé architecte-en-chef du projet Euralille, en 1988. Etant donnée sa considérable notoriété, il est étonnant qu'il n'ait pas construit davantage, mais c'est le cas pour de nombreuses réputations actuelles qui reposent plus sur la théorie que sur la pratique. Une harmonie existe cependant entre ses idées et ses bâtiments récents. Comme le critique du «New York Times» a pu l'écrire: «M. Koolhaas cherche une mythologie lyrique pour la cité telle qu'elle existe aujourd'hui.»

Detail of the façade of the Grand Palais, Lille, France.

Fassadendetail des Grand Palais in Lille, Frankreich.

Détail de la façade du Grand Palais, à Lille.

Kunsthal Rotterdam, Rotterdam
1987–1992

The first building of its kind in Holland, the Kunsthal Rotterdam opened on October 31, 1992. Within its 3 300 m^2 interior, it is possible to organize five to six exhibitions simultaneously for a total of 25 exhibitions per year. Rem Koolhaas and the late French landscape architect Yves Brunier designed the Museum Park which connects the Kunsthal to the Netherlands Architecture Institute and to the nearby Boymans-van Beuningen Museum, thus offering Rotterdam an up-to-date cultural complex as sophisticated as anything Amsterdam has to offer. The Kunsthal itself is full of surprises – like the corrugated plastic or black concrete used for some façades. The characteristics of both these materials as they age may present some drawbacks. Then too, the entrance ramp which bisects the building, and indeed encourages passers-by to wander through, apparently renders access difficult for handicapped persons. Other details such as the wide metal grating used on the floor of one gallery are not appreciated by female visitors. It thus might not be possible to say that the Kunsthal is a total success, but it did draw approximately 120 000 visitors in its first year of operation (October 1992 – October 1993).

These two views of the Kunsthal Rotterdam show how the building deals with the considerable difference of level between the park and street sides, with a street-sized passage slicing through the structure.

Diese beiden Ansichten der Kunsthal Rotterdam zeigen, wie das Gebäude den beträchtlichen Niveauunterschied zwischen Park und Straßenbereich ausgleicht. Durch die Kunsthalle führt eine straßenähnliche Passage.

Ces deux vues du Kunsthal Rotterdam montrent la manière dont le bâtiment s'accommode de la considérable différence de niveau entre le parc et les rues avoisinantes. Un passage, de la largeur d'une rue, se glisse à travers le bâtiment.

Die am 31. Oktober 1992 eröffnete Kunsthal Rotterdam gilt als erstes Gebäude dieser Art in den Niederlanden. In den 3 300 m^2 großen Innenräumen lassen sich gleichzeitig bis zu sechs verschiedene Ausstellungen organisieren, so daß pro Jahr etwa 25 Wechselausstellungen möglich sind. Gemeinsam mit dem verstorbenen französischen Landschaftsarchitekten Yves Brunier entwarf Rem Koolhaas auch den Museumspark, der die Kunsthalle mit dem Niederländischen Architekturinstitut und dem nahegelegenen Museum Boymans-van Beuningen verbindet. Auf diese Weise entstand in Rotterdam ein moderner Kulturkomplex, der den Kunsttempeln Amsterdams in nichts nachsteht. Die Kunsthalle selbst steckt voller Überraschungen – wie etwa den Kunststoffwellplatten oder den Fassadenverkleidungen aus schwarzem Beton. Allerdings könnten die Eigenschaften dieser beiden Materialien noch einige Probleme mit sich bringen, da sie nicht witterungsbeständig sind. Auch der Eingangsbereich, der das Gebäude in zwei Teile teilt und zufällige Passanten zu einer Besichtigung ermutigt, ist für Behinderte und Rollstuhlfahrer nicht leicht zu erreichen. Andere Details wie das breite Metallgitter auf dem Boden einer Galerie stoßen insbesondere bei weiblichen Besuchern nicht gerade auf Begeisterung. Obwohl man die Kunsthalle aus den obengenannten Gründen nicht als einen hundertprozentigen Erfolg bezeichnen kann, zog sie bereits im ersten Jahr nach ihrer Eröffnung (Oktober 1992 – Oktober 1993) etwa 120 000 Besucher an.

Premier bâtiment de ce type construit aux Pays-Bas, le Kunsthal Rotterdam a ouvert le 31 octobre 1992. Ses 3 300 m^2 peuvent accueillir 25 expositions par an, dont cinq à six simultanément. Rem Koolhaas et l'architecte-paysagiste disparu, Yves Brunier, ont dessiné le Museum Park qui relie le Kunsthal à l'Institut National d'Architecture et au Boymans-van Beuningen Museum, offrant ainsi à Rotterdam un complexe ultramoderne sophistiqué qui peut rivaliser avec les équipements culturels d'Amsterdam. Le Kunsthal lui-même réserve de multiples surprises, comme le plastique ondulé ou le béton noir de certaines façades, matériaux qui risquent cependant de mal vieillir. La ruelle en pente qui divise en deux parties le bâtiment, et encourage les passants à le traverser, rend en réalité difficile l'accès aux handicapés. D'autres détails comme les grilles métalliques servant de sol à l'une des galeries ne sont pas appréciés des visiteuses. On ne peut donc dire que le Kunsthal soit un succès total, mais il a attiré environ 120 000 visiteurs au cours de sa première année de fonctionnement (octobre 1992 – octobre 1993).

Page 102/103: Unusual materials like corrugated plastic walls and the slant imposed by the site assure that the Kunsthal is a visually vibrant building. Above: The auditorium.

Seite 102/103: Ungewöhnliche Materialien wie Kunststoffwellplatten sowie die durch das Gelände bedingte Neigung machen die Kunsthalle zu einem optisch sehr lebendigen Bauwerk. Oben: Das Auditorium, das in die entgegengesetzte Richtung geneigt ist.

Page 102/103: Des matériaux inhabituels, comme le plastique ondulé, et le dénivellement imposé par le site, font que le Kunsthal ne laisse pas indifférent. En haut: L'auditorium, incliné dans le sens opposé à celui du site.

Grand Palais, Lille
1990–1994

Rem Koolhaas and the Office for Metropolitan Architecture (OMA) were chosen to design the master plan of the Euralille complex in November 1988. Physically separated from the rest of the buildings designed by Jean Nouvel or Christian de Portzamparc, the Grand Palais by Koolhaas is surrounded by heavily traveled roads. With a total of 50 000 m^2 of usable space and a 350 million franc budget, the Grand Palais certainly deserves its name. The 300 meter long oval structure includes a 15 000 seat rock concert hall (Zénith), three auditoriums, an 18 000 m^2, wide open exhibition hall, and parking for 1 200 cars. The first impression of any visitor who enters the building is one of surprise. A great deal of exposed concrete, and a large corrugated plastic "column of light" lead to an astonishing double staircase. Plastic, plywood and other inexpensive materials are indeed the hallmark of the Grand Palais, for budgetary reasons, but it is a measure of the talent of Koolhaas that he has turned this problem into an interesting design feature of the structure. As for the master plan of Euralille, Koolhaas has explained that the internal complexity of the Grand Palais means that it has urban design on the inside.

1988 wurden Rem Koolhaas und das Office for Metropolitan Architecture (OMA) mit der Gestaltung des Bebauungsplans für den Euralille-Komplex beauftragt. Das von den übrigen (von Jean Nouvel und Christian de Portzamparc entworfenen) Gebäuden getrennte Grand Palais liegt inmitten stark befahrener Straßen und wird mit einer Nettonutzfläche von 50 000 m^2 und einem Budget von 350 Millionen Francs seinem Namen gerecht. Die 300 Meter lange ovale Struktur umfaßt eine Rockkonzerthalle (Zénith) mit 15 000 Plätzen, drei Auditorien, eine 18 000 m^2 große, offene Ausstellungshalle und Parkplätze für 1 200 Wagen. Beim Betreten des Gebäudes erwartet den Besucher eine Überraschung: Ein Großteil des Sichtbetons und eine große »Lichtsäule« aus Kunststoffwellplatten führen zu einer erstaunlichen Doppeltreppe. Tatsächlich wurden Kunststoff, Sperrholz und andere preiswerte Materialien zum Markenzeichen des Grand Palais – nicht nur aus finanziellen Gründen. Sie gelten auch als Maßstab für Koolhaas' Talent, der ein Problem in eine interessante Designkomponente seines Bauwerks verwandelt. In bezug auf den Bebauungsplan von Euralille erklärte Koolhaas, daß die innere Komplexität des Grand Palais als urbanes Design im Inneren des Gebäudes zu verstehen sei.

Rem Koolhaas et son Office for Metropolitan Architecture (OMA) ont été retenus pour la conception du plan de masse du complexe Euralille en novembre 1988. Physiquement indépendant des bâtiments de Jean Nouvel ou de Christian de Portzamparc, le Grand Palais de Koolhaas est encerclé de voies très fréquentées. Avec sa surface de 50 000 m^2 d'espace utile et son coût de 350 millions de francs, il mérite certainement son nom. Cette structure ovale de 300 m de long comprend une salle de concerts rock de 15 000 places (le Zénith), trois auditoriums, un hall d'exposition de 18 000 m^2 et un parking pour 1 200 véhicules. La première impression du visiteur pénétrant dans le bâtiment est la surprise. Après une débauche de béton brut et une énorme «colonne de lumière» en plastique ondulé, il découvre un étonnant double-escalier. Plastique, contre-plaqué et autres matériaux bon marché sont la marque de ce Grand Palais, pour des raisons budgétaires, certes, mais aussi par choix de l'architecte, qui a réussi à tourner la difficulté en originalité. De même que pour le plan de masse d'Euralille, il a expliqué que la complexité apparente de ce Grand Palais reflétait une conception urbaine interne.

Page 105: As in Rotterdam, unusual materials and unexpected angles mark the Lille Grand Palais. Page 104: An aerial view shows how the enormous oval shape of the structure stands off from the rest of Euralille, on the upper left of the image.

Seite 105: Wie die Rotterdamer Kunsthalle zeichnet sich auch das Grand Palais in Lille durch die Verwendung ungewöhnlicher Materialien und Neigungswinkel aus. Seite 104: Die Luftansicht zeigt, wie sich die gewaltige ovale Form des Palais vom übrigen Euralille-Komplex (im oberen linken Bereich der Abbildung) abhebt.

Page 105: Comme pour Rotterdam, des matériaux peu usités et des angles inattendus marquent le Grand Palais de Lille. Page 104: Vue aérienne de l'énorme ovale de la construction qui se détache du reste d'Euralille, en partie supérieure gauche de l'image.

Alessandro **Mendini**

Born in Milan in 1931, Alessandro Mendini received his doctorate in architecture from the Milan Polytechnic University in 1959. Editor of the magazine *Casabella* from 1970 to 1976, member of the Archizoom and Superstudio groups, and editor of *Domus* from 1980 to 1985, he is the artistic director of Alessi and Swatch. In the case of the Groninger Museum too, Mendini has acted as a sort of artistic director, coordinating his own contribution with those of the French designer Philippe Starck, the Italian designer Michele de Lucchi, the Austrian architects Coop Himmelblau, and a number of Dutch collaborators. The broad range of Mendini's creativity, from journalism to architecture and design, places him in a long Italian tradition of artistic production. His radical ideas about the function of museums, and the generosity of his Dutch patrons have permitted Mendini to carry out the project of a lifetime in Groningen.

Der 1931 in Mailand geborene Architekt Alessandro Mendini erhielt 1959 an der Polytechnischen Hochschule in Mailand den Doktortitel der Architektur. Der ehemalige Herausgeber der Zeitschriften »Casabella« (1970–76) und »Domus« (1980–85) war Mitglied der Architektengruppen Archizoom und Superstudio und ist heute als Art Director von Alessi und Swatch tätig. Auch beim Groninger Museum hatte Mendini die Funktion eines künstlerischen Art Directors inne, der seinen eigenen architektonischen Beitrag mit denen des französischen Designers Philippe Starck, des italienischen Designers Michele De Lucchi, der österreichischen Architekten Coop Himmelblau und einer Reihe von niederländischen Mitarbeitern koordinierte. Mendinis breitgefächerte Kreativität – vom Journalismus bis hin zu Architektur und Design – ist typisch für die alte italienische Tradition künstlerischer Tätigkeit und Produktivität. Dank seiner radikalen Ansichten zur Aufgabe eines Museums und der Großzügigkeit seiner niederländischen Auftraggeber erhielt Mendini in Groningen die einmalige Gelegenheit, dieses wichtige Projekt zu verwirklichen.

Né à Milan en 1931, Alessandro Mendini est fait docteur en architecture de l'Université polytechnique de Milan, en 1959. Editeur du magazine «Casabella», de 1970 à 1976, membre des groupes Archizoom et Superstudio, éditeur de «Domus» de 1980 à 1985, il est directeur artistique d'Alessi et de Swatch. Pour le Groninger Museum, il a également joué en quelque sorte un rôle de directeur artistique, coordonnant sa propre contribution à celles du designer français Philippe Starck, de l'Italien Michele de Lucchi, des architectes autrichiens Coop Himmelblau, et d'un certain nombre de collaborateurs néerlandais. L'étendue de la créativité de Mendini, du journalisme à l'architecture et au design, le rattache à une longue tradition artistique italienne. Ses conceptions radicales sur la fonction des musées, et la générosité de ses clients néerlandais, lui ont permis de mener à bien, à Groningue, le projet le plus important de sa vie.

The "treasure house" tower of the Groninger Museum.

Die »Schatzkammer« des Groninger Museums.

La tour du «trésor» du Groninger Museum.

Groninger Museum, Groningen
1990–1994

An unusual project in more respects than one, the Groninger Museum forms an artificial island linked to land by a bridge over the Verbindings-kanaal. The most direct route between the central railroad station and the old town, the bridge is an obligatory point of passage for almost two million people a year, which fits in well with the museum's ambition to be as open as possible. Designed by Alessandro Mendini, former editor of the magazine *Domus,* the Groninger is also the work of Michele de Lucchi, Philippe Starck, and the Austrian architects Coop Himmelblau. Together with museum director Frans Haks, Mendini's ambition is nothing less than the creation of a "total" work of art, since both believe that no distinction should be made between art, architecture and design. The 60 meter high central tower or "treasury" is covered in gold plastic laminate, signaling the joyous or even humorous approach of Mendini. Intended as a place of display for the "old" art of the museum, the Coop Himmelblau pavilion, a last-minute replacement for a pavilion designed by the artist Frank Stella which was judged too complex and costly, may be less well adapted to its declared task than to making a statement about the unusual ways in which space can be handled. The total cost of the 8 062 m² building was 47 million florins, of which more than half was denotated by N.V. Nederlandse Gasunie in celebration of its 25th anniversary.

Das Groninger Museum, das in vielerlei Hinsicht als außergewöhnlich bezeichnet werden kann, bildet eine künstliche Insel, die mit Hilfe einer Brücke über den Verbindingskanaal mit dem Land verbunden ist. Diese Brücke stellt den direkten Verbindungsweg zwischen dem Hauptbahnhof und der Altstadt dar, den jährlich fast zwei Millionen Menschen nutzen – was gut zum Selbstverständnis des Museums paßt, das möglichst offen und zugänglich sein möchte. Für das von Alessandro Mendini (dem ehemaligen Herausgeber der Zeitschrift »Domus«) entworfene Groninger Museum zeichneten aber auch Michele de Lucchi, Philippe Starck und die österreichischen Architekten Coop Himmelblau verantwortlich. In Übereinstimmung mit Museumsdirektor Frans Haks beabsichtigt Mendini nichts weniger als die Schaffung eines Gesamtkunstwerks, da beide die Ansicht vertreten, daß zwischen Kunst, Architektur und Design kein Unterschied gemacht werden solle. Der 60 Meter hohe Mittelturm, die »Schatzkammer« mit dem Kunstdepot, ist in goldgelbes Laminat gehüllt und signalisiert Mendinis heiteren oder sogar humorvollen Ansatz. Der als Ausstellungsraum für die Alten Meister geplante Pavillon von Coop Himmelblau, der in letzter Minute als Ersatz für den als zu komplex und kostspielig empfundenen Pavillon des Künstlers Frank Stella konzipiert wurde, wird seiner eigentlichen Aufgabe nicht hundertprozentig gerecht, demonstriert dafür aber beispielhaft, auf welch ungewöhnliche Weise Raum gestaltet werden kann. Die Gesamtkosten für das 8 062 m² große Gebäude beliefen sich auf 47 Millionen Gulden, zu denen die N.V. Nederlandse Gasunie anläßlich ihres 25jährigen Jubiläums mehr als die Hälfte beisteuerte.

Projet inhabituel, le Groninger Museum forme une île artificielle sur le Verbingdingskanaal (canal de liaison). Elle est reliée aux rives par un pont, route la plus directe entre la gare centrale et la vieille ville, et passage obligé pour deux millions de personnes. Le souhait d'ouverture par an maximale du musée en est facilité d'autant. Conçu par Alessandro Mendini, ancien éditeur du magazine «Domus», cet ensemble est également dû à Michele de Lucchi, Philippe Starck et aux architectes autrichiens du groupe Coop Himmelblau. L'ambition commune à Mendini et au directeur du musée, Frans Haks, qui pensent qu'aucune distinction ne devrait être faite entre art, architecture et design, n'était rien moins que la création d'une œuvre d'art «totale». La tour centrale de 60 m de haut, le «trésor», est recouverte de plastique lamifié doré, et donne le ton de l'approche joyeuse, et même humoristique, de Mendini. Lieu d'exposition pour les collections d'art «ancien» du musée, le pavillon de Coop Himmelblau, commandé en catastrophe à la place d'une proposition de l'artiste Frank Stella, jugée trop complexe et coûteuse, remplit peut-être moins bien la tâche qu'on lui avait assignée qu'une brillante démonstration de la façon la plus étrange de découper l'espace. Le coût: de cet ensemble de 8 062 m² 40 millions de florins, dont plus de la moitié a été offerte par la société N.V. Nederlandse Gasunie, pour son 25ème anniversaire.

This skewed passageway is located in the Coop Himmelblau wing of the Groninger Museum, which houses the museum's collections of traditional painting.

Diese schräge Passage führt durch den Pavillon des Groninger Museums, der von Coop Himmelblau gestaltet wurde und kurioserweise die Sammlung der »alten Meister« beherbergt.

Ce passage en biais est situé dans l'aile du Groninger Museum construite par Coop Himmelblau, curieusement consacrée aux collections de peinture classique du musée.

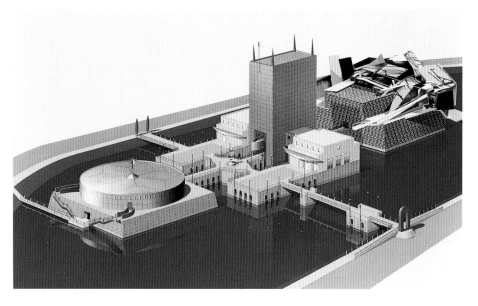

Page 110: Above, this overall drawing of the museum shows its similarity to temples like that at Philae in Egypt. The Coop Himmelblau pavilion is visible at the upper right, interior view below.

Seite 110: Oben: Der Gesamtplan des Museums zeigt dessen Ähnlichkeit mit alten Tempelanlagen wie etwa der auf der ägyptischen Nilinsel Philae. In der oberen rechten Bildhälfte ist der Pavillon von Coop Himmelblau sichtbar. Unten: Innenansicht.

Page 110: Ci-dessus, cette représentation générale du musée montre sa similitude avec des temples tels que celui de Philae, en Egypte. Le pavillon de Coop Himmelblau est visible dans la partie supérieure droite; ci-dessous, vue intérieure.

Page 111: Above, a view across the Verbindingskanaal shows Mendini's tower to the left, with
the Coop Himmelblau pavilion in the foreground.
Below, an interior view gives an idea of Mendini's use of vibrant color.

Seite 111: Oben: Die Ansicht über den Verbindingskanaal zeigt Mendinis Turm auf der linken
Bildseite und den Pavillon von Coop Himmelblau
im Vordergrund. Unten: Eine Innenansicht des
Museums, die eine Vorstellung von Mendinis
leuchtender Farbgestaltung vermittelt.

Page 111: Ci-dessus, vue prise de la rive du Verbindingskanaal montrant la tour de Mendini, à
gauche, et le pavillon de Coop Himmelblau, au
premier plan. Ci-dessous, cette vue intérieure
témoigne du sens de la vibration des couleurs
de Mendini.

Enric **Miralles**

Interior view of Els Hostalets de Balenyá.

Innenansicht des Els Hostalets de Balenyá.

Vue intérieure de l'Els Hostalets de Balenyá.

Born in Barcelona in 1955, Enric Miralles received his degree from the ETSA in that city in 1978. He has lectured there, at Columbia University in New York, at Harvard, and at the Architectural Association in London. He formed a partnership with Carme Pinós in 1983, and won a competition for the Igualada Cemetery Park on the outskirts of Barcelona in 1985 (completed in 1992). Contrary to the minimalism of other local architects like Viaplana and Piñón with whom he worked from 1974 to 1984, or Estève Bonnel, Miralles has become known for the exuberance of his style, whose odd angles sometimes resemble those seen in "deconstructivist" architecture. While interested in deconstruction as it is applied to literature, Miralles is skeptical about its application to architecture. The raw power of the forms conceived by Miralles makes it clear that he is not an imitator. Given the current return to fashion of a "clean" modernism, he looks more like a rebel than a follower.

Enric Miralles wurde 1955 in Barcelona geboren und promovierte 1978 an der dortigen Hochschule (ETSA), an der er auch als Dozent tätig war. Darüber hinaus hielt er Vorlesungen an der Columbia University in New York, an der Harvard University und an der Architectural Association in London. 1983 tat er sich mit Carme Pinós zusammen und gewann 1985 den Architekturwettbewerb für die Igualada-Friedhofsanlage am Stadtrand von Barcelona (fertiggestellt 1992). Im Gegensatz zum Minimalismus anderer örtlicher Architekten, wie Viaplana und Piñón – mit denen er von 1974 bis 1984 zusammenarbeitete – oder Estève Bonnel, wurde Miralles für seinen expressiven Stil bekannt, dessen seltsame Neigungswinkel manchmal an Elemente »dekonstruktivistischer« Architektur erinnern. Während Miralles eine »Dekonstruktion« der Literatur für denkbar hält, begegnet er der Anwendung eines vergleichbaren Verfahrens bei der Architektur mit Skepsis. Die ursprüngliche Kraft der von ihm entworfenen Formen zeigt deutlich, daß er kein Imitator ist. In Anbetracht der momentanen Rückbesinnung auf eine »klare« Moderne ist Miralles eher ein Rebell als ein Mitläufer.

Né à Barcelone, en 1955, Enric Miralles est diplômé de l'ETSA de cette ville en 1978. Il y enseigne, ainsi qu'à Columbia University, à New York, Harvard, et à l'Architectural Association de Londres. Il s'associe à Carme Pinós en 1983, et remporte le concours du cimetière d'Igualada, dans la banlieue de Barcelone, en 1985 (terminé en 1992). Contrairement au minimalisme d'autres architectes locaux, comme Viaplana et Piñón, avec lesquels il collabore de 1974 à 1984, ou d'Estève Bonnel, Miralles se fait remarquer par l'exubérance de son style, dont les angles étranges rappellent parfois une certaine architecture déconstructiviste. Bien qu'intéressé par la déconstruction en littérature, il est sceptique sur ses applications à l'architecture. La puissance brutale des formes qu'il conçoit montre qu'il n'est pas un imitateur. Compte tenu du retour actuel à un modernisme clean, il semble plus un rebelle qu'un suiveur.

Els Hostalets de Balenyá, Civic Center, Hostalets de Balenyá (Barcelona) 1988–1994

This 1 100 m² center designed by Enric Miralles with Carme Pinós, houses twenty different functions, including a 300 seat auditorium, a library, studios, a bar and a reading room. Located on an unattractive peripheral road encircling the town of Hostalets, near Barcelona, the structure has been compared to the work of the Russian Constructivists, in particular that of Konstantin Melnikov, because of his use of rough, industrial materials. Although not easily linked to the "deconstructivist" trend, the 100 million peseta Hostalets Center does make use of a fragmented geometry usually associated with that movement. In this instance, the design is also a response to the disorganized industrial suburban environment, as the architect says, the building was born of a desire to "make it disappear from this place." The access ramps which make the terraces accessible from the garden "give form to the building, creating a complex wall." Internal spaces are intentionally disconnected, as are the intended functions, which according to Miralles, "allows the light to enter."

Dieses 1 100 m² große Zentrum, von Enric Miralles und Carme Pinós entworfen, beherbergt zwanzig verschiedene Einrichtungen, einschließlich eines Auditoriums mit 300 Plätzen, einer Bücherei, verschiedener Studios, einer Bar und einem Lesesaal. Der an einer Umgehungsstraße der Stadt Hostalets bei Barcelonas gelegene Gebäudekomplex wurde aufgrund der verwendeten groben Industriematerialien bereits mit den russischen Konstruktivisten und insbesondere mit Konstantin Melnikows Arbeiten verglichen. Obwohl eigentlich keine direkte Verbindung zum »Dekonstruktivismus« besteht, weist das 100 Millionen Peseta teure Gebäude dennoch eine zerstückelte Geometrie auf, die im allgemeinen mit dieser Bewegung assoziiert wird. Außerdem stellt das Design in diesem besonderen Fall eine Reaktion auf die zerrüttete industrielle Vorstadtumgebung dar. Nach Aussage der Architekten entstand dieses Gebäude aus dem Bedürfnis, »es von diesem Ort verschwinden zu lassen«. Die Auffahrtsrampen, die die Terrassen vom Garten her zugänglich machen, »verleihen dem Gebäude Form und strukturieren es durch eine komplexe Wandfläche.« Selbst die Innenräume sind absichtlich voneinander getrennt – entsprechend ihren unterschiedlichen Funktionen – so daß laut Miralles »viel Licht einfallen kann«.

Ce bâtiment municipal de 1 100 m², conçu par Enric Miralles et Carme Pinós, pour remplir une vingtaine de fonctions différentes, dont une salle de 300 places, une bibliothèque, des studios, un bar et une salle de lecture. Situé en bordure d'une voie périphérique peu engageante de la ville d'Hostalets, près de Barcelone, on a pu le rapprocher des projets des Constructivistes russes, en particulier ceux de Konstantin Melnikov, pour son recours à des matériaux industriels bruts. Même s'il est difficile de le ranger dans la catégorie du déconstructivisme, ce centre de 100 millions de pesetas fait référence à la géométrie éclatée généralement associée à ce mouvement. D'une certaine façon, il reflète l'environnement désarticulé de cette banlieue. Comme l'ont déclaré les architectes, il est né d'un désir «de le faire disparaître du lieu». Les rampes d'accès qui relient les terrasses au jardin «donnent forme au bâtiment, en créant une muraille complexe». Les espaces intérieurs sont volontairement déconnectés les uns des autres, de même que les fonctions, ce qui, selon Miralles, «permet à la lumière de pénétrer».

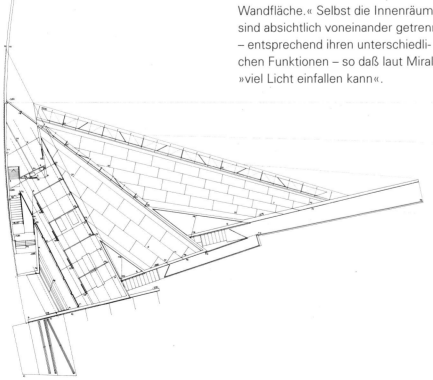

Page 114/115: First conceived in 1986–88, this project was completed eight years later, yet it retains a feeling, in its fractured plan which is very much in the spirit of the architecture of the early 1990s.

Seite 114/115: Obwohl die erste Planungsphase bereits 1986–88 verlief und das Projekt erst acht Jahre später fertiggestellt wurde, besitzt das Gebäude eine Ausstrahlung, die sehr an die Architektur der frühen 90er Jahre erinnert.

Page 114/115: Conçu en 1986–88, ce projet fut terminé huit ans plus tard, ce qui explique que son plan éclaté soit bien dans l'esprit de l'architecture du début des années 90.

National Training Center for Rhythmic Gymnastics, Alicante 1989–1993

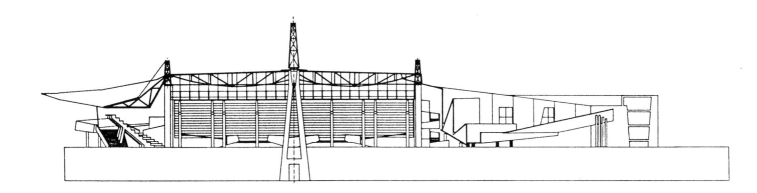

Enric Miralles's own description of this structure is short enough to be quoted: "It's a building with a very complex program: Competition sport hall, training spaces, and a school for professional rhythmic gymnastics. The complexity of the program is unified by a unique roof and ramps in the main façade which transform the enormous building into an extensive balcony." Although the project was awarded to 40 year old Miralles and his former partner Carme Pinós in 1989, it was built in nine months beginning in early 1993, at a cost of $9,5 million. Alicante in southern Spain is the capital of the province of the same name, and has a population of about 260 000 persons. The Center was the site of the 1993 World Gymnastics Championships. The main hall for public performances seats 4 000 persons. Despite its apparent density, the roof structure was mounted in the space of one month, and it clearly serves to free the use of vast internal spaces. Again the deconstructivist style comes to mind, but Miralles himself believes that the "deconstruction" of literature is feasible, whereas the application of a similar procedure to architecture is impossible.

Enric Miralles beschreibt dieses Projekt mit den Worten: »Hierbei handelt es sich um ein Gebäude mit einem sehr komplexen Aufgabenbereich: eine Wettkampfhalle, Trainingsräume und eine Schule für professionelle rhythmische Gymnastik. Die Komplexität dieses Programms wird durch ein einziges Dach und mehrere Rampen in der Hauptfassade, die das gewaltige Gebäude in einen ausladenden Balkon verwandeln, vereint.« Den Auftrag zu diesem Projekt erhielten Miralles und Pinós bereits 1989. Die neunmonatigen Bauarbeiten begannen allerdings erst im Frühjahr 1993 und verschlangen 9,5 Millionen Dollar. Das in Südspanien gelegene Alicante mit ca. 260 000 Einwohnern ist die Hauptstadt der Provinz Alicante. 1993 fand hier die Gymnastik-Weltmeisterschaft statt. Die Haupthalle bietet 4 000 Zuschauern Platz. Trotz der offensichtlichen Komplexität wurde die Dachkonstruktion innerhalb eines Monats errichtet und ermöglicht (durch ihre Form) eine ungehinderte Nutzung der Räumlichkeiten. Auch hier fällt der dekonstruktivistische Stil auf; Miralles selbst meint allerdings, daß eine »Dekonstruktion« der Literatur zwar denkbar wäre, die Anwendung eines vergleichbaren Verfahrens bei der Architektur aber unmöglich sei.

La description par Enric Miralles de cette construction est assez brève pour être citée : «C'est un bâtiment au programme très complexe : salle de sports de compétition, espaces d'entraînement, et école de gymnastique rythmique professionnelle. La complexité de ce programme est tempérée par la présence d'un toit unique et des rampes en façade principale qui transforment cette énorme construction en un vaste balcon.» Bien que Miralles – 40 ans – et son ancien associé Carme Pinós, aient obtenu cette commande en 1989, elle ne fut édifiée en neuf mois qu'à partir du début de 1993, au coût de 9,5 millions de dollars. Alicante, dans le sud de l'Espagne, est la capitale de la province du même nom, et possède une population de 260 000 habitants. Ce centre a été le site des championnats du monde de gymnastique en 1993. La grande salle de compétition peut accueillir 4 000 personnes. Malgré son apparente complexité, la structure du toit a été montée en un mois seulement. Elle permet de libérer de vastes espaces intérieurs. Une fois encore le style déconstructiviste vient à l'esprit, mais pour Miralles, si la déconstruction est possible en littérature, elle lui semble tout à fait inapplicable à l'architecture.

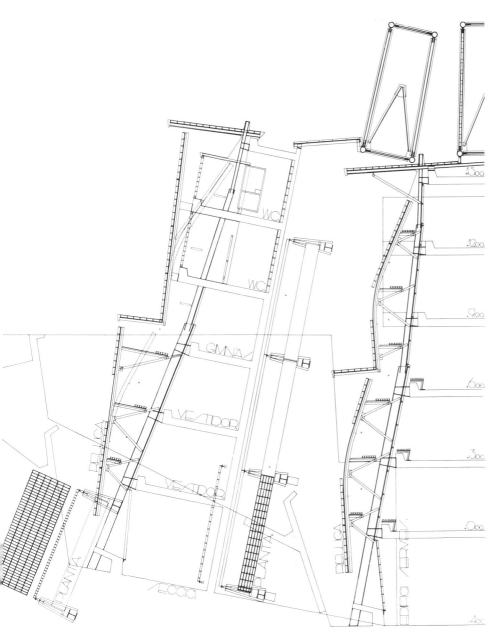

Page 116/117: Above, the main public entrance on the north side of the building. The auditorium is located to the right. Left hand page, a cross section of the rehearsal hall, and on this page to the left, a plan.

Seite 116/117: Oben: Der Haupteingangsbereich auf der Nordseite des Gebäudes. Die Wettkampfhalle liegt rechts. Linke Seite: Querschnitt der Trainingshalle. Diese Seite links: Ein Grundriß.

Page 116/117: En haut, l'entrée principale sur la façade Nord du bâtiment. La salle des spectacles est située à droite. Page de gauche, coupe de la salle de répétition et, sur cette page à gauche, le plan.

A view of the practice hall, with the supports of
the structural spine of the building visible in the
center. A public ramp leading to the auditorium
is located on the right of the image.

Ansicht der Trainingshalle; in der Mitte die tra-
genden Elemente der Gebäudekonstruktion. Auf
der rechten Bildseite der Publikumseingang zur
Wettkampfhalle.

Vue de la salle de répétitions, avec les supports
de la structure du bâtiment, bien visibles au
centre. A droite, la rampe qui conduit à la salle
de spectacles.

José Rafael **Moneo**

Interior view of the Davis Museum,
Wellesley College, Wellesley,
Massachusetts.

Innenansicht des Davis Museum,
Wellesley College, Wellesley,
Massachusetts.

Vue intérieure du Davis Museum,
Wellesley College, Wellesley,
Massachussets.

José Rafael Moneo was born in Tudela, Navarra in 1937. He graduated from the ETSA in Madrid in 1961. The following year, he went to work with Jørn Utzon in Denmark. Rafael Moneo has taught extensively, including at the ETSA in Madrid and Barcelona. He was chairman of the Department of Architecture at the Graduate School of Design at Harvard from 1985 to 1990 and is well-known in architectural circles for such buildings as his National Museum of Roman Art in Merida (1980–86) which includes the foundations of part of the old Roman city, or more recently his San Pablo Airport Terminal in Seville (1989–91) built for Expo '92, the new structure of the Miró Foundation in Palma (1992) or the interior architecture of the Thyssen-Bornemisza Collection in Madrid (1992). Often incorporating subtle links to the existing environments, Moneo's buildings represent an effective adaptation of modernity to the lessons of history.

José Rafael Moneo wurde 1937 in Tudela in der spanischen Provinz Navarra geboren. 1961 schloß er sein Studium an der ETSA in Madrid ab und bereits im darauffolgenden Jahr ging er nach Dänemark, um dort mit Jørn Utzon zusammenzuarbeiten. Darüber hinaus war Moneo an zahlreichen Hochschulen als Dozent tätig, darunter auch an der ETSA in Madrid und Barcelona. Zwischen 1985 und 1990 stand er dem Department of Architecture an der Graduate School of Design in Harvard vor und ist in architektonischen Kreisen aufgrund solcher Bauwerke wie dem Nationalen Museum für römische Kunst in Merida (1980–86) bekannt, das einen Teil der antiken römischen Stadtmauern umfaßt. Aber auch sein San Pablo Airport-Terminal in Sevilla (1989–91), den er für die Expo '92 errichtete, oder sein Gebäude für die Miró-Stiftung in Palma (1992) sowie die Innenarchitektur des Museums Thyssen-Bornemisza in Madrid (1992) erregten in der Fachwelt Aufsehen. Moneos Bauwerke, die häufig eine subtile Verbindung zu ihrer Umgebung eingehen, repräsentieren eine effektive Adaption der Moderne an die Lehren der Vergangenheit.

José Rafael Moneo est né à Tudela, province de Navarre, en 1937. Il est diplômé de l'ETSA de Madrid en 1961. L'année suivante, il part travailler pour Jørn Utzon au Danemark. Il a beaucoup enseigné, y compris dans les ETSA de Madrid et de Barcelone. Directeur du département d'architecture de la Graduate School of Design d'Harvard, de 1985 à 1990, il est très connu dans les cercles architecturaux pour son Musée national d'art romain de Mérida (1980–86) qui englobe les fondations d'une partie de la vieille cité romaine ou, plus récemment, le terminal San Pablo de l'aéroport de Séville (1989–91), construit pour Expo '92, le nouveau bâtiment de la Fondation Miró à Palma (1992), ou l'architecture intérieure du bâtiment abritant la Collection Thyssen-Bornemisza à Madrid (1992). En incorporant souvent des liaisons subtiles avec leur environnement, les constructions de Moneo illustrent une adaptation efficiente de la modernité aux leçons de l'histoire.

Davis Museum, Wellesley, Massachusetts 1989–1993

The first building outside Spain designed by Rafael Moneo, former chairman of the Department of Architecture at Harvard, the Davis Museum was intended as a necessary addition to the Jewett Arts Center, built on the beautiful Wellesley campus by Paul Rudolph in 1958. Moneo, who completed the rehabilitation of the Villahermosa Palace in Madrid for the Thyssen-Bornemisza Museum in 1992, chose a muted brick box-like structure in order to defer to the adjacent building. The focus of his $11.7 million museum is on the inside, with the double staircase and exhibition galleries. African art, modern painting and contemporary art are shown on the ground floor, a mezzanine provides offices and a study room, with a connection to the Jewett Center. On the second floor, Renaissance, Baroque and Oriental art are shown, with sculpture exhibited on the top, skylit level. A 200 seat movie theater, café and a temporary exhibition hall are housed in the basement. For Paul Goldberger, architecture critic at *The New York Times*, the galleries and stairs of the Davis Museum are "nothing short of magnificent."

Das Davis Museum ist das erste von Moneo (dem ehemaligen Vorsitzenden des Department of Architecture an der Universität Harvard) entworfene Gebäude, das außerhalb Spaniens entstand. Es erweitert das von Paul Rudolph 1958 auf dem Wellesley Campus errichtete Jewett Arts Center. Moneo, der 1992 die Sanierung des Villahermosa Palastes in Madrid für das Thyssen-Bornemisza-Museum abgeschlossen hatte, entwarf einen ruhigen, kubischen Ziegelbau, mit dem er den angrenzenden Gebäude seinen Respekt erweist. Den Mittelpunkt des 11,7 Millionen Dollar teuren Museums bilden die Doppeltreppe und die Ausstellungsgalerien. Im Erdgeschoß befinden sich die Ausstellungsräume mit afrikanischer Kunst, moderner Malerei und zeitgenössischer Kunst, während das Zwischengeschoß die Verwaltungsbüros und Arbeitsräume beherbergt und eine Verbindung zum Jewett Center besitzt. Im zweiten Geschoß sind Werke der Renaissance und des Barocks sowie orientalische Kunst ausgestellt. Die Skulpturensammlung ist im obersten, mit Oberlichtern versehenen Geschoß. Im Untergeschoß wurden ein Kinosaal mit 200 Plätzen, ein Café und Räumlichkeiten für Wechselaustellungen untergebracht. Der Architekturkritiker der »New York Times«, Paul Goldberger, bezeichnete die Galerien und Treppen des Davis Museum als »geradezu brillant«.

Premier édifice réalisé en dehors d'Espagne par Rafael Moneo, ancien directeur du département d'architecture d'Harvard, le Davis Museum est l'extension longtemps attendue du Jewett Arts Center, construit sur le magnifique campus de Wellesley par Paul Rudolph, en 1958. Moneo, auteur de la réhabilitation du palais de Villahermosa à Madrid pour la collection Thyssen-Bornemisza, en 1992, s'est déterminé pour une forme de boîte aveugle et en brique afin de se distinguer radicalement du bâtiment adjacent. L'intérêt principal de ce musée de 11,7 millions de dollars se trouve à l'intérieur, dans son escalier à double révolution et ses galeries d'exposition. L'art africain, l'art moderne et contemporain sont présentés au rez-de-chaussée, les bureaux et une salle d'étude occupent une mezzanine, d'où l'on rejoint le Jewett Center. Le second niveau est réservé à l'art de la Renaissance, au Baroque et à l'Orient, les sculptures étant exposées au dernier niveau, sous verrière. Un auditorium de 200 places, un café et une salle pour les expositions temporaires sont aménagés en sous-sol. Pour Paul Goldberger, critique d'architecture au «The New York Times», les galeries et les escaliers du Davis Museum sont «tout simplement magnifiques».

Although visually unspectacular, the Davis Museum fits well into the calm atmosphere of the Wellesley campus and makes no attempt to detract attention from the neighboring Jewett Arts Center.

Obwohl es optisch keine spektakulären Ansichten bietet, fügt sich das Davis Museum hervorragend in die ruhige Atmosphäre des Wellesley College ein und lenkt nicht vom benachbarten Jewett Arts Center ab.

Bien qu'il ne soit pas très spectaculaire, le Davis Museum s'intègre parfaitement à l'atmosphère calme du campus de Wellesley, et ne tente pas de rivaliser avec le Jewett Arts Centre tout proche.

Jean **Nouvel**

Born in Fumel in 1945, Jean Nouvel is probably the best known contemporary French architect outside his own country, although most of his built work is in France. Part of the reason for his celebrity is undoubtedly his strong physical presence – always dressed in black he is easily recognizable, and he is, to say the least, outspoken. It was probably the Institut du Monde Arabe in Paris which did the most to create his reputation, though it is not often pointed out that he collaborated with Architecture Studio on this structure. Although the Opéra de Lyon and the Fondation Cartier in Paris carried his reputation to new heights, as did an unbuilt scheme for a 400 meter high tower in the Défense area of Paris, Jean Nouvel was also in the news in France late in 1994 because although he won the competition for a large new stadium to be built near Paris for the 1998 World Cup competition, another group, headed by Michel Macary was given the job, an outcome which Nouvel vigorously contested.

Jean Nouvel, 1945 in Fumel geboren, ist wahrscheinlich der weltweit bekannteste französische Architekt seiner Zeit. Zu diesem Ruhm trug sicher auch seine starke physische Präsenz bei – seine stets schwarze Kleidung, die ihm einen hohen Wiedererkennungswert verleiht, kombiniert mit einem – vorsichtig ausgedrückt – freimütigen Auftreten. Aber den größten Beitrag zu seiner Reputation lieferte vermutlich das Institut du Monde Arabe in Paris, obwohl selten auf seine Zusammenarbeit mit dem Architecture Studio bei diesem Bauwerk hingewiesen wird. Die Opéra de Lyon, die Fondation Cartier in Paris und die Konstruktionspläne eines nicht ausgeführten 400 Meter hohen Turms im Pariser Viertel La Défense verhalfen Nouvels Ruf zu ungeahnten Höhen. Ende des Jahres 1994 füllte er die Schlagzeilen seiner Heimat, weil er die Ausschreibung für den Bau eines großen Stadions gewonnen hatte, das für die Fußballweltmeisterschaft 1998 in der Nähe von Paris errichtet werden soll. Der Bauauftrag wurde jedoch einer anderen Architektengruppe unter Leitung von Michel Macary erteilt, was zu heftigen Protesten Nouvels führte.

Né en 1945 à Fumel, Jean Nouvel est aujourd'hui sans doute l'architecte français le plus connu en dehors de son pays, même s'il a essentiellement construit en France. Une raison partielle de sa célébrité tient sans doute à sa forte présence physique. Pour le moins extraverti et toujours vêtu de noir, il est facilement reconnaissable. C'est probablement l'Institut du Monde Arabe, à Paris, qui a fait le plus pour le lancer, même si l'on oublie souvent de mentionner pour cet édifice la collaboration d'Architecture Studio. Bien que l'Opéra de Lyon et la Fondation Cartier aient porté sa réputation à de nouveaux sommets, de même qu'une tour de 400 m non réalisée pour le quartier de La Défense, Nouvel a encore fait la une des journaux en 1994. Alors qu'il avait remporté le concours du nouveau stade de Saint-Denis, près de Paris, pour la Coupe du Monde de football 1998, une autre équipe, dirigée par Michel Macary, a hérité du contrat, ce qu'il a vigoureusement contesté.

Interior view of the Opéra de Lyon.

Innenansicht der Opéra de Lyon.

Intérieur de l'Opéra de Lyon.

Opéra de Lyon, Lyon
1987–1993

By hollowing out the original Lyon Opéra house, built by Chenavard and Pollet in 1831, Jean Nouvel managed to triple the interior volume of the structure. He achieved this by digging below the building, but also by adding a twenty meter high semi-cylindrical drum to the top, which is used for the rehearsal areas of the opera ballet company. Situated just opposite the town hall and fifty meters from the Lyon art museum, the Opéra has become a readily recognizable feature of the city skyline, all the more so since lighting specialist Yann Kersalé was called in by Nouvel to give a distinctive red glow to the building, whose intensity depends on the number of people within. The cultural activity of Lyon has been highlighted by the renovation of the museum and the square in front of it (Place des Terreaux), which was redesigned by the artist Daniel Buren. Nouvel's favorite color is certainly black as the entrance lobby and the interior of the main theater attest in this project, but his taste for disorienting spaces (again, the entrance) is not shared by all of the visitors.

Durch die Entkernung des ursprünglichen, von Chenavard und Pollet 1831 errichteten Opernhauses in Lyon gelang es Jean Nouvel, den Innenraum des Gebäudes zu verdreifachen. Dazu schachtete er nicht nur den Boden unterhalb der Oper aus, sondern versah das ursprüngliche Bauwerk auch mit einem 20 Meter hohen, halbzylindrischen Aufsatz, der als Proberaum für das Opernballet dient. Die Oper liegt genau gegenüber dem Rathaus und 50 Meter vom Lyoner Kunstmuseum entfernt. Sie ist inzwischen zu einem prägnanten Element der städtischen Skyline geworden, das sich – dank des von Nouvel beauftragten Beleuchtungsexperten Yann Kersalé – durch einen rotglühenden Farbton auszeichnet (wobei die farbliche Intensität von der Anzahl der Personen im Gebäude abhängt). Die kulturelle Bedeutung der Stadt Lyon wurde durch die Renovierung des Museums und die Umgestaltung des davor gelegenen Platzes (Place des Terreaux) besonders hervorgehoben, für die der Künstler Daniel Buren verantwortlich zeichnete. Nouvels bevorzugte Farbe ist Schwarz, wie der Eingangsbereich und die Innenausstattung des großen Theatersaals dieses Projektes belegen; allerdings teilen nicht alle Besucher seine Vorliebe für eine verwirrende Raumaufteilung.

En vidant entièrement l'ancien Opéra de Lyon, construit par Chenavard et Pollet en 1831, Jean Nouvel a réussi à tripler son volume intérieur. Il y est parvenu en creusant en sous-sol, mais aussi en remplaçant la toiture classique par un demi-cylindre de 20 mètres de haut, réservé aux salles de répétition de la troupe de ballet. Situé juste en face de l'hôtel de ville, et à cent mètres du musée des Beaux-Arts, l'Opéra s'est vite intégré au paysage urbain lyonnais, d'autant plus que Nouvel a appelé Yann Kersalé, spécialiste de la lumière, qui a créé un éclairage rougeoyant, dont l'intensité varie selon le nombre de personnes présentes dans l'édifice. L'activité culturelle de la ville a été réveillée par la rénovation du musée et de la Place des Terreaux qui lui fait face, redessinée par l'artiste Daniel Buren. La couleur favorite de Nouvel est le noir, comme en atteste une fois de plus l'entrée et l'intérieur de la salle, mais son goût des espaces suprenants (l'entrée) ne fait pas l'unanimité parmi les visiteurs.

Page 126: The enormous barrel vault which Jean Nouvel added to the existing 1831 façades of the Opéra accommodates studio space for the dance school.

Seite 126: Das gewaltige Zylindergewölbe, das Jean Nouvel dem bereits seit 1831 existierenden Operngebäude hinzufügte, dient als Proberaum für das Opernballet.

Page 126: L'énorme voûte en tonneau dont Jean Nouvel a surmonté les façades de l'Opéra de Lyon abrite les salles de répétition de l'école de danse.

Page 128/129: A sophisticated lighting system designed by Yann Kersalé is meant to glow more when the building is fully occupied. In any case, its shape, with the dance studios high in the barrel vault (right) stands out distinctly on the Lyon skyline.

Seite 128/129: Ein ausgeklügeltes, von Yann Kersalé entwickeltes Beleuchtungssystem leuchtet je nach personeller Besetzung des Gebäudes mehr oder weniger intensiv. Die Oper mit den Ballet-Proberäumen im oberen Teil des Zylindergewölbes (rechts) ist zu einem herausragenden Kennzeichen der Lyoner Skyline geworden.

Page 128/129: Un système d'éclairage sophistiqué imaginé par Yann Kersalé traduit par son intensité le niveau d'activité du bâtiment. La forme en tonneau et cet éclairage (à droite) font remarquer le bâtiment sur le panorama des quais du Rhône.

Palais des Congrès, Tours
1989–1993

Located opposite the modest Tours TGV station, this congress center includes three rooms with a respective capacity of 2 000, 700 and 350 persons. The 2 000 seat theater borrows its design concept from that of hi-fi according to Nouvel, "dark and clean with recessed equipment." There is also a restaurant for up to 800 people, with the whole complex, measuring some 22 000 m², set on a long, narrow site, The largest of the three meeting areas is recessed into the ground, permitting the relatively low-rise external appearance, which is nonetheless rendered dramatic by the curving sweep of the facade and the extended baseball-cap like overhang. The architect placed emphasis on "the external simplicity and internal complexity of the building." He says with pride of the outside, "This is the lightest facade I have designed, it doesn't express its technology." The effect of Nouvel's intervention in this otherwise very traditional town is assured by the fact that he also designed the tourism office located across the street. Unloading areas for the congress center are situated in the basement of the tourism office.

Das gegenüber dem schlichten TGV-Bahnhof gelegene Kongreßzentrum von Tours verfügt über drei Tagungs- und Veranstaltungsräume für jeweils 2 000, 700 bzw. 350 Personen. Bei der Gestaltung des Theatersaals mit seinen 2 000 Plätzen handelt es sich um eine Adaption des Designs von Hi-Fi-Anlagen: »Dunkel und schlicht, mit versenkter Ausstattung« wie Nouvel es formulierte. Darüber hinaus besitzt das Kongreßzentrum ein Restaurant für bis zu 800 Personen und hat eine Nutzfläche von 22 000 m², die sich über ein schmales, langgezogenes Gelände verteilt. Der größte der drei Kongreßsäle ist in den Boden eingelassen und ermöglicht dadurch ein relativ flaches Erscheinungsbild des Gebäudekomplexes, das nichtsdestotrotz durch die geschwungene Fassade und die an eine Baseballkappe erinnernde Auskragung dramatisch wirkt. Der Architekt legte besonderen Wert auf »äußere Schlichtheit und innere Komplexität des Gebäudes.« Stolz bezeichnet er die Fassade als »die transparenteste Fassade, die ich je entworfen habe und die ihre eigene Konstruktion verbirgt«. Der Eindruck, den Nouvels Eingriff in dieser an sich eher traditionellen Stadt erzeugte, wird durch das ebenfalls von ihm entworfene Fremdenverkehrsbüro auf den anderen Straßenseite bekräftigt. Im Untergeschoß dieses Gebäudes befinden sich weitere Lagerräume des Kongreßzentrums.

Situé en face de la modeste gare de TGV de Tours, ce centre de congrès comprend trois salles de 2 000, 700, et 350 places. Selon Jean Nouvel, l'auditorium de 2 000 sièges, emprunte son concept à la Hi-Fi, «sombre, net, dissimulant sa technique». On y trouve également un restaurant de 800 places. L'ensemble de 22 000 m² a été implanté sur un terrain tout en longueur. La plus vaste des trois salles est enterrée, ce qui a permis de réduire le volume extérieur apparent (qui n'en est pas moins spectaculaire pour autant), grâce aux courbes des façades et à l'important porte-à-faux en forme de casquette de l'entrée principale. L'architecte a mis l'accent sur «la simplicité externe et la complexité interne». Il déclare avec satisfaction que, de l'extérieur, «c'est le bâtiment le plus léger que j'aie dessiné, il n'exprime pas sa technologie». L'effet de l'intervention de Nouvel sur cette ville assez conservatrice est renforcé par l'office de tourisme, qu'il a construit de l'autre côté de la rue. Les aires de déchargement pour le centre de congrès sont d'ailleurs situées dans les sous-sols de ce bâtiment.

The protruding hood of the Palais des Congrès and its smooth glass façade set it apart in the otherwise very conservative city of Tours.

Die Dachauskragung des Palais des Congrès und seine glatte Glasfassade bilden einen interessanten Kontrast zur ansonsten sehr konservativen Stadt Tours.

L'avancée proéminente du palais des Congrès et sa façade de verre profilée tranchent sur le style architectural de la très conservatrice ville de Tours.

Page 132/133: Interior views of the Palais des Congrès give an idea of the flexibility of its spaces and the ways in which the sophisticated exterior design is echoed within the building.

Seite 132/133: Die Innenansichten des Palais des Congrès vermitteln einen Eindruck von der Vielseitigkeit seiner Räume und zeigen, auf welch raffinierte Weise die Innenausstattung die kunstvolle Gestaltung der Außenfassaden widerspiegelt.

Page 132/133: Vues intérieures du Palais des Congrès permettant de comprendre la souplesse des aménagements et la façon dont la sophistication de la conception des façades se retrouve dans le bâtiment lui-même.

Fondation Cartier, Paris
1991–1994

"I place art in architecture, and architecture in the city," says Jean Nouvel, chosen by the GAN insurance company (owner of the site) and Cartier to build the new Fondation Cartier building at 261 Boulevard Raspail in Paris in 1991. The structure includes no fewer than 16 levels, of which 8 are below grade. There are 4 000 m² of offices for Cartier France, 1 600 m² of exhibition space for the Foundation, 800 m² of technical space, and 4 000 m² of gardens. Most importantly, the Fondation Cartier is made up of some 5 000 m² of glass façades. As Nouvel, says, "It is an architecture whose game is to make the tangible limits of the structure disappear in a poetically evanescent manner. When the virtual and the real are no longer distinct, architecture must have the courage to assume such a contradiction." Nouvel, whose own striking black silhouette seems carefully calculated to contribute to his image as a living legend certainly thinks highly of his own work, but his excellent opinion of himself does seem to be borne out by the Fondation Cartier, one of the most innovative and striking buildings erected in France in recent years.

»Ich plaziere die Kunst in die Architektur und die Architektur in die Stadt«, sagt Jean Nouvel, der 1991 von der GAN-Versicherungsgesellschaft (Eigentümerin des Grundstücks) und Cartier beauftragt wurde, das neue Fondation Cartier-Gebäude am Boulevard Raspail Nr. 261 in Paris zu errichten. Dieser Gebäudekomplex umfaßt nicht weniger als 16 Geschosse (von denen sich acht unterhalb des Geländeniveaus befinden), die insgesamt 4 000 m² Bürofläche für Cartier France, 1 600 m² Ausstellungsfläche für die Stiftung und 800 m² für technische Räumlichkeiten aufweisen. Hinzu kommen weitere 4 000 m² Gartenfläche und – das Wichtigste – 5 000 m² Glasfassade. Laut Nouvel handelt es sich hierbei um »eine Architektur, deren Ziel es ist, die materiellen Beschränkungen des Gebäudes auf eine poetisch vergängliche Weise verschwinden zu lassen. Wenn Virtualität und Realität nicht länger voneinander zu trennen sind, muß die Architektur den Mut aufbringen, solche Widersprüche auf sich zu nehmen.« Zweifelsohne besitzt Nouvel (dessen außergewöhnliches schwarzes Erscheinungsbild zur Unterstreichung seines Images als lebende Legende sorgfältig gewählt wirkt) eine hohe Meinung von seiner eigenen Arbeit, und das Fondation Cartier-Gebäude, eines der innovativsten und aufsehenerregendsten französischen Bauwerke der vergangenen Jahre, gibt ihm darin durchaus recht.

«J'introduis l'art dans l'architecture et l'architecture dans la ville», aime à déclarer Jean Nouvel, choisi, en 1991, par la compagnie d'assurances GAN (propriétaire du terrain) et Cartier pour construire le nouveau siège de la Fondation Cartier, 261 boulevard Raspail à Paris. Le bâtiment ne compte pas moins de 16 niveaux dont 8 en sous-sol. Il abrite 4 000 m² de bureaux pour Cartier France, 1 600 m² d'espace d'exposition pour la Fondation, 800 m² de locaux techniques et 4 000 m² de jardins. Le tout se dissimule derrière quelque 5 000 m² de façades de verre. Comme le dit encore Nouvel: «Le jeu de cette architecture est de faire disparaître les limites tangibles de la construction d'une manière évanescente et poétique. Lorsque le réel et le virtuel ne se distinguent plus, l'architecture doit avoir le courage d'assumer une telle contradiction.» L'architecte, dont l'intrigante silhouette noire semble soigneusement calculée pour cultiver son image de légende vivante, pense à l'évidence beaucoup de bien de ses œuvres. L'excellente opinion qu'il a de lui-même ne peut qu'être confortée par la Fondation Cartier, l'un des édifices les plus innovateurs et les plus frappants construits en France au cours de ces dernières années.

The glass façades of the Fondation Cartier on the Boulevard Raspail in Paris recall the alignment of existing buildings on the street, allow a view into the structure itself, and naturally permit ample natural lighting within.

Die Glasfassade der Fondation Cartier am Boulevard Raspail in Paris bewirkt nicht nur eine optische Übereinstimmung mit den bereits existierenden Gebäuden an dieser Straße, sondern erlaubt auch einen Blick in das Innere des Gebäudes und läßt darüber hinaus ausreichend Tageslicht einfallen.

Les façades de verre de la Fondation Cartier, boulevard Raspail à Paris, rappellent l'alignement des autres immeubles, et laissent pénétrer le regard dans le bâtiment lui-même, dont l'intérieur est baigné de lumière naturelle.

Jean Nouvel 135

Page 136/137: The main exhibition space of the Fondation Cartier, on the ground level, is extremely high and entirely surrounded by glass, which poses a problem for some artists invited to exhibit there. To the right, eight views of the interior of the building with works by Raymond Hains and Richard Artschwager seen during temporary exhibitions.

Seite 136/137: Der Hauptausstellungsraum der Fondation Cartier im Erdgeschoß liegt extrem hoch und ist mit Absicht vollkommen mit Glas umschlossen, was für manchen Künstler, der hier seine Werke präsentiert, ein Problem darstellt. Rechts: Acht Innenansichten mit Arbeiten von Raymond Hains und Richard Artschwager, aufgenommen während einer Ausstellung.

Page 136/137: De très grande hauteur, le principal espace d'exposition de la Fondation, au rez-de-chaussée, est par principe, entièrement vitré, ce qui pose un problème à certains artistes exposants. A droite, huit plans de l'intérieur du bâtiment, avec des œuvres de Raymond Hains et Richard Artschwager, présentées à l'occasion d'une exposition temporaire.

Renzo **Piano**

The massive, undulating façade of Kansai Airport, Osaka Bay, Japan.

Die massive, geschwungene Fassade des Kansai Airport in der Bucht von Osaka, Japan.

La façade ondulée et massive de l'aéroport de Kansai, dans la baie d'Osaka, au Japon.

Born in 1937 in Genoa, Renzo Piano, in association with Richard Rogers, completed the Centre Georges Pompidou in Paris in 1977. This was the project which brought him almost instantly to international attention. Since that time, he has become one of the most active "stars" of the world of architecture, completing the Menil Collection Museum in Houston (1986), or the San Nicola stadium in Bari (1987–90). Although he has no regrets about the aggressive design of the Centre Georges Pompidou, he does say, "We were young and we wanted the building to be noticed," opting in his more recent work for a more sophisticated and subtle kind of technologically oriented architecture. He is capable of a wide variety of stylistic expressions, as evidenced by his Centre Culturel Canaque Jean-Marie-Tjibaou, being built in New Caledonia, his 1989 extension for the IRCAM, a calm brick structure, just opposite the multi-colored tubes and pipes of the Centre Georges Pompidou, and, in a different context, the renovation of the Lingotto complex in Turin.

Der 1937 in Genua geborene Architekt Renzo Piano stellte 1977 in Zusammenarbeit mit Richard Rogers das Centre Georges Pompidou in Paris fertig, das ihm zu internationaler Bekanntheit verhalf. Seit dieser Zeit zählt er zu den aktivsten »Stars« der Architekturwelt und errichtete u.a. das Menil Collection Museum in Houston (1986) und das San Nicola-Stadion in Bari (1987–90). Obwohl er das aggressive Design des Centre Georges Pompidou keinesfalls bedauert, bekannte Piano: »Wir waren jung und wollten erreichen, daß das Gebäude Aufmerksamkeit erregt.« Bei seinen jüngeren Bauwerken entschied er sich statt dessen für eine mit allen Raffinessen versehene Variante technisch orientierter Architektur. Piano beherrscht eine breit gefächerte Stilpalette – wie sich bei seinem Centre Culturel Canaque Jean-Marie-Tjibaou in Neukaledonien, seinem Erweiterungsbau für das IRCAM (Institut für akustische und musikalische Forschungen) von 1989 (eine ruhige Ziegelsteinkonstruktion genau gegenüber den mehrfarbigen Röhren und Leitungen des Centre Georges Pompidou) oder der von ihm durchgeführten Renovierung des Lingottokomplexes in Turin deutlich zeigt.

Né en 1937 à Gênes, Renzo Piano, associé à Richard Rogers, est l'auteur du Centre Georges Pompidou, à Paris (1977). Ce projet attire immédiatement sur lui l'attention internationale. Depuis cette époque, il est devenu l'une des «stars» les plus actives du monde de l'architecture, réalisant le Menil Collection Museum à Houston (1986), ou le stade San Nicola à Bari (1987–90). S'il n'éprouve aucun regret pour l'agressivité de la conception du Centre Georges Pompidou, il écrit: «Nous étions jeunes, et nous voulions leur en mettre plein la figure.» Dans ses plus récents travaux, il opte pour une architecture technologique plus sophistiquée et plus subtile. Il est capable d'une impressionnante variété de styles, comme le montre son Centre Culturel Canaque Jean-Marie-Tjibaou, actuellement en construction en Nouvelle-Calédonie, ou son extension pour l'IRCAM (1989), calme petit immeuble de brique, face aux tuyauteries multicolores du Centre Georges Pompidou ou, dans un contexte différent, la rénovation du complexe de Lingotto, à Turin.

Kansai Airport, Osaka
1988–1994

The idea of building an airport in the Bay of Osaka was first proposed in 1971. Fifteen invited groups of architects participated in the 1988 competition, including Ricardo Bofill, Jean Nouvel and Kazuhiro Ishii. Piano's winning design, a megastructure 1.7 kilometers long was built on an artificial island 4.37 by 1.27 kilometers long, for a total surface of 511 hectares. An essential feature of Piano's building is the 90 000 m² roof, covered with 82 400 ferrite type stainless steel panels, each measuring 1800 mm by 600 mm, a size chosen so that each panel could be carried by a single person. As Piano points out, the roof often has considerable importance in Japanese architecture. Although 180 million cubic meters of earth and sand were used to create the island, with as many as 80 boats unloading per day, the problem known as "differential settlement" or the uneven settling of different parts of the ground, required the use of 900 pillars with jacks at their base used to adjust height. A sophisticated level monitoring system checks the horizontal status of the building accordingly. A connecting bridge 3 750 meters long was also built between the airport island and the shore of Osaka Bay, making Kansai Airport one of the greatest engineering and architectural feats of the late 20th century.

Die Idee zu einem Flughafen in der Bucht von Osaka enstand bereits 1971. Zu dem 1988 ausgeschriebenen Wettbewerb hatte man fünfzehn Architektengruppen eingeladen, ihre Entwürfe weiter auszuarbeiten: u.a. Ricardo Bofill, Jean Nouvel und Kazuhiro Ishii. Pianos preisgekrönter Entwurf, eine 1,7 Kilometer lange Megastruktur, wurde auf einer künstlichen, 4,37 Kilometer langen und 1,27 Kilometer breiten Insel angelegt, die eine Gesamtfläche von 511 Hektar aufweist. Zu den herausragendsten Kennzeichen von Pianos Gebäude zählt die 90 000 m² große Dachkonstuktion: Sie besteht aus 82 400, jeweils 180 cm langen und 60 cm breiten Platten aus ferritischem, nichtrostendem Stahl, die problemlos von einem Arbeiter getragen werden konnten. Piano wies explizit darauf hin, daß der Dachkonstruktion in der japanischen Architektur häufig besondere Bedeutung beigemessen wird. Obwohl die Insel aus 180 Millionen Kubikmetern Erde und Sand entstand (täglich von 80 Transportschiffen angeliefert), erforderte das »Problem der unterschiedlichen Setzung« – einige Teile der künstlichen Insel setzen sich schneller als andere – den Einsatz von 900 Pfählen mit Hebeböcken, um den Höhenunterschied auszugleichen. Darüber hinaus wurde zwischen der Bucht von Osaka und der Flughafeninsel eine 3,75 Kilometer lange Verbindungsbrücke angelegt, wodurch der Kansai Airport als eine der herausragendsten Meisterleistungen der Ingenieurskunst und der Architektur des späten 20. Jahrhunderts bezeichnet werden kann.

L'idée de construire un aéroport dans la baie d'Osaka date de 1971. Quinze équipes d'architectes participèrent au concours de 1988, dont Ricardo Bofill, Jean Nouvel et Kazuhiro Ishii. Le projet lauréat, signé Piano, est un bâtiment géant de 1,7 km de long, édifié sur une île artificielle de 4,37 x 1,27 km de long, et de 511 ha. Une de ses caractéristiques est la toiture de 90 000 m², recouverte de panneaux d'acier inoxydable de type ferrite, de 1,80 x 0,60 m chacun, taille étudiée pour qu'ils puissent être manipulés par un seul individu. Comme le fait remarquer Piano, le toit revêt souvent une importance considérable dans l'architecture japonaise. Bien que 180 millions de m³ de terre et de sable aient été utilisés pour créer l'île (déchargés par une noria de 80 bateaux quotidiens) le problème «d'ajustement différentiel», ou de tassement inégal du sol a exigé la plantation de 900 piliers sur vérins réglables. Un système sophistiqué de contrôle de niveau vérifie l'horizontalité du bâtiment. Un pont de 3,75 km a été construit pour relier l'aéroport à la côte de la baie d'Osaka, faisant de Kansai l'une des plus brillantes réussites d'ingénierie et d'architecture de cette fin du XXᵉ siècle.

Despite its vast scale, Kansai Airport offers a friendly, light-filled interior, where the high-tech nature of its design does not overly encumber open spaces.

Trotz seines großen Ausmaßes besitzt der Kansai Airport eine freundliche, lichtdurchflutete Innenausstattung, bei der die technischen Elemente des Designs die offenen Räume nicht zu sehr in Beschlag nehmen.

Malgré son énorme échelle, le l'aéroport de Kansai offre des halls intérieurs accueillants, éclairés par la lumière du jour. Les détails high-tech de la construction ont su ne pas encombrer l'espace.

An aerial view of the artificial island built for Kansai Airport. 4.37 by 1.27 kilometers long, it is connected to Osaka by the bridge visible to the upper right. Above, a view from the interior of the passenger area toward the waiting aircraft.

Luftaufnahme der künstlich angelegten Insel für den Flughafen Kansai Airport. Dieses 4,37 Kilometer lange und 1,27 Kilometer breite Areal ist über eine Brücke (oben rechts) mit der Stadt Osaka verbunden. Oben: Blick vom Innenraum auf die wartenden Flugzeuge.

Vue aérienne de l'île artificielle créée pour l'aéroport de Kansai. De 4,37 km de long et 1,27 km de large, elle est reliée à Osaka par un pont, visible en haut à droite. En haut, l'intérieur de la zone passagers à proximité des avions.

Christian **de Portzamparc**

Born in Casablanca in 1944, Christian de Portzamparc studied at the Ecole des Beaux-Arts from 1962 to 1969. From the time of his earliest projects, such as the water tower he built in Marne-la-Vallée near Paris (1971–74) or his Hautes Formes public housing in Paris (1975–79), Portzamparc has developed a lyrical vocabulary which has been compared to a musical approach to modernity. Despite the almost baroque aspect of his compositions, Portzamparc steered his own path, clear of associations with the postmodern movement, and was given the large Cité de la Musique project on the outskirts of Paris in 1984. The significance of this project was recognized when he was awarded the 1994 Pritzker Prize. Another recently completed project is the boot-shaped tower he built over the new Lille-Europe railway station in Lille. His current work includes an addition to the Palais des Congrès in Paris, a tower for the Bandai toy company in Tokyo, and a courthouse building for Grasse in the south of France.

Christian des Portzamparc wurde 1944 in Casablanca geboren und studierte von 1962 bis 1969 an der Ecole des Beaux-Arts. Zu seinen ersten Projekten zählten der Wasserturm in Marne-la-Vallée bei Paris (1971–74) und seine städtische Wohnanlage Hautes Formes in Paris (1975–79). Seit dieser Zeit entwickelte Portzamparc ein lyrisches Architekturvokabular, das mit einer musikalischen Annäherung an die Moderne verglichen wurde. Ungeachtet der nahezu barock anmutenden Aspekte seiner Entwürfe ging Portzamparc seinen eigenen Weg – weitab von allen Strömungen der Postmoderne – und erhielt 1984 den Auftrag für das große Cité de la Musique-Projekt am Rande von Paris. Die Bedeutung dieses Projektes zeigte sich, als ihm 1994 der Pritzker Preis verliehen wurde. Ein weiteres, erst kürzlich fertiggestelltes Projekt ist der stiefelförmige Turm, den Portzamparc über den neuen Bahnhof Lille-Europe in Lille stülpte. Zur Zeit beschäftigt er sich mit einem Erweiterungsbau für das Palais des Congrès in Paris, einem Turm für den Spielzeughersteller Bandai in Tokio und einem Gerichtsgebäude für die Stadt Grasse in Südfrankreich.

Christian de Portzamparc est né à Casablanca en 1944, et a fait ses études à l'Ecole des Beaux-Arts de Paris, de 1962 à 1969. Depuis ses premiers projets – le château d'eau de Marne-la-Vallée, près de Paris (1971–74), ou les immeubles de logement social des Hautes-Formes, à Paris (1975–79) – il a développé un vocabulaire lyrique qui a pu être comparé à une approche musicale de la modernité. Malgré les aspects presque baroques de ses compositions, il trace sa propre voie, clairement à l'écart du mouvement post-moderne. Le grand projet de la Cité de la Musique, à Paris, lui est confié en 1984 et lui vaut le Prix Pritzker 1994. Une de ses autres réalisations récentes est la tour en forme de botte, élevée au-dessus de la gare Lille-Europe, à Lille. Parmi ses travaux actuels, une extension du Palais des Congrès de Paris, une tour pour la société de jouets Bandaï à Tokyo, et le palais de justice de Grasse, en Provence.

The entrance of the western section of the Cité de la Musique, Paris.

Eingang zum westlichen Teil der Cité de la Musique, Paris.

L'entrée de la partie Ouest de la Cité de la Musique, à Paris.

To the right an overall view of the western
section of the Cité de la Musique. Below, the
façade of the eastern section of the project,
opened in 1990. At the bottom of the page, the
street-side façade of the western section. Both
of these façades face the Boulevard Jean-
Jaurès.

Rechts: Gesamtansicht des westlichen Teils der
Cité de la Musique. Unten: Die Fassade des öst-
lichen Teils dieses Projektes, der 1990 eröffnet
wurde. Am unteren Rand der Seite: Die zur
Straße gewandte Fassade des westlichen Teils.
Beide Fassaden blicken auf den Boulevard Jean-
Jaurès.

A droite, vue générale de la partie Ouest de la
Cité de la Musique. En dessous, façade de la
partie Est, ouverte en 1990. En bas de page,
façade sur la rue de la partie Ouest. Ces deux
façades donnent sur le boulevard Jean-Jaurès.

Cité de la Musique Ouest, La Villette, Paris 1985–1995

Christian de Portzamparc was chosen by competition to design this "Beaubourg for music" in January 1985. The total budget for the two halves of the complex was one billion francs, but that works out at only 6 500 francs per square meter, a relatively low sum. Integrated into the much larger La Villette complex which includes an exhibition hall (Grande Halle), a rock concert hall (Zénith) an enormous science museum (Cité des Sciences), and a garden with "follies" designed by Bernard Tschumi, the Cité de la Musique's eastern half containing the National Conservatory of music was inaugurated on December 7, 1990. The other half of the Cité, situated to the west, and containing a large, flexible oval concert hall, was opened on January 12, 1995. A museum of musical instruments, which has fallen behind schedule, was to be completed by the Fall of 1995. Fragmented into numerous pieces which correspond at least in part to their function, the Cité de la Musique Ouest is a testimony to the subtlety and the variety of which the 1994 Pritzker Prize winner is capable. The oval concert hall, part of an overall spiral design including an internal street, is the only one of its shape in the world.

Im Januar 1985 wurde Christian de Portzamparc als Architekt für dieses »Beaubourg der Musik« ausgewählt. Das Gesamtbudget für die beiden Hälften dieses Komplexes belief sich zwar auf eine Milliarde Francs, aber das bedeutete nur einen Betrag von 6 500 Francs pro Quadratmeter – eine relativ niedrige Summe. Die im viel größeren Parc de La Villette gelegene östliche Hälfte der Cité de la Musique, die das Nationalkonservatorium für Musik beherbergt, konnte am 7. Dezember 1990 eröffnet werden, während die im Westen plazierte andere Hälfte der Cité mit einem großen, ovalen Mehrzweck-Konzertsaal am 12. Januar 1995 der Öffentlichkeit übergeben wurde. Der Zeitplan für das ebenfalls geplante Musikinstrumenten-Museum hatte sich jedoch auf den Herbst 1995 verschoben. Die in zahllose Teile untergliederte Cité de la Musique Ouest, deren einzelne Elemente zumindest in bezug auf ihre Funktion miteinander übereinstimmen, ist ein Beweis für die Finesse und Vielseitigkeit des Architekten Portzamparc, der 1994 den Pritzker Preis erhielt. Der ovale Konzertsaal – Teil eines übergreifenden Spiraldesigns mit einer internen Straße – ist aufgrund seiner Form weltweit einzigartig.

Christian de Portzamparc a été sélectionné par concours pour construire ce «Beaubourg de la musique» en janvier 1985. Le budget total de ce complexe en deux parties est de 1 milliard de francs, ce qui ne représente guère que 6 500 francs par m², somme relativement raisonnable. Intégrée dans l'ensemble encore plus vaste de La Villette, qui comprend un hall d'exposition, la Grande Halle, une salle de concert rock, le Zénith, un énorme musée des Sciences, et un parc agrémenté des «folies» de Bernard Tschumi, la partie Est de la Cité de la Musique contenant le Conservatoire national de Musique a ouvert le 7 décembre 1990. L'autre partie, à l'Ouest, qui contient une grande salle de concert ovale et modulable, a été inaugurée le 12 janvier 1995. Un musée d'instruments de musique, qui a connu quelques retards, sera terminé à l'automne 1995. Fragmentée en nombreux éléments qui correspondent chacun en partie à une fonction, la Cité de la Musique Ouest illustre la subtilité et l'imagination dont le lauréat du Pritzker Prize 1994 est capable. Le plan en spirale, qui comprend la salle de concert et une rue intérieure, est sans équivalent dans le monde.

To the right, this protruding metal frame crosses the entire western section of the Cité. On the far right, the undulating openings created by Portzamparc are to some extent related to the musical function of the building.

Rechts: Dieser hervorspringende Metallrahmen überragt den westlichen Teil der Cité. Rechts außen: Die wellenförmigen Öffnungen stellen eine Verbindung zur Funktion des Gebäudes als Musikzentrum her.

A droite, cette structure métallique en avancée traverse toute la partie Ouest de la Cité de la Musique. A l'extrême droite, les ouvertures ondulantes dessinées par Portzamparc évoquent la fonction musicale du bâtiment.

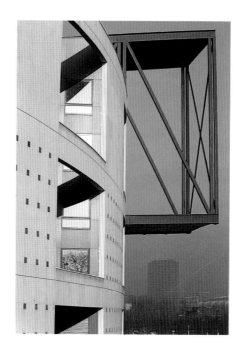

Page 148/149: Within the complex, the internal "street" and the main concert hall. Below, the main entrance, incorporating a structure echoing the Villette Park "follies" designed by Bernard Tschumi. A floor plan shows the spiral design of the whole, and the oval concert hall.

Seite 148/149: Die interne »Straße« und der große Konzertsaal innerhalb des Komplexes. Unten: Der Haupteingang, dessen Konstruktionsweise an die von Bernard Tschumi entworfenen »Follies« im Parc de la Villette erinnert. Der Grundriß zeigt das spiralförmige Design sowie den ovalen Mehrzweck-Konzertsaal.

Page 148/149: Intérieur du complexe: la «rue» interne et le grand auditorium. Ci-dessous, l'entrée principale intègre une structure qui rappelle les «folies» dessinées par Bernard Tschumi pour le Parc de La Villette. Le plan de masse montre la conception en spirale et l'ovale de la salle de concert.

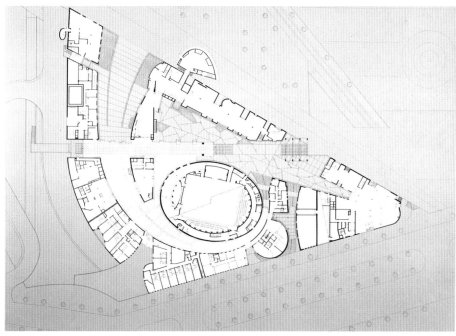

Axel **Schultes**

Born in Dresden in 1943, Axel Schultes graduated from the Technical University of Berlin in 1969. He worked in partnership with Dietrich Bangert, Bernd Jansen and Stephan Scholz from 1974 to 1991 (BJSS). After planning the Kunstmuseum Bonn he created his own firm, and participated in both the Reichstag and Spreebogen competitions in 1993, as well as numerous other competitions before that such as that for the Deutsche Historische Museum in Berlin (1988), or the Alexandria Library in 1989. His built work also includes the Büropark am Welfenplatz in Hannover (1993). Aside from the Spreebogen and Chancellory projects, which undoubtedly will make Schultes a well-known figure outside of Germany, he is working on the extension of the "Yenidze" tobacco-mosque in Dresden and the Baumschulenweg Crematorium in Berlin. The Spreebogen design was executed in collaboration with Charlotte Frank, born in Kiel in 1959, who, together with Christoph Witt, has been his associate since 1992.

Der 1943 in Dresden geborene Architekt Axel Schultes beendete 1969 sein Studium an der Technischen Hochschule von Berlin. Von 1974 bis 1991 arbeitete er mit Dietrich Bangert, Bernd Jansen und Stephan Scholz (BJSS) zusammen. Nach der Planung für das Kunstmuseum Bonn gründete er sein eigenes Büro und beteiligte sich ein Jahr später an den Ausschreibungen für den Reichstag und das Spreebogen-Projekt. Zuvor hatte Schultes bereits an vielen Architekturwettbewerben teilgenommen – wie etwa an der Ausschreibung für das Deutsche Historische Museum in Berlin (1988) oder für die Alexandria-Bibliothek (1989). Für den Büropark am Welfenplatz in Hannover (1993) zeichnete Schultes ebenfalls verantwortlich. Zur Zeit beschäftigt er sich – neben seiner Arbeit am Spreebogen-Projekt und am Kanzleramt, das ihn zweifellos über die Grenzen Deutschlands bekannt machen wird – mit einem Erweiterungsbau der »Yenidze«-Tabakmoschee in Dresden und dem Krematorium Baumschulenweg in Berlin. Der Entwurf für das Spreebogen-Projekt entstand in Zusammenarbeit mit Charlotte Frank (1959 in Kiel geboren), die zusammen mit Christoph Witt seit 1992 Büropartnerin ist.

Né à Dresde en 1943, Axel Schultes obtient son diplôme de l'Université technique de Berlin en 1969. Il travaille en association avec Dietrich Bangert, Bernd Jansen et Stephan Scholz, de 1974 à 1991 (BJSS). Après avoir élaboré les plans du Kunstmuseum Bonn, il crée sa propre agence et participe à de nombreux concours comme celui du Deutsche Historische Museum (1988) à Berlin, et de la Bibliothèque d'Alexandrie (1989). Son œuvre construite comprend également le Büropark am Welfenplatz, à Hanovre (1993). En dehors du Spreebogen et de ses travaux à la Chancellerie, qui lui ont assuré une notoriété indiscutable en dehors de l'Allemagne, il travaille à une extension de la mosquée Yenidze de Dresde, et au crématorium de Baumschulenweg, à Berlin. Le projet du Spreebogen a été conçu en collaboration avec Charlotte Frank, qui est avec Christoph Witt son associée depuis 1992.

A detail of the exterior arcade of the Kunstmuseum Bonn.

Detail der Außenarkade des Kunstmuseum Bonn.

Détail de la façade extérieure du Kunstmuseum Bonn.

Kunstmuseum Bonn, Bonn
1985–1992

Designed before the fall of the Berlin Wall, this museum was originally intended to form a homogeneous whole, on a 100 by 300 meter site between Bonn and Bad Godesberg, with the adjacent Bundeskunsthalle (Federal Art Gallery), but as often happens in such "integrated" projects, the two entities were separated, breaking with the concept of a Berlin-like museum "island," and the Austrian architect Gustav Peichl was called on to design the second structure. According to the architect, the required top lighting was provided in the galleries through a "development of the glazed roof to be found in the hall of the German Protestant Church in Hanover". The architect's intention here was not to erect an art temple, a Domus Aurea," says Schultes, "the aim was to create a Domus Lux, a house of light." Significantly, Axel Schultes also quotes the artist Markus Lüpertz in his description of the Kunstmuseum: "Architecture must have the greatness to present itself in such a way that it can accomodate art, and that it does not drive art away through its own claims."

Das vor dem Fall der Berliner Mauer konzipierte Kunstmuseum war ursprünglich als homogenes Ganzes auf einem 100 Meter breiten und 300 Meter langen Gelände zwischen Bonn und Bad Godesberg, zusammen mit der Bundeskunsthalle, geplant. Aber wie so oft bei »integrierten« Projekten wurden auch hier die beiden Teile voneinander getrennt, wodurch das Konzept einer Berlinähnlichen Museums-»Insel« überholt war. Für den Entwurf des zweiten Baus wählte man den österreichischen Architekten Gustav Peichl. Das erforderliche, von oben einfallende Licht in den Galerien wurde – so der Architekt – durch eine »Weiterentwicklung des Glasdaches der Zentralkanzlei der Evangelischen Kirche Deutschlands« in Hannover erreicht. Schultes erklärte, daß »das Ziel des Architekten hierbei nicht darin bestand, einen Kunsttempel, ein Domus Aurea zu errichten, sondern ein Domus Lux, ein Haus des Lichts.« Bezeichnenderweise zitiert Schultes bei seiner Beschreibung des Kunstmuseums auch den Künstler Markus Lüpertz: »..., daß Architektur die Größe haben müßte, sich so angelegt darzustellen, daß Kunst in ihr möglich wird; daß sie eben nicht durch eigenen Anspruch Kunst vertreibt.«

Conçu avant la chute du Mur de Berlin, ce musée construit sur un terrain de 300 x 100 m entre Bonn et Bad Godesberg devait à l'origine former un ensemble homogène avec la Bundeskunsthalle toute proche. Mais comme il arrive souvent dans ce genre de projets «intégrés», les deux entités furent séparées, réduisant à néant le concept d'une «île-musée», à la berlinoise, et l'on appela l'architecte autrichien Gustav Peichl pour dessiner le second bâtiment. Selon Schultes, l'éclairage zénithal demandé pour les galeries lui a été inspiré par «la verrière de l'église protestante de Hanovre». L'intention, ici, n'était pas «d'ériger un temple à l'art, une Domus Aurea, explique Schultes, mais de créer une domus lux, une maison de lumière». Il est significatif qu'il cite également l'artiste Markus Lüpertz dans sa description du Kunstmuseum: «... que l'architecture devrait avoir la grandeur de se présenter de telle manière qu'elle puisse s'ouvrir à l'art, et qu'elle ne gêne pas celui-ci par ses propres revendications.»

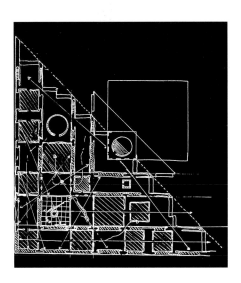

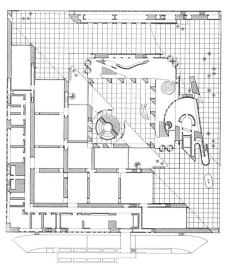

Page 152/153: According to Axel Schultes, the Kunstmuseum "recalls features from a number of buildings – the Villa Imperiale in Tivoli, Le Corbusier's endless museum, a wharf in Barcelona, Cordoba's great mosque – without conforming to a particular type".

Seite 152/153: Laut Axel Schultes erinnern einige Elemente des Kunstmuseums »an eine Reihe von anderen Gebäuden – die Villa Imperiale in Tivoli, Le Corbusiers endloses Museum, eine Werft in Barcelona, Córdobas große Moschee – ohne sich jedoch auf einen bestimmten Typus festzulegen«.

Page 152/153: Selon Axel Schultes, le Kunstmuseum «rappelle les caractéristiques d'un certain nombre de monuments – la Villa Impériale de Tivoli, le musée sans fin de Le Corbusier, une jetée de Barcelone, la grande mosquée de Cordoue – sans se conformer à un type particulier».

Page 154/155: The architect emphasizes his attempt to reconcile the different forces which form a museum: "the political need for prestige versus the necessities of urban planning, the public nature of exhibitions versus the personal and private experience of art."

Seite 154/155: Der Architekt unterstreicht seinen Versuch, die verschiedenen Kräfte, die ein Museum bilden, miteinander in Einklang zu bringen: »Das politische Prestigebedürfnis gegen die Zwänge der Stadtplanung; der öffentliche Charakter der Ausstellungen gegen das persönliche und private Erleben von Kunst.«

Page 154/155: L'architecte a mis l'accent sur sa tentative de réconciliation des différentes forces qui contribuent à la vie d'un musée: «La recherche politique du prestige face aux nécessités de l'urbanisme, la nature publique des expositions face à l'expérience artistique, personnelle et intime».

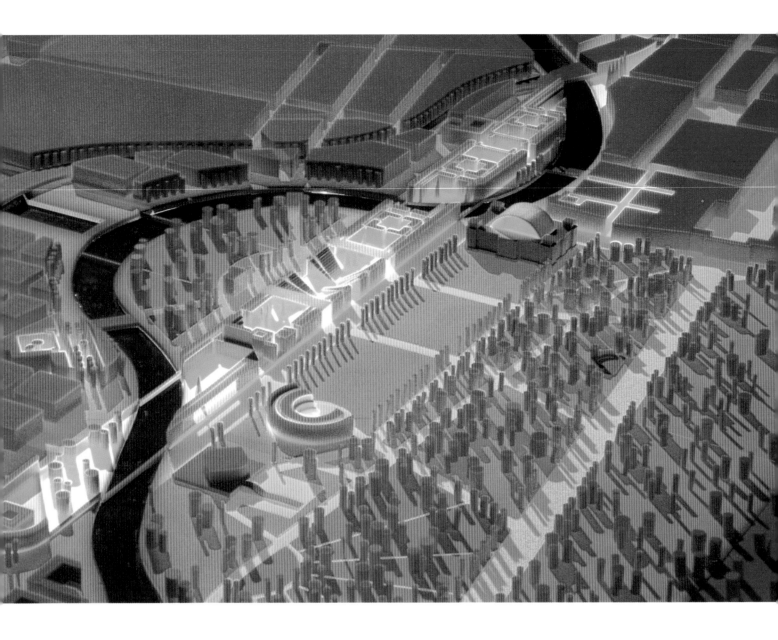

Two views of the strong line of buildings proposed by Axel Schultes for the bend in the Spree nearest the Reichstag, creating a new heart for official Berlin.

Zwei Ansichten des Gebäudekomplexes, den Axel Schultes für ein Gelände im Spreebogen neben dem Reichstag entwarf, um so ein neues Zentrum des offiziellen Berlin zu schaffen.

Deux vues du puissant alignement de bâtiments proposé par Axel Schultes pour le méandre de la Spree, très proche du Reichstag, créant un nouveau cœur pour le Berlin officiel.

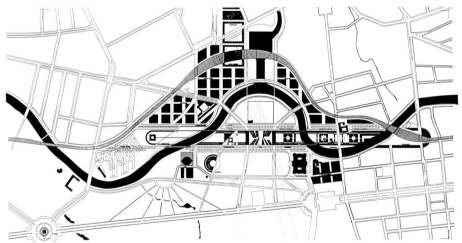

Spreebogen Project
1993–

Some 835 architects from 44 different countries submitted entries to the competition for this site in what is soon to become the administrative heart of Germany. The project of Axel Schultes and Charlotte Frank was chosen in February 1993. According to Schultes, the project aims to "create an urban fabric where it would appear even without planning: in the terrain between the railway track and the river, with the park sprawled across two bends in the Spree, forming a magnificent contrast. The federal government is the third factor, the factor that lends the city its special status and provides the missing link in the urban fabric." The idea of a chain of federal and parliamentary buildings, stepping over the limits which in principle were set for this competition and creating a highly symbolic link between the former eastern and western parts of the once and future capital, that persuaded the jury. One criticism levelled at the project was that it did not give enough prominence to the Chancellory. The clear spatial structure of the project and its sense of permanence contrast with what Rossi has described as "today's fragmented sense of synthesis" and set a counterpoint to this historically charged place.

An der Ausschreibung für dieses Gelände, auf dem der Regierungs- und Verwaltungssitz der Bundesrepublik Deutschland entstehen soll, beteiligten sich 835 Architekten aus 44 Ländern. Im Februar 1993 entschied man sich für einen Entwurf von Axel Schultes und Charlotte Frank. Laut Schultes handelt es sich bei diesem Projekt um den Versuch, der »Stadt stattzugeben, da, wo sie sowieso hineinwachsen würde, in das Gelände zwischen Stadtbahnviadukt und Spreeufer, – und dem Park, in großzügigstem Kontrast über zwei Spreebögen hinweg Landschaftsraum zu lassen. Der Bund, der dritte im Bunde, ist das Ausgezeichnete, das Besondere, das Stadt und Land Verbindende, das ›missing link‹ in der Stadtgestalt.« Die Idee dieser Kette von Regierungs- und Parlamentsbauten, das Überschreiten von Grenzen, durch die sich der Entwurf von den anderen Wettbewerbsbeiträgen unterschied und eine stark symbolische Verbindung zwischen den vormals östlichen und westlichen Stadtteilen kreierte, überzeugte die Jury. Kritisiert wurde lediglich, daß das Projekt dem Sitz des Kanzlers nicht genügend Bedeutung einräume. Die klare räumliche Struktur des Projektes, sein »langer Atem«, stellt sich dem »zerbrochenen Synthesevermögen unserer Zeit« (Rossi) und dem historisch so belasteten Ort entgegen.

Quelque 835 architectes de 44 pays ont participé au concours pour l'aménagement de ce site en centre administratif de l'Allemagne réunifiée. Le projet d'Axel Schultes et de Charlotte Frank fut retenu en février 1993. Selon Schultes, celui-ci s'inscrit dans un effort pour «laisser la ville être, là où elle se serait développée de toute façon, dans le terrain compris entre le viaduc du métro et la rive de la Sprée – et le parc, en laissant un espace au paysage sur deux méandres de la Sprée, ce qui forme un contraste généreux. Le Bund, le troisième associé, est ce qu'il y a de remarquable, de particulier, le lien entre la ville et la campagne, le ‹chaînon marquant› dans l'apparence de la ville». C'est certainement cette idée de chaîne de bâtiments gouvernementaux et parlementaires, franchissant les limites géographiques fixées par le cahier des charges et créant un lien hautement symbolique entre les parties Est et Ouest de l'ancienne et future capitale, qui convainquit le jury. Une critique adressée au projet fut de ne pas donner suffisamment d'importance au siège de la Chancellerie. La nature spatiale affirmée du projet, son «souffle», s'oppose à la force de synthèse rompue de notre époque» (Rossi) et à ce lieu, lourd de tout un passé historique.

Otto **Steidle + Partner**

Façade of the Ulm University Engineering Sciences Building.

Fassade des Gebäudes für Inge-nieurswissenschaften der Universität Ulm West.

Façade du bâtiment des sciences de l'ingénierie de l'Université d'Ulm.

Born in Munich in 1943, Otto Steidle studied at the Akademie der Bildenden Künste in that city from 1965 to 1969. In 1966, he created the firm Muhr + Steidle, and in 1969, Steidle + Partner. He has taught extensively, in Munich, Kassel, Berlin, Amsterdam and at MIT in Cambridge, Massachusetts (1991, 1993). He has been the Rector of the Munich Akademie der Bildenden Künste since 1993. Otto Steidle is best known for his work on housing which he feels should always be informal and open to evolution, and for large projects such as the headquarters of Gruner + Jahr in Hamburg (1983–91). His last building, created in association with Uwe Kiessler, has been described as a "horizontal skyscraper," or a "spatial city." Built for some 2 500 employees, intended for creative and productive edi-torial work as opposed to administration, the struc-ture was intended not only to be flexible, but also to fit into its neighborhood, since it was "developed on the lines of old buildings destroyed in the war."

Otto Steidle, 1943 in Mün-chen geboren, studierte von 1965 bis 1969 an der Akademie der Bildenden Künste. 1966 gründete er das Architekturbüro Muhr + Steidle und 1969 das Büro Steidle + Partner. Steidle war u.a. in München, Kas-sel, Berlin, Amsterdam und am MIT (Massachusetts Institute of Technology) in Cambridge, Massachusetts (1991, 1993) als Dozent tätig und ist seit 1993 Rektor an der Münchner Akademie der Bildenden Künste. Be-kannt wurde Steidle durch seine Wohnungsbaupro-jekte, die seines Erachtens immer ungezwungen und für eine Entwicklung offen sein sollten, und durch sol-che Großprojekte wie das Gruner + Jahr-Gebäude in Hamburg (1983–91). Dieser Bau, den er zusammen mit Uwe Kiessler errichtete, wurde beschrieben als »ein horizontaler Wolkenkratzer« oder »eine Raum-Stadt«. Gebaut wurde er für 2 500 Angestellte, die sich – im Gegensatz zu reinen Ver-waltungsangestellten – mit kreativer und produktiver Redaktionsarbeit beschäfti-gen. Das Gebäude mußte nicht nur flexibel konzipiert sein, sondern auch in die Umgebung eingefügt wer-den, da es »auf dem ehe-maligen Gelände im Krieg zerstörter Häuser« ent-stand.

Né à Munich en 1943, Otto Steidle y fait ses études, à l'Akademie der Bildenden Künste, de 1965 à 1969. En 1966, il crée l'agence Muhr + Steidle, et en 1969, Steidle + Partner. Il a beau-coup enseigné à Munich, Kassel, Berlin, Amsterdam, et au MIT, à Cambridge, Massachusetts (1991, 1993). Il est recteur de l'Akademie der Bildenden Künste depuis 1993. Il est surtout connu pour son tra-vail sur l'habitat, dont il pense qu'il devrait toujours rester informel et ouvert à l'évolution, et pour certains grands projets comme le siège de Gruner + Jahr, à Hambourg (1983–91). Il décrit cet immeuble, réalisé en collaboration avec Uwe Kiessler, comme un «gratte-ciel horizontal», ou une «cité de l'espace». Construit pour les 2 500 employés des départe-ments de la création et de la production éditoriale, et non pour des services ad-ministratifs, cet immeuble a été voulu adaptable, mais également adapté à son environnement, «un aligne-ment d'anciens bâtiments détruits pendant la guerre».

Ulm University, Ulm
1990–1991

Like a town wall, this very large group of buildings with sodded roofs and provisions for collecting and distributing rainwater to ensure that the ecosystem is damaged as little as possible, creates a division between the urban Ulm and the forested Oberer Eselsberg. The research equipment is installed in the concrete basement, while above, the "thinking rooms" are formed with lighter, inexpensive materials. The outer layer of the façades consists of "cemented extruded particle board or fiber cement panels with wooden strips covering the joints, inside are marine quality laminated panels treated with linseed oil." The bright colors visible on the outside of the university buildings are based visually on a rhythmic diagram of Bach's Fugue in C Minor. According to Steidle, this is "not a world for specialists, but more an indicator of the links between and the closeness of art and science," highlighting his own rejection of buildings which have only one possible function. The rapid building time and limited budget are certainly a factor in the appearance of this complex, which obviously seeks to make the most of its inherent limitations. Those interested in architecture can easily observe the marked stylistic contrasts between the Ulm University buildings and the neighboring Research Center for Daimler-Benz designed by the American architect Richard Meier.

Diesem großen Gebäudekomplex (mit seinen Gründächern und Vorrichtungen zur Sammlung und Retardierung des Regenwassers, um das Ökosystem »Oberer Eselsberg« so wenig wie möglich zu beeinträchtigen) liegt der bereits im Wettbewerbstitel proklamierte Begriff »Stadt« zu Grunde. Die Stadt als geordnetes, strukturelles Gefüge aus Wegen und Gebäuden, im Gegensatz zur Landschaft als naturbelassene Fläche. Die hochinstallierten Forschungseinrichtungen befinden sich im Erdgeschoß, das als Stahlbetonskelettbau angelegt ist, während die darüberliegenden »Denk-Räume« aus Holz errichtet wurden. Die äußerste Fassadenschicht besteht aus »zementgebundenen Spanplatten, deren Elementstöße Holzleisten überdecken. Innen kamen leinölbehandelte Seekieferschichtplatten zur Anwendung.« Die leuchtenden Farben der unterschiedlich gefärbten Quartiershöfe werden durch die 400 Meter lange Promenade (Erschließungsbaumarkt) ähnlich eines Musikstücks moduliert und variiert. Laut Steidle ist dies »keine Spezialistenwelt, vielmehr ein Hinweis auf die Zusammenhänge und Nähe zwischen Kunst und Wissenschaft«. Gleichzeitig betont der Architekt dadurch noch einmal seine ablehnende Haltung gegenüber Gebäuden, die nur eine einzige Funktion erfüllen können. Aber auch die kurze Bauzeit und das beschränkte Budget bildeten bestimmende Faktoren bei der architektonischen Gestaltung dieses Gebäudekomplexes, die das Beste aus den begrenzten Möglichkeiten zu machen sucht. Architekturinteressierte werden den stilistischen Kontrast zwischen den Gebäuden der Universität Ulm West und dem benachbarten, von dem amerikanischen Architekten Richard Meier entworfenen Forschungszentrum von Daimler-Benz leicht erkennen können.

Comme le rempart d'une cité, ce très vaste ensemble de bâtiments aux toits recouverts de gazon et à système écologique de collecte et de redistribution de l'eau de pluie, sépare la ville du massif forestier de l'Oberer Eselsberg. Les installations de recherche sont logées dans les sous-sols en béton, tandis qu'au-dessus, les «salles de réflexion» sont édifiées en matériaux légers et économiques. Le revêtement des façades est en «plaques de particules extrudées et panneaux de fibrociment cimentés à couvre-joints de bois et, à l'intérieur, en panneaux de contre-plaqué marine traités à l'huile de lin». Les couleurs vives de l'extérieur s'inspirent d'un diagramme de la fugue en ut mineur de J.S. Bach. Pour Steidle, qui souligne son rejet des bâtiments réduits à une unique fonction, il ne s'agit pas ici «d'un univers de spécialistes, mais davantage d'un témoin des liens entre l'art et la science et de leur proximité». La brève durée de la construction et son budget limité ont certainement contribué à l'apparence de cet ensemble qui a tenté de tirer le meilleur parti de ces contraintes. Le contraste entre ces bâtiments universitaires et le centre de recherches de Daimler-Benz voisin, dû à Richard Meier, est on ne peut plus frappant.

The two story structure is designed without false floors and shafts. The research equipment is installed in the basement, and large corridors encourage free circulation within the complex. The color scheme is based on a visual interpretation of J.S. Bach's Fugue in C Minor.

Das zweigeschossige Gebäude wurde ohne Zwischendecken und Schächte konstruiert. Alle Forschungseinrichtungen befinden sich im Erdgeschoß, und die offenen, galerieartigen Flure dienen der kommunikativen Verbindung innerhalb des Gebäudekomplexes. Das Farbschema basiert auf einer visuellen Interpretation von J.S. Bachs Fuge in c-moll.

Le bâtiment à deux niveaux ne comporte ni faux-plafonds ni gaines techniques. Les installations de recherche sont implantées dans les sous-sols, et de grands corridors facilitent la libre circulation à l'intérieur du complexe. La coloration repose sur une interprétation visuelle de la fugue de J.S. Bach en ut mineur.

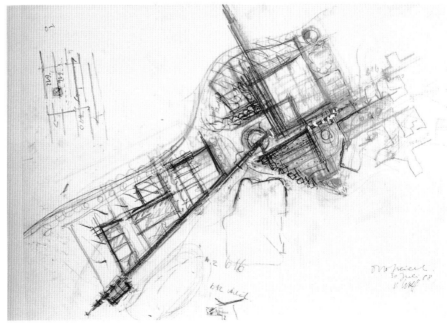

Intended as an ecologically sound design within a limited budget, the Ulm University buildings use color and innovative forms to break the institutional monotony which might be expected in such a structure.

Mit Hilfe von Farbe und innovativen Gestaltungselementen durchbricht die Universität Ulm (trotz eines beschränkten Budgets) auf ökologisch vertretbare Weise die Einheits-Monotonie, die man sonst bei einem solchen Bauwerk erwartet.

Réalisés dans le cadre d'un budget à l'évidence limité, voulus écologiques, les nouveaux bâtiments de l'Université d'Ulm utilisent la couleur et des formes innovantes pour rompre la monotonie généralement de mise dans ce type de bâtiment.

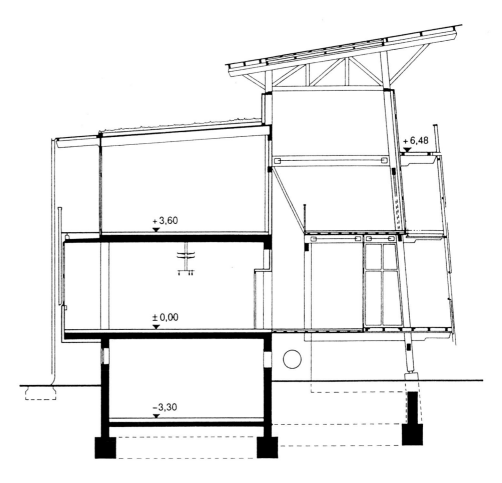

Jean-Michel **Wilmotte**

An interior view of the Chiado Museum, Lisbon.

Innenansicht des Chiado Museum in Lissabon.

Vue intérieure du Musée Chiado à Lisbonne.

Born in 1948, a graduate of the Ecole Camondo in Paris, Jean-Michel Wilmotte created his own firm, Governor, in 1975. Although he is best known for his work in interior design, including private apartments for François Mitterrand in the Elysée Palace, Wilmotte joined the Order of Architects in France in 1993. With approximately 60 employees, his office works on industrial and furniture design, such as the new lighting fixtures and benches recently installed on the Champs-Elysées, but he also participated in the recent competition for the British Museum, making use of the experience he had gathered as architect of the Decorative Arts Department of the Louvre for the Richelieu wing, completed in 1993. As an architect, Jean-Michel Wilmotte recently completed two buildings in Tokyo, the International Executive Office Building in the Shinjuku area, and the New N° 3 Arai Building, while he also carried out the furniture design for the Bank of Luxembourg building, completed by Arquitectonica in 1994.

Jean-Michel Wilmotte – 1948 geboren – studierte an der Ecole Camondo in Paris und gründete 1975 das Architekturbüro Governor. Obwohl er eher für seine innenarchitektonischen Arbeiten bekannt ist – wie die Ausgestaltung der Privaträume François Mitterrands im Palais de l'Elysée –, trat Wilmotte 1993 dem französischen Architektenbund bei. Sein mit etwa 60 Angestellten besetztes Büro beschäftigt sich mit Industrie- und Möbeldesign wie etwa den neuen Beleuchtungskörpern und Sitzbänken, die vor kurzem auf den Champs-Elysées aufgestellt wurden. Darüber hinaus nahm Wilmotte am kürzlich ausgeschriebenen Architekturwettbewerb des British Museum teil, wobei ihm die Erfahrungen zugute kamen, die er als Architekt der Abteilung Angewandte Kunst im Richelieu-Flügel des Louvre sammeln konnte, der 1993 vollendet wurde. Zu seinen weiteren architektonischen Werken zählen zwei vor kurzem vollendete Gebäude in Tokio – das International Executive Office Building im Viertel Shinjuku und das New N° 3 Arai Building. Außerdem entwarf er die Möbel für die Banque de Luxembourg, die 1994 von Arquitectonica gebaut worden war.

Né en 1948, et diplômé de l'Ecole Camondo, à Paris, Jean-Michel Wilmotte crée son propre studio, Governor, en 1975. Surtout connu pour ses réalisations en architecture intérieure, comme les appartements privés de F. Mitterrand au Palais de l'Elysée, il s'inscrit à l'Ordre des Architectes en 1993. Son agence, qui compte environ 60 collaborateurs, intervient dans les domaines du design industriel et du meuble, comme les nouveaux éclairages et bancs publics des Champs-Elysées, mais a également participé au récent concours pour le British Museum, pour mettre à profit son expérience d'architecte du département des Arts décoratifs du Louvre, pour l'aile Richelieu (1993). En tant qu'architecte, Wilmotte a récemment signé deux immeubles à Tokyo, le International Executive Office Building dans le quartier de Shinjuku, et le New N° 3 Arai Building. A Luxembourg, il a conçu le mobilier du siège de la Banque de Luxembourg, achevé par Arquitectonica en 1994.

Chiado Museum, Lisbon
1990–1994

Following the catastrophic fires which swept through the historic Chiado district of Lisbon on August 25, 1988, Jean-Michel Wilmotte, perhaps best known for his extensive work in the Grand Louvre together with I.M. Pei, was called on to renovate and expand this museum of Portuguese art. Subtle and respectful of historic buildings, Wilmotte was undoubtedly an ideal choice to restructure the existing spaces and to add new exhibition areas, bringing the total up to 2 700 m², for a budget of 40 million francs. The bulk of this sum was provided by the French ministries of Foreign Affairs, Culture, Tourism and Housing. The challenge, which consisted in the creation of a logical sequence for the visit of five buildings dating from the 16th to the 18th centuries, the whole on a steeply inclined site, was met by Wilmotte with his usual ability to blend the modern and the traditional. Here, he has skillfully inserted a suspended steel stairway and two metal passageways, to make the visit more coherent. A modern temporary exhibition module was added by the architect in an effort to propose a new standard for museum presentations.

Nach der katastrophalen Feuersbrunst, die am 25. August 1988 den historischen Chiado-Bezirk in der Altstadt von Lissabon fast vollständig zerstörte, wurde Jean-Michel Wilmotte – bekannt für seine Arbeiten am Grand Louvre (zusammen mit I.M. Pei) – mit der Renovierung und Erweiterung des Museu Nacional de Arte Contemporânea beauftragt. Bekannt für seinen Respekt gegenüber historischer Bausubstanz, war er der ideale Architekt für eine Rekonstruktion der vorhandenen Räume und eine Erweiterung der Ausstellungsflächen, wodurch das Museum eine Gesamtfläche von 2 700 m² erhielt – bei einem Budget von 40 Millionen Francs. Diese Summe wurde größtenteils vom französischen Außenministerium, dem Kulturministerium sowie den Ministerien für Tourismus und Wohnungsbau aufgebracht. Wilmotte löste die an ihn herangetragene Aufgabe, eine logische Abfolge für einen Besuch der fünf aus verschiedenen Jahrhunderten stammenden Gebäude zu schaffen, die zudem auf einem steil abfallenden Gelände liegen – durch seine wiederholt bewiesene Fähigkeit, Altes mit Neuem zu verbinden. Um dem Museumsbesuch einen logischen Zusammenhang zu verleihen, entwarf er für dieses Museum eine Hängetreppe aus Stahl sowie zwei Verbindungsgänge aus Metall. Darüber hinaus bemühte sich der Architekt, neue Maßstäbe in der Präsentation von Museen und ihrer Exponate zu setzen, indem er das Museum durch einen modernen Gebäudeteil mit Wechselausstellungen ergänzte.

C'est à la suite de l'incendie catastrophique qui ravagea le quartier historique du Chiado, au cœur de Lisbonne, le 25 août 1988, que fut appelé Jean-Michel Wilmotte, plus connu pour son importante intervention sur le Grand Louvre en compagnie de I.M.Pei. Il fut chargé de restaurer et d'agrandir ce musée d'art portugais. Respectueux des bâtiments historiques, le subtil Wilmotte était sans doute le choix idéal pour traiter ces 2 700 m². Le financement de 40 millions de francs a été fourni pour l'essentiel par les ministères français des affaires étrangères, de la culture, du tourisme et du logement. Le défi – créer une séquence de visite logique à travers cinq constructions datant des XVIe au XVIIIème siècles, sur un site fortement incliné – a été relevé par Wilmotte dont le talent à mêler l'ancien et le moderne est bien connu. Pour rendre le parcours plus cohérent, il a inséré avec art un escalier d'acier suspendu, et deux passerelles de métal. Il a également ajouté un module moderne, pour les expositions temporaires et dynamiser les présentations du musée.

Page 166/167: A specialist in the subtle transformation of the interiors of historic monuments such as the Louvre, Jean-Michel Wilmotte is also an accomplished architect, as his work in the Chiado Museum, where he has both created new space and redesigned old areas, proves.

Seite 166/167: Als Spezialist für respektvolle, innenarchitektonische Umgestaltungen historischer Bausubstanz (wie etwa beim Louvre) machte Jean-Michel Wilmotte seinem Namen als hervorragender Architekt auch im Falle des Chiado Museum alle Ehre, bei dem er sowohl neue Räume schuf als auch vorhandene Räume rekonstruierte.

Page 166/167: Spécialiste des transformations subtiles et des aménagements intérieurs de bâtiments historiques comme le Louvre, Jean-Michel Wilmotte est également un architecte accompli, comme le prouve le travail réalisé pour le musée Chiado, pour lequel il a créé un nouvel espace et redessiné les anciens.

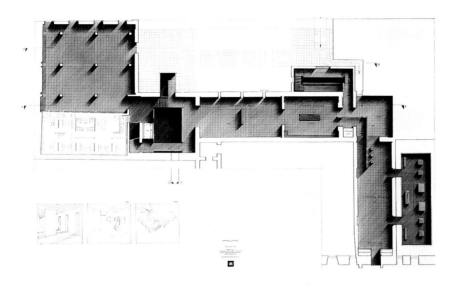

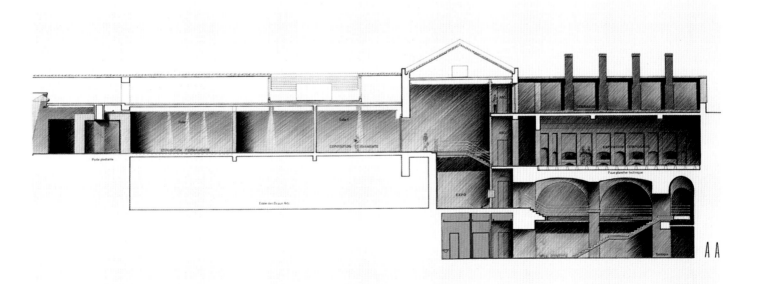

Page 168/169: Although the Chiado Museum does not have a very substantial art collection and it is spread between several different spaces, including a new exhibition pavilion, Wilmotte has given a unified tone to the whole.

Seite 168/169: Obwohl das Chiado Museum keine besonders herausragende Kunstsammlung besitzt und die Exponate in verschiedenen Gebäuden untergebracht sind (darunter auch ein neuer Ausstellungspavillon), verlieh Wilmotte dem gesamten Museum eine gewisse Einheitlichkeit.

Page 168/169: Le musée Chiado ne possède pas une collection très importante. Wilmotte a réussi à unifier l'ensemble, réparti entre plusieurs espaces, dont un nouveau pavillon d'exposition.

Biographies
Biographien

Bolles+Wilson

Peter Wilson was born in Melbourne in 1950. He studied at the University of Melbourne (1968–70) and at the Architectural Association in London (1972–74). Julia Bolles Wilson, was born in 1948 in Münster and studied at the University of Karlsruhe (1968–76) and at the A. A. in London (1978–79) while Wilson was Unit Master (1978–88). Since 1994 Peter Wilson lectures at the Weissensee Kunsthochschule in Berlin. Bolles+Wilson was formed in 1980. Their projects include a "garden folly" at Expo '90 in Osaka. They built the Suzuki House (1993), Tokyo, and the Technologiehof in Münster. Other current projects include the WLV Office Building in Münster, and Quay Rotterdam.

Peter Wilson wurde 1950 in Melbourne geboren. Er studierte an der University of Melbourne (1968–70) und an der Architectural Association in London (1972–74). Julia Bolles Wilson wurde 1948 in Münster geboren; sie studierte an der Universität Karlsruhe (1968–76) sowie an der A. A. in London (1978–79), während Wilson dort als Dozent tätig war (1978–88). Seit 1994 ist Peter Wilson Professor an der Weissensee Kunsthochschule, Berlin. 1980 gründeten sie gemeinsam Bolles+Wilson. Ihre Bauprojekte umfassen u.a. die Gestaltung einer »garden folly« für die International Garden and Greenery Expo '90 in Osaka sowie das Suzuki House in Tokio sowie Technologiehof Münster. Zu den aktuellen Projekten dieses Architekturbüros zählen das WLV-Verwaltungsgebäude in Münster und die Kaianlagen im Rotterdamer Hafen.

Peter Wilson est né à Melbourne en 1950. Il étudie à l'Université de Melbourne (1968–70), et à l'Architectural Association de Londres (1972–74). Julia Bolles Wilson (1948, née à Münster, Allemagne), fait ses études à l'Université de Karlsruhe (1968–76) puis à l'A. A. à Londres (1978–79), alors que Wilson y est responsable d'unité (1978–88). Depuis 1994, Peter Wilson est professeur à la Weissensee Kunsthochschule de Berlin. Ils créent le Bolles+Wilson en 1980. Parmi leurs projets, une «folie» de jardin pour l'Expo '90 d'Osaka. Peter Wilson construit en 1993 la Suzuki House à Tokyo. Ils travaillent actuellement sur un projet d'immeuble de bureaux pour WLV à Münster, et Quai Rotterdam.

Architekturbüro Bolles+Wilson
Alter Steinweg 17
D–48143 Münster
Tel: 49-251-44204
Fax: 49-251-44504

Mario Botta

Born in 1943 in Mendrisio, Switzerland, Mario Botta left school at the age of 15 to become an apprentice in a Lugano architectural office. He designed his first house the following year. After completing his studies in Milan and Venice, Botta worked briefly in the entourage of Le Corbusier, Louis Kahn and Luigi Snozzi. He built numerous private houses in Cadenazzo (1970–71), Riva San Vitale (1971–73) and Ligornetto (1975–76). The culturalcenter in Chambéry (1982-87) and the Médiathèque in Villeurbanne (1984-88) followed. Current projects include the Evry Cathedral (1988–95), the Tamaro Chapel with the artist Enzo Cucchi in Switzerland, a church in Mogno, and a telecommunications center in Bellinzona.

Der 1943 im Schweizerischen Mendrisio geborene Mario Botta verließ die Schule bereits mit 15 Jahren, um als Lehrling in einem Architekturbüro in Lugano zu arbeiten. Im darauffolgenden Jahr entwarf er sein erstes Haus. Nach seinem Studium in Mailand und Venedig war er kurzfristig für Le Corbusier, Louis Kahn und Luigi Snozzi tätig. Botta errichtete zahlreiche Privathäuser in Cadenazzo (1970–71), Riva San Vitale (1971–73) und Ligornetto (1975–76), denen das Kulturzentrum in Chambéry (1982-87) und die Médiathèque in Villeurbanne (1984-88) folgten. Zu seinen aktuellen Bauprojekten gehören die Kathedrale von Evry (1988–1995), die Tamaro-Kapelle in der Schweiz (in Zusammenarbeit mit dem Künstler Enzo Cucchi), eine Kirche in Mogno sowie ein Fernmeldezentrum in Bellinzona.

Né en 1943 à Mendrisio, en Suisse, Mario Botta quitte l'école à 15 ans pour devenir apprenti dans une agence d'architecture de Lugano. Il dessine sa première maison l'année suivante. Après avoir complété ses études à Milan et à Venise, il travaille brièvement dans l'entourage de le Corbusier, de Louis Kahn et de Luigi Snozzi. Il construit de nombreuses résidences privées à Cadenazzo (1970–71), Riva San Vitale (1971–73), ou Ligornetto (1975–76), puis édifie la Maison de la culture de Chambéry (1982–87), et la Médiathèque de Villeurbanne (1984–88). Parmi ses projets actuels, la cathédrale d'Evry (1988–95), la Chapelle de Tamaro, en Suisse, en collaboration avec le peintre Enzo Cucchi, une église à Mogno, et un centre de télécommunications à Bellinzona.

Mario Botta
Via Ciani 16
CH–6904 Lugano
Tel.: 41-91-528625
Fax.: 41-91-531454

Santiago Calatrava

Born in Valencia in 1951, Santiago Calatrava studied art at the Art School in Valencia (1968-69) and architecture at the Escuela Técnica Superior de Arquitectura in Valencia (1969-74) and engineering at the ETH in Zurich (doctorate in Technical Science, 1981). He opened his own architecture and civil engineering office the same year. His built work includes Gallery and Heritage Square, BCE Place, Toronto (1987-92), the Bach de Roda Bridge, Barcelona (1985–87), the Torre de Montjuic, Barcelona, (1989–92), the Kuwait Pavilion at Expo '92, Seville, and the Alamillo Bridge for the same exhibition. He was a finalist in the competition for the Reichstag in Berlin, and plans to build a museum of science and communications tower in Valencia.

Santiago Calatrava wurde 1951 in Valencia geboren, wo er von 1968 bis 1969 an der Kunstschule und von 1969 bis 1974 an der Escuela Tecnica Superior de Arquitectura studierte, bevor er zur ETH (Eidgenössischen Technischen Hochschule) nach Zürich wechselte und dort 1981 in Technischer Wissenschaft promovierte und den Titel »Bauingenieur« erhielt. Im gleichen Jahr gründete er dort auch sein eigenes Architektur- und Bauingenieurbüro. Zu seinen Bauprojekten zählen u.a. der Gallery and Heritage Square, der BCE Place in Toronto (1987–92), die Bach-de-Roda Brücke in Barcelona (1985–87), der Torre de Montjuic in Barcelona (1989–92), der Pavillon Kuwaits sowie die Alamillo-Brücke (beide für die Expo '92 in Sevilla). Auch bei der Ausschreibung für den Reichstag in Berlin gelangte Calatrava in die Endrunde; zur Zeit plant er den Bau eines Museums für Wissenschaft und Kommunikation in Valencia.

Né à Valence en 1951, Santiago Calatrava étudie l'art à l'école d'art (1968-69) et l'architecture à la Escuela Técnica Superior de Arquitectura de cette ville (1969-74), et l'ingénierie à l'ETH de Zurich (docteur ès Sciences et Techniques en 1981). Il ouvre sa propre agence d'architecture et d'ingénierie la même année. Son œuvre construite comprend Gallery et Heritage Square, Toronto (1987–92), le pont Bach de Roda, à Barcelone (1985–87), la Torre de Monjuic, Barcelone (1989–92), le Pavillon du Koweit à Expo 92 et le pont Alamillo, à Séville. Il est finaliste du concours pour le Reichstag, à Berlin, et projette la construction d'un musée des sciences et d'une tour de télécommunications à Valence.

Calatrava Valls Sa
Höschgasse 5
CH–8008 Zürich
Tel: 41-1-4227500
Fax: 41-1-4225600

Chemotov/Huidobro

Paul Chemetov was born in 1928 in Paris and graduated from the Ecole des Beaux Arts in 1959. His early work was concentrated in low-cost housing, or in sports facilities (skating rink, Saint-Ouen, 1979) built on the outskirts of Paris, particularly in Saint-Ouen, but also in Reims and L'Isle-d'Abeau. In 1964, he built the Hammamet Theater in Tunisia with Jean Deroche. Since his association in 1983 with Borja Huidobro, who was born in Santiago, Chile in 1936, he has designed the French embassy in New Delhi, the underground galleries in the Halles district of Paris (1986) and, most notably, the 900 meter long, 225 000 m² Ministry of Finance building at the eastern limit of Paris at Bercy (1982–90). Recent work includes the Evreux Médiathèque, situated next to the city's cathedral.

Paul Chemetoff wurde 1928 in Paris geboren und beendete 1959 sein Studium an der Ecole des Beaux Arts. Seine ersten Arbeiten konzentrierten sich auf den sozialen Wohnungsbau und Sporteinrichtungen in den Vorstädten von Paris, insbesondere in Saint-Ouen (Kunsteisbahn, 1979), aber auch in Reims und L'Isle-d'Abeau. 1964 errichtete er in Zusammenarbeit mit Jean Deroche das Hammamet Theater in Tunesien. Nach seinem Zusammenschluß im Jahre 1983 mit Borja Huidobro – der 1936 in Santiago geboren wurde – entwarf er die französische Botschaft in Neu Delhi, die unterirdischen Passagen in Les Halles (Paris) sowie das 900 Meter lange, 225.000 m² große Gebäude des Finanzministeriums am Ostrand von Paris bei Bercy (1982–90). Zu seinen jüngsten Arbeiten zählt die Evreux Médiathèque, direkt neben der Pariser Kathedrale.

Paul Chemetov naît en 1928 à Paris, et est diplômé de l'Ecole des Beaux-Arts en 1959. Il réalise pour commencer des H.L.M. et des installations sportives (Patinoire, Saint-Ouen 1979), dans la banlieue parisienne, en particulier à Saint-Ouen, mais également à Reims et l'Isle-d'Abeau. En 1964, il construit le théâtre d'Hammamet, en Tunisie, avec Jean Deroche. Depuis son association, en 1983, avec Borja Huidobro (né à Santiago-du-Chili en 1936), il a conçu l'ambassade de France à New Delhi, l'extension du Forum des Halles à Paris (1986) et, plus particulièrement, le nouveau ministère des Finances à Bercy (900 m de long, 225 000 m²), à la limite Est de la capitale (1982–90). Parmi ses récents travaux figure la médiathèque d'Evreux, à côté de la cathédrale.

Chemetov/Huidobro
4, square Massena
F–75013 Paris
Tel: 33-1-45828548
Fax: 33-1-45868914

Jo Coenen

Born in 1949 in Heerlen, Jo Coenen graduated from the Eindhoven University of Technology in 1979. Between 1976 and 1979, he lectured both in Eindhoven and in Maastricht, and worked with Luigi Snozzi, James Stirling and Aldo van Eyck. He opened his own office in 1979, and built his first project, a library and exhibition gallery in Heerlen in 1983. Other built works include the Chamber of Commerce, Maastricht (1988), and offices for the Haans Company, Tilburg (1989). He also designed a Library for the Delft University of Technology (1992), an arts college and city concert hall for Tilburg (1992), and a master plan for Treptow, Berlin (1993).

Der 1949 in Heerlen geborene Architekt Jo Coenen beendete 1979 sein Studium an der technischen Hochschule in Eindhoven. Von 1976 bis 1979 war er in Eindhoven und Maastricht als Dozent tätig und arbeitete mit Luigi Snozzi, James Stirling und Aldo van Eyck. Im Jahre 1979 gründete er auch sein eigenes Architekturbüro. 1983 errichtete Coenen sein erstes Bauprojekt, eine Bibliothek und Kunstgalerie in Heerlen. Zu seinen weiteren Bauten zählen die Handelskammer in Maastricht (1988) und das Verwaltungsgebäude der Handelsgesellschaft Haans in Tilburg (1989). Außerdem entwarf er eine Bibliothek für die Technische Hochschule in Delft (1992), eine Kunstakademie und einen Konzertsaal für die Stadt Tilburg (1992) sowie einen Bebauungsplan für den Berliner Stadtteil Treptow (1993).

Né en 1949 à Heerlen, Jo Coenen est diplômé de l'Université de technologie d'Eindhoven en 1979. De 1976 à 1979, il enseigne à Eindhoven et Maastricht, et collabore avec Luigi Snozzi, James Stirling et Aldo van Eyck. Il ouvre sa propre agence en 1979, et réalise son premier projet, une bibliothèque et une galerie d'exposition à Heerlen, en 1983. Parmi ses autres travaux, la Chambre de commerce de Maastricht (1988), un immeuble de bureaux pour la société Haans à Tilburg (1989), la bibliothèque de l'Université de technologie de Delft (1992), un collège pour les arts et une salle de concert municipale à Tilburg (1992), ainsi que le plan de masse de Treptow, à Berlin (1993).

Jo Coenen
Bouillonstraat 14
NL–6211 LH Maastricht
Tel: 31-43-25 60 44
Fax: 31-43-25 65 33

Sir Norman Foster

Born in Manchester in 1935, Norman Foster studied at the University of Manchester and at Yale in 1963. After working briefly with Buckminster Fuller, he founded "Team 4" with Richard Rogers, and created Foster Associates in 1967. Knighted in 1990, Sir Norman Foster has built the Sainsbury Center at the University of East Anglia, Norwich (1978), the Renault Distribution Center, Swindon (1983), the Hong Kong and Shanghai Bank tower in Hong Kong (1986), and the terminal for Standsted Airport (1981–91). Current projects are the Commerzbank in Frankfurt, the tallest building in Europe, Hong Kong's new airport, and King's Cross Station in London.

Norman Foster wurde 1935 in Manchester geboren und studierte bis 1963 an der University of Manchester und an der Yale University. Nach einer kurzen Zusammenarbeit mit Buckminster Fuller gründete Foster zusammen mit Richard Rogers das »Team 4« und 1967 »Foster Associates«. 1990 wurde er in den Adelsstand erhoben. Zu den herausragendsten Bauten Sir Norman Fosters zählen das Sainsbury Center der University of East Anglia in Norwich (1978), die Renault Vertriebszentrale in Swindon (1983), das Gebäude der Hongkong and Shanghai Bank in Hongkong (1986) sowie der Terminal des Standsted Airport (1981–1991). Zur Zeit arbeitet sein Büro an der Fertigstellung des Commerzbankgebäudes in Frankfurt (dem höchsten Gebäude Europas), Hongkongs neuem Flughafen und King's Cross Station in London.

Né à Manchester en 1935, il fait ses études à l'Université de cette ville et à Yale (1963). Après avoir brièvement collaboré avec Buckminster Fuller, il fonde «Team 4» avec Richard Rogers, et crée Foster Associates en 1967. Anobli en 1990, Sir Norman Foster a en particulier construit le Sainsbury Center de l'Université d'East Anglia, Norwich (1978), le Centre de distribution Renault, Swindon (1983), la tour de la Hong Kong and Shanghai Bank, Hong Kong (1986), et le terminal de l'aéroport de Standsted (1981–91). Il travaille actuellement sur la tour de la Commerzbank, à Francfort sur le Main – la plus haute d'Europe –, le nouvel aéroport de Hong Kong, et la gare de King's Cross à Londres.

Sir Norman Foster and Partners
Riverside 3,
22 Hester Road
GB–London SW11 4AN
Tel: 44-171-738 0455
Fax: 44-171-738 1107

Nicholas Grimshaw

A 1965 graduate of the Architectural Association, Nicholas Grimshaw was born in London in 1939. He created his present firm, Nicholas Grimshaw and Partners Ltd. in 1980. His numerous factory structures include those built for Herman Miller in Bath (1976), BMW at Bracknell (1980), the furniture maker Vitra at Weil am Rhein, Germany (1981) and for *The Financial Times* in London in 1988. He also built houses associated with the Sainsbury Supermarket Development in Camden Town (1989), and the British Pavilion at the 1992 Universal Exhibition in Seville.

Der 1939 in London geborene Architekt Nicholas Grimshaw beendete 1965 sein Studium an der Architectural Association. Seine heutige Firma – Nicholas Grimshaw and Partners Ltd. – gründete er im Jahre 1980. Zu seinen zahlreichen Industriebauten gehören auch die Fabrikanlagen für Herman Miller in Bath (1976), für BMW in Bracknell (1980), für den Möbelhersteller Vitra in Weil am Rhein (1981) oder für die »Financial Times« in London (1988). Darüber hinaus war er an der Errichtung des Sainsbury Supermarket Development in Camden Town (1989) beteiligt und errichtete den Pavillon Großbritanniens für die Weltausstellung '92 in Sevilla.

Diplômé en 1965 de l'Architectural Association, Nicholas Grimshaw est né à Londres en 1939. Il crée son agence actuelle, Nicholas Grimshaw and Partners Ltd. en 1980. Il édifie de nombreuses usines, dont celles d'Herman Miller à Bath (1976), de BMW à Bracknell (1980), du fabricant de meubles Vitra, à Weil am Rhein (1981), ou l'imprimerie du «Financial Times» à Londres (1988). Il a également construit des maisons dans le cadre du Sainsbury Supermarket Development, à Camden Town (1989), et le pavillon britannique d'Expo 92, à Séville (1992).

Nicholas Grimshaw
and Partners Ltd.
1 Conway Street
Fitzroy Square
GB–London W1P 6LR
Tel: 44-171-6310869
Fax: 44-171-6364866

Herzog & de Meuron

Jacques Herzog and Pierre de Meuron were both born in Basel in 1950. They received degrees in architecture at the ETH in Zurich in 1975, after studying with Aldo Rossi, and founded their firm Herzog & de Meuron Architecture Studio in Basel in 1978. Their built work includes the Antipodes I Student Housing at the Université de Bourgogne, Dijon (1991–92), the Ricola Europe Factory and Storage Building in Mulhouse (1993) and a gallery for a private collection of contemporary art in Munich (1991–92). Most notably they were chosen early in 1995 to design the new Tate Gallery extension for contemporary art, to be situated in the Bankside Power Station, on the Thames, opposite Saint Paul's Cathedral.

Jacques Herzog und Pierre de Meuron wurden beide 1950 in Basel geboren. Nachdem die beiden ehemaligen Schüler von Aldo Rossi 1975 ihr Architekturstudium an der ETH in Zürich beendet hatten, gründeten sie drei Jahre später ihr Architekturbüro Herzog & de Meuron in Basel. Zu ihren Bauprojekten gehören das Studentenwohnheim Antipodes I der Université de Bourgogne in Dijon (1991–92), das Fabrik- und Lagergebäude von Ricola Europe in Mulhouse (1993) sowie eine Galerie für eine private Sammlung zeitgenössischer Kunst in München (1991–92). Aber ihr wohl wichtigstes Bauvorhaben ist die Erweiterung der Ausstellungsräume für zeitgenössische Kunst der Tate Gallery, die in der Bankside Power Station – direkt an der Themse gegenüber von St. Paul's Cathedral gelegen – untergebracht werden sollen.

Jacques Herzog et Pierre de Meuron, sont tous deux nés à Bâle en 1950. Diplômés en architecture de l'ETH de Zurich (1975), après avoir étudié avec Aldo Rossi comme professeur, ils fondent leur agence, Herzog & de Meuron Architecture Studio, à Bâle en 1978. Parmi leurs œuvres: le foyer d'étudiants Antipodes 1 pour l'Université de Bourgogne, à Dijon (1991–92), l'usine-entrepôt Ricola Europe à Mulhouse (1993), et une galerie pour une collection privée d'art contemporain à Munich (1991–92). Ils viennent d'être sélectionnés, en 1995, pour l'extension de la Tate Gallery consacrée à l'art contemporain, qui sera aménagée dans l'ancienne centrale thermique Bankside Power Station, au bord de la Tamise, face à la cathédrale Saint-Paul.

Herzog & de Meuron Architekten
Rheinschanze 6
CH–4056 Basel
Tel: 41-61-3225737
Fax: 41-61-3224515

Rem Koolhaas

Rem Koolhaas was born in The Hague in 1944. Before studying at the Architectural Association in London, he tried his hand as a journalist for the *Haagse Post* and as a screenwriter. He founded the Office for Metropolitan Architecture in London in 1975, and became well-known after the 1978 publication of his book *Delirious New York*. His built work includes a group of apartments at Nexus World, Fukuoka (1991), the Villa dall'Ava, Saint-Cloud (1985–91). He was named head architect of the Euralille project in Lille in 1988, and has worked on a design for the new Jussieu University Library in Paris. His recent 1400 page book *S,M,L,XL* (Monacelli Press, 1995) promises to maintain his reputation as an influential writer.

Rem Koolhaas wurde 1944 in Den Haag geboren. Bevor er sein Studium an der Architectural Association in London aufnahm, versuchte er sein Glück als Journalist für die »Haagse Post« und als Drehbuchautor. 1975 gründete er das Office for Metropolitan Architecture (OMA) in London und wurde durch die Veröffentlichung seines Buches »Delirious New York« 1978 zu einer international bekannten Persönlichkeit der Architekturwelt. Zu seinen Bauprojekten gehören u.a. ein Apartmentblock in Nexus World, Fukuoka (1991) und die Villa dall'Ava in Saint-Cloud (1985–91). 1988 ernannte man ihn zum Chefarchitekten des Euralille-Projekts in Lille. Danach beschäftigte er sich mit dem Entwurf für die neue Jussieu-Universitätsbibliothek in Paris. Sein erst kürzlich veröffentlichtes Buch »S,M,L,XL« (Monacelli Press, 1995) scheint seinen Ruf als einflußreicher Theoretiker zu bestätigen.

Rem Koolhaas est né à La Haye en 1944. Avant d'étudier à l'Architectural Association de Londres, il s'essaye au journalisme pour le «Haagse Post», et aux scenarii de films. Il crée son Office for Metropolitan Architecture, à Londres en 1975 et se fait connaître par son livre «Delirious New York» (1978). Il a construit, entre autres, un ensemble d'appartements à Nexus World, Fukuoka (1991), la villa dall'Ava, Saint-Cloud (1985–91). Il est nommé architecte-en-chef du projet Euralille, à Lille, en 1988, et a travaillé sur la conception de la nouvelle bibliothèque de l'université de Jussieu, à Paris. Son dernier livre «S,M,L,X,L» (Monacelli Press, 1995) confirmera sans doute son influence de théoricien.

Office for Metropolitan Architecture
Boompjes 55
NL–Rotterdam 3011XB
Tel: 31-10-4111216
Fax: 31-10-4114195

Alessandro Mendini

Born in Milan in 1931, Alessandro Mendini, received his doctorate in architecture from the Milan Polytechnic University in 1959. Editor of the magazine *Casabella* from 1970 to 1976, he was a member of the Archizoom and Superstudio groups, and editor of *Modo* from 1977 to 1980, where he defended decorative arts and the value of kitsch. Editor of *Domus* from 1980 to 1985, he created the Domus Academy in 1982. Mendini collaborated with Studio Alchymia from 1979 to 1991 and is the artistic director of Alessi and Swatch. Although Alessandro Mendini has worked on numerous architectural projects such as "La Casa della Felicità" (1980–88), he is best known as a figure of the world of design.

Der 1931 in Mailand geborene Alessandro Mendini erhielt 1959 an der Polytechnischen Hochschule von Mailand den Doktortitel der Architektur. Dieser ehemalige Herausgeber der Zeitschriften »Casabella« (1970–76), »Modo« (1977–80) – bei der er die Bildenden Künste und den Wert des Kitsches verteidigte – und »Domus« (1980–85). Er gründete 1982 die Domus Akademie und war Mitglied der Architektengruppen Archizoom und Superstudio. Von 1979 bis 1991 arbeitete er mit dem Studio Alchymia zusammen und ist heute als künstlerischer Direktor von Alessi und Swatch tätig. Obwohl Alessandro Mendini an zahlreichen Architekturprojekten beteiligt war – u.a. an der »Casa della Felicità« (1980–88) – kennt man ihn eher als Designer denn als Architekten.

Né à Milan en 1931, Alessandro Mendini devient docteur en architecture de l'Université polytechnique de Milan en 1959. Editeur du magazine «Casabella», de 1970 à 1976, membre des groupes Archizoom et Superstudio, est aussi éditeur de «Modo», de 1977 à 1980, où il défend les arts décoratifs et la valeur du kitsch. Editeur de «Domus», de 1980 à 1985, il crée Domus Academy en 1982. Il collabore avec Studio Alchymia de 1979 à 1991, et devient directeur artistique d'Alessi et de Swatch. Bien qu'il ait travaillé sur d'innombrables projets d'architecture, comme la «Casa della Felicità» (1980–88), il est surtout connu pour être l'une des grandes figures du monde du design.

Atelier Mendini
Via Sannio 24
I-20137 Milano
Tel: 39-02-59901508
Fax: 39-02-59900974

Enric Miralles

Born in Barcelona in 1955, Enric Miralles received his degree from the Escuela Técnica Superior de Arquitectura in that city in 1978. He worked with Helio Piñón and Albert Viaplana (1974–84) before forming his partnership with Carme Pinós in 1983. He has lectured at Columbia University in New York, at Harvard, and at the Architectural Association in London. His work includes the Igualada Cemetery Park on the outskirts of Barcelona (1985–92), the Olympic Archery Ranges, Barcelona (1989–91), the La Mina civic center, Barcelona (1987–92), the Morella Boarding School, Castelló, (1986–94), and the Huesca Sports Hall (1988–94).

Enric Miralles wurde 1955 in Barcelona geboren und promovierte 1978 an der dortigen Hochschule (Escuela Técnica Superior de Arquitectura). Bevor er sich 1983 mit Carme Pinós zusammentat, hatte er bereits mit Helio Piñón und Albert Viaplana (1974–84) zusammengearbeitet. Darüber hinaus war er als Dozent an der Columbia University in New York, an der Harvard University sowie an der Architectural Association in London als Dozent tätig. Zu seinen Bauwerken gehören die Igualada-Friedhofsanlage am Stadtrand von Barcelona (1985–92), die olympische Bogenschützenanlage, ebenfalls in Barcelona (1989–91), das Bürgerzentrum »La Mina« in Barcelona (1987–92), das Morella-Internat in Castelló (1986–94) und die Huesca-Sporthalle (1988–94).

Né à Barcelone, en 1955, Enric Miralles est diplômé de l'Escuela Técnica Superior de Arquitectura de sa ville en 1978. Il travaille avec Helio Piñón et Albert Viaplana (1974–84), avant de s'associer à Carme Piños en 1983. Il enseigne à Columbia University, New York, à Harvard et l'Architectural Association de Londres. Il a construit le cimetière d'Igualada, dans la banlieue de Barcelone (1985–92), les installations d'archerie pour les jeux Olympiques de Barcelone (1989–91), le centre municipal La Mina à Barcelone (1987–92), le pensionnat Morella, Castello (1986–94), et le palais des sports de Huesca (1988–94).

Enric Miralles
52 Avinyo St.
E–08002 Barcelone
Tel: 34-3-4125342
Fax: 34-3-4123718

José Rafael Moneo

José Rafael Moneo was born in Tudela, Navarra in 1937. He graduated from the Escuela Técnica Superior de Arquitectura in Madrid in 1961. The following year, he went to work with Jørn Utzon in Denmark. Rafael Moneo has taught extensively, including at the ETSA in Madrid and Barcelona. He was chairman of the Department of Architecture at the Graduate School of Design at Harvard from 1985 to 1990. His recent work includes the National Museum of Roman Art, Merida (1980–86), the San Pablo Airport Terminal in Seville (1989–91) built for Expo '92, the Atocha railway station in Madrid (1991), the Miró Foundation in Palma (1992) and the interior architecture of the Thyssen-Bornemisza Collection in Madrid (1992).

José Rafael Moneo wurde 1937 in Tudela in der spanischen Provinz Navarra geboren. 1961 schloß er sein Studium an der Escuela Tecnica Superior de Arquitectura in Madrid ab, und bereits im darauffolgenden Jahr ging er nach Dänemark, um dort mit Jørn Utzon zusammenzuarbeiten. Darüber hinaus war Moneo an zahlreichen Hochschulen als Dozent tätig, darunter auch an der ETSA in Madrid und Barcelona. Zwischen 1985 und 1990 leitete er das Department of Architecture an der Graduate School of Design in Harvard. Zu seinen Bauwerken zählen das Nationale Museum für römische Kunst in Merida (1980–86), der San Pablo Airport-Terminal in Sevilla (1989–91), den er für die Expo '92 errichtete, der Bahnhof Atocha in Madrid (1991), das Gebäude für die Miró-Stiftung in Palma (1992) sowie die Innenarchitektur der Thyssen-Bornemisza-Sammlung in Madrid (1992).

José Rafael Moneo naît à Tuleda, province de Navarre, en 1937. Il est diplômé de l'Escuela Técnica de Arquitectura de Madrid en 1961. En 1962, il part travailler avec Jørn Utzon. Il enseigne beaucoup, y compris aux ETSA de Madrid et de Barcelone. Directeur du département d'architecture de la Graduate School of Design d'Harvard de 1985 à 1990. Parmi ses récents travaux: le Musée national d'art romain de Merida (1980–86), le terminal de l'aéroport de San Pablo à Séville (1989–91), édifié pour Expo 92, la gare d'Atocha à Madrid (1991), la Fondation Miró à Palma (1992), et l'architecture intérieure du palais de la Collection Thyssen-Bornemisza, à Madrid (1992)

José Rafael Moneo
Cinca 5
E–28002 Madrid
Tel: 34-1-5642257
Fax: 34-1-5635217

Jean Nouvel

Born in Fumel in 1945, Jean Nouvel was admitted to the Ecole des Beaux-Arts in Bordeaux in 1964. In 1970, he created his first office with François Seigneur. His first widely noticed project was the Institut du Monde Arabe in Paris (1981–87, with Architecture Studio). Other recent projects include his Nemausus housing, Nîmes, 1985–87, offices for the CLM/BBDO advertising firm, Issy-les-Moulineaux, 1988–92, and his unbuilt projects for the 400 meter tall "Tours sans fins", La Défense, Paris, 1989, or Grand Stade for the 1998 World Cup, Paris, 1994. Current work includes a store for the Galeries Lafayette, Friedrichstrasse, Berlin, and a project for a cultural center in Lucerne.

Jean Nouvel, der 1945 in Fumel geboren wurde, nahm 1964 sein Studium an der École des Beaux-Arts in Bordeaux auf. 1970 gründete er zusammen mit François Seigneur sein erstes Architekturbüro. Das Institut du Monde Arabe in Paris (1981–87, in Zusammenarbeit mit Architecture Studio) war sein erstes Bauprojekt, das international Aufsehen erregte. Zu seinen kürzlich fertiggestellten Bauprojekten zählen seine »Nemausus«-Wohnanlage in Nîmes (1985–87), das Verwaltungsgebäude der Werbeagentur CLM/BBDO in Issy-les-Moulineaux (1988–92), sein (nicht ausgeführter) 400 Meter hoher Turm »Tours sans fins« im Pariser Viertel La Défense (1989) sowie seine Konstruktionspläne des Grand Stade (1994) für die Fußballweltmeisterschaft 1998 in Frankreich. Zur Zeit beschäftigt sich Jean Nouvel mit einem Ladengeschäft für die Galerie Lafayette auf der Friedrichstraße in Berlin und einem Projekt für ein Kulturzentrum in Luzern.

Né en 1945 à Fumel, Jean Nouvel est admis à l'Ecole des Beaux-Arts de Bordeaux en 1964. En 1970, il crée une première agence avec François Seigneur. Son premier projet vraiment remarqué estl'Institut du Monde Arabe à Paris (1981–87, avec Architecture Studio). Parmi ses autres récents chantiers, les immeubles d'appartements Nemausus à Nîmes (1985–87), les bureaux de l'agence de publicité CLM/BBDO (Issy-les-Moulineaux, 1988–92), et les projets non réalisés pour une tour de 400 m «La tour sans fin» (La Défense, Paris, 1989) et le Grand Stade de la Coupe du monde de football 1998 (Paris, 1994). Actuellement, il travaille à un grand magasin pour les Galeries Lafayette à Berlin (Friedrichstrasse), et à un centre culturel pour Lucerne.

Jean Nouvel
4, Cité Grissset
F–75011 Paris
Tel: 33-1-49238383
Fax: 33-1-43553561

Renzo Piano

Born in Genoa in 1937, Renzo Piano studied at the University of Florence and at the Polytechnic Institute in Milan. He formed his own practice (Studio Piano) in the 1960's, then associated with Richard Rogers (Piano & Rogers, 1971–78). They completed the Pompidou Center in Paris in 1977. From 1978 to 1980, Piano worked with Peter Rice (Piano & Rice Associates). He created the Renzo Piano Building Workshop in 1981 in Genoa and Paris. His work includes the Menil Collection Museum, Houston (1986), the San Nicola stadium, Bari (1987–90), the 1989 extension for the IRCAM, Paris, and the renovation of the Lingotto complex, Turin. Current work includes the Centre Culturel Canaque, Nouméa, and projects near Potsdamer Platz in Berlin.

Der 1937 in Genua geborene Architekt Renzo Piano studierte an der Universität von Florenz sowie am polytechnischen Institut in Mailand. In den 60er Jahren gründete er sein eigenes Architekturbüro (Studio Piano), bevor er sich in den 70er Jahren mit Richard Rogers zusammentat (1971–78). Gemeinsam errichteten sie 1977 das Centre Pompidou in Paris. Von 1978 bis 1980 arbeitete Piano mit Peter Rice zusammen (Piano & Rice Associates); ein Jahr später gründete er den Renzo Piano Building Workshop in Genua und Paris (1981). Zu seinen Bauwerken zählen u.a. das Menil Collection Museum in Houston (1986), das San Nicola-Stadion in Bari (1987–90), der Erweiterungsbau für das Pariser IRCAM (1989) und die Renovierung des Lingotto-komplexes in Turin. Seine aktuellen Bauprojekte umfassen ein Centre Culturel Canaque in Nouméa und Projekte in der Nähe des Potsdamer Platzes in Berlin.

Né en 1937 à Gênes, Renzo Piano, étudie à l'Université de Florence et au Politecnico de Milan. Il crée son propre cabinet Studio Piano dans les années 60, puis s'associe à Richard Rogers (Piano & Rogers, 1978–78). Ensemble, ils construisent le Centre Pompidou (Paris, 1977). De 1978 à 1980, Piano travaille avec Peter Rice (Piano & Rice Associates). Il crée le Renzo Piano Building Workshop en 1981, à Gênes et Paris. Il a réalisé le Menil Collection Museum à Houston (1986), le stade San Nicola à Bari (1987–90), l'extension de l'IRCAM (1989), la rénovation de l'usine du Lingotto, à Turin. Actuellement, il travaille sur le Centre Culturel Canaque Jean-Marie-Tjibaou à Nouméa, et sur des projets autour de la Potsdamer Platz, à Berlin.

Renzo Piano Building Workshop
34, rue des Archives
F–75004 Paris
Tel: 33-1-42780082
Fax: 33-1-42780198

Christian de Portzamparc

Born in Casablanca in 1944, Christian de Portzamparc studied at the Ecole des Beaux Arts in Paris from 1962 to 1969. Early projects include a water tower at Marne-la-Vallée, (1971–74) and the Hautes Formes public housing, Paris (1975–79). He won the competition for the Cité de la Musique on the outskirts of Paris in 1984, completing the project in 1995. He was awarded the 1994 Pritzker Prize. He participated in the Euralille project with a tower built over the new Lille-Europe railway station in Lille, and built housing for the Nexus World project in Fukuoka (1992). Current work includes an addition to the Palais des Congrès in Paris, a tower for the Bandai toy company in Tokyo, and a courthouse for Grasse in the south of France.

Christian de Portzamparc wurde 1944 in Casablanca geboren und studierte von 1962 bis 1969 an der École des Beaux Arts in Paris. Zu seinen ersten Projekten zählten der Wasserturm in Marne-la-Vallée bei Paris (1971–74) und seine städtische Wohnanlage Hautes Formes in Paris (1975–79). 1984 gewann er den Architekturwettbewerb für die Cité de la Musique am Rande von Paris, die er 1995 fertigstellte. Ein Jahr zuvor (1994) verlieh man ihm den Pritzker Preis. Darüber hinaus war Portzamparc mit einem Turm über dem neuen Bahnhof Lille-Europe am Euralille-Projekt beteiligt und errichtete eine Wohnanlage für das Nexus World-Projekt in Fukuoka (1992). Zur Zeit beschäftigt er sich mit einem Erweiterungsbau für das Palais des Congrès in Paris, einem Turm für den Spielzeughersteller Bandai in Tokio und einem Gerichtsgebäude für die Stadt Grasse in Südfrankreich.

Christian de Portzamparc est né à Casablanca en 1944, et a fait ses études à l'Ecole des Beaux-Arts de Paris de 1962 à 1969. Ses premiers projets comprennent les châteaux d'eau de Marne-la-Vallée (1971–74), ou les H.L.M. des Hautes-Formes à Paris (1975–79). Il a remporté le concours pour la Cité de la Musique à Paris (1984), dont la construction a été achevée en 1995. En 1994, il reçoit le Prix Pritzker. Il participe au projet Euralille, à Lille, avec une tour au-dessus de la gare Lille-Europe, et construit un immeuble pour Nexus World à Fukuoka (1992). Actuellement, il travaille à l'agrandissement du Palais des Congrès de Paris, à une tour pour la société de jouets Bandaï à Tokyo, et au futur palais de justice de Grasse, en Provence.

Christian de Portzamparc
1, rue de l'Aude
F–75014 Paris
Tel: 33-1-43271197
Fax: 33-1-43277479

Axel Schultes

Born in Dresden in 1943, Axel Schultes graduated from the Technical University of Berlin in 1969. He worked in partnership with Dietrich Bangert, Bernd Jansen and Stefan Scholz from 1974 to 1991 (BJSS). He created his own firm in 1992, and participated in both the Reichstag and Spreebogen competitions in 1993, as well as numerous other competitions before that such as that for the Deutsche Historische Museum in Berlin (1988), or the Alexandria Library in 1989. His built work includes the Büropark am Welfenplatz, Hanover (1993). Current projects are the extension of the "Yenidze" tobacco-mosque, Dresden and the Baumschulenweg Crematorium, Berlin.

Der 1943 in Dresden geborene Architekt Axel Schultes schloß 1969 sein Studium an der Technischen Hochschule von Berlin ab. Von 1974 bis 1991 arbeitete er mit Dietrich Bangert, Bernd Jansen und Stefan Scholz (BJSS) zusammen. 1992 gründete er seine eigene Firma und beteiligte sich ein Jahr später an den Ausschreibungen für den Reichstag und das Spreebogen-Projekt. Auch zuvor hatte Schultes bereits an zahlreichen Architekturwettbewerben teilgenommen – wie etwa an der Ausschreibungen für das Deutsche Historische Museum in Berlin (1988) oder für die Alexandria-Bibliothek (1989). Zu seinen Bauprojekten gehören u.a. der Büropark am Welfenplatz in Hannover (1993). Zur Zeit beschäftigt sich Schultes mit einem Erweiterungsbau der »Yenidze«-Tabakmoschee in Dresden und dem Krematorium Baumschulenweg in Berlin.

Né à Dresde en 1943, Axel Schultes obtient son diplôme de l'Université technique de Berlin en 1969. Il travaille en association avec Dietrich Bangert, Bernd Jansen et Stefan Scholz, de 1974 à 1991 (BJSS). Il crée sa propre agence en 1992 et participe à de nombreux concours comme celui du Deutsche Historische Museum à Berlin (1988) et de la Bibliothèque d'Alexandrie (1989). Son œuvre construit comprend également le Büropark am Welfenplatz à Hanovre (1993). Il travaille actuellement à une extension de la mosquée Yenidze de Dresde, et au crématorium de Baumschulenweg à Berlin.

Axel Schultes
Lützowplatz 7
D–10785 Berlin
Tel.: 49-30-2651080
Fax: 49-30-2651188

Otto Steidle

Born in Munich in 1943, Otto Steidle studied at the Akademie der Bildenden Künste in that city from 1965 to 1969. In 1966, he created the firm Muhr + Steidle, and in 1969, Steidle + Partner. He has taught extensively, in Munich, Kassel, Berlin, Amsterdam and at MIT in Cambridge, Massachusetts (1991,1993). He has been the Rector of the Munich Akademie der Bildenden Künste since 1993. Built work includes housing on the Genter Strasse in Munich where he has his offices (1969–75), the Kreuzgassen Quarter, Nuremberg (1986–92), and the headquarters of Gruner + Jahr, Hamburg (1983–91). Work under construction includes a residential and commercial building, Landshut, and the Pensions Fund Building of the Wacker Chemie Corporation in Munich.

Otto Steidle wurde 1943 in München geboren, wo er von 1965 bis 1969 an der Akademie der Bildenden Künste studierte. Bereits 1966 gründete er das Architekturbüro Muhr + Steidle und 1969 das Büro Steidle + Partner. Steidle war u.a. in München, Kassel, Berlin, Amsterdam und am MIT (Massachusetts Institute of Technology) in Cambridge, Massachusetts (1991, 1993) als Dozent tätig und ist seit 1993 Rektor der Münchner Akademie der Bildenden Künste. Zu seinen Bauprojekten zählen u.a. die Wohnanlage an der Genter Straße in München (1969–73), wo sich auch sein Büro befindet, das Kreuzgassen-Viertel in Nürnberg (1986–92) und das Gruner + Jahr-Gebäude in Hamburg (1983–91, in Zusammenarbeit mit Uwe Kiessler & Partner sowie Schwäge & Partner). Zur Zeit beschäftigt Steidle sich mit einem Wohn- und Geschäftshaus in Landshut und dem Gebäude für die Pensionskasse der Wacker Chemie AG in München.

Né à Munich en 1943, Otto Steidle y fait ses études à l'Akademie der Bildenden Künste, de 1965 à 1969. En 1966, il crée l'agence Muhr + Steidle, et en 1969, Steidle + Partners. Il a beaucoup enseigné à Munich, Kassel, Berlin, Amsterdam, et au MIT, à Cambridge, Massachusetts (1991, 1993). Il est recteur de l'Akademie der Bildenden Künste depuis 1993. Parmi ses réalisations: un immeuble Genter Strass à Munich, où il a ses bureaux (1969–75), le quartier de Kreuzgasse à Nuremberg (1986–92), et le siège de Gruner + Jahr à Hambourg (1983–91). Actuellement, il travaille sur un immeuble résidentiel et commercial à Landshut, et le siège de la caisse de retraite de la société Wacker Chemie à Munich.

Steidle + Partner
Genter Strasse 13
D–80805 München
Tel: 49-89-36090722
Fax: 49-89-3617906

Jean-Michel Wilmotte

Born in 1948, a graduate of the Camondo school in Paris, Jean-Michel Wilmotte created his own firm, Governor in 1975. Although he is best known for his work in interior design, including private apartments for François Mitterrand in the Elysée Palace, Wilmotte joined the Order of Architects in France in 1993. His recent work includes the architecture and interior design of the Decorative Arts Department of the Louvre, Richelieu Wing, (1989–93), and the Museum of Fashion, Marseille. As an architect, Jean-Michel Wilmotte recently completed the International Executive Office building, Tokyo, and the New N°3 Arai Building, also in Tokyo, while he also carried out the furniture design for the Banque de Luxembourg building, completed by Arquitectonica in 1994.

Jean-Michel Wilmotte wurde 1948 in Paris geboren und gründete 1975 sein eigenes Architekturbüro Governor, nachdem er das Studium an der École Camondo in Paris erfolgreich abgeschlossen hatte. Obwohl er eher für seine innenarchitektonischen Arbeiten bekannt ist – wie etwa den Privaträumen François Mitterrands im Palais de l'Elysée – trat Wilmotte 1993 dem französischen Architektenbund bei. Zu seinen jüngsten Arbeiten zählen die Architektur und Innenausstattung des Départements des Beaux Arts des Louvre (Richelieu-Flügel, 1989–93) und das Museum für Mode in Marseille sowie zwei vor kurzem vollendete Gebäude in Tokio – das International Executive Office Building im Viertel Shinjuku und das New N°3 Arai Building. Außerdem zeichnete Wilmotte für das Möbeldesign der Banque de Luxembourg verantwortlich, die 1994 von Arquitectonica errichtet wurde.

Né en 1948 et diplômé de l'Ecole Camondo à Paris, Jean-Michel Wilmotte crée son propre studio, Governor, en 1975. Surtout connu pour ses réalisations en architecture intérieure, comme les appartements privés de F. Mitterrand au Palais de l'Elysée, il s'inscrit à l'Ordre des Architectes en 1993. Il a réalisé l'architecture et les aménagements intérieurs du département des Arts Décoratifs du Louvre, pour l'aile Richelieu (1989–93). En tant qu'architecte, Wilmotte a récemment signé deux immeubles à Tokyo, l'International Executive Office Building dans le quartier de Shinjuku, et le New N°3 Arai Building. A Luxembourg, il a conçu le mobilier du siège de la Banque du Luxembourg, achevé par Arquitectonica en 1994.

Jean-Michel Wilmotte, architecte
68, rue du Faubourg
Saint-Antoine
F–75012 Paris

Bibliography
Bibliographie

Bauwelt (ed.): *Hauptstadt Berlin – Parlamentsviertel im Spreebogen.* Birkhäuser: Berlin, 1993

Bezombes, Dominique: *La Grande Galerie du Muséum national d'histoire naturelle.* Le Moniteur: Paris, 1994

Bouman, Ole: *The Invisible in Architecture.* Academy Editions: London, 1994

Cullen, Michael: *Calatrava Berlin, 5 Projects.* Birkhäuser: Berlin, 1994

Deutsches Architekturmuseum (ed.): *Architektur Jahrbuch 1992, 1993, 1994.* Prestel: München

Feireiss, Kristin (ed.): *Reichstag Berlin.* Aedes, Galerie und Architekturforum: Berlin, 1994

Feldmeyer, Gerhard; Sack, Manfred; Mathewson, Casey C.M.: *The New German Architecture.* Rizzoli: New York, 1993

Goulet, Patrice: *Jean Nouvel.* Editions du Regard: Paris, 1994

Koolhaas, Rem: *Delirious New York.* The Monacelli Press: New York, 1994, originally published in 1978

Koolhaas, Rem: *S, M, L, XL.* The Monacelli Press: New York, 1995

Kossak, F. (ed.): *Otto Steidle – Bewohnbare Bauten.* Artemis: Zürich, 1994

"Lignes étirées, Université des science à Ulm". In: *Techniques & Architecture,* Octobre-Novembre 1992

Muschamp, Herbert: *"Rem Koolhaas's State of Mind".* In: The New York Times, November 4, 1994

NAi Publishers (ed.): *The Netherlands Architecture Institute.* Rotterdam, 1993

Oxenaar, Aart; van der Vlugt, Ger: *Jo Coenen.* Uitgeverij 010: Rotterdam, 1993

Peter Blum Edition (ed.): *Architectures of Herzog & de Meuron.* New York, 1994

Petit, Jean: *Botta, traces d'architecture.* Fidia Edizioni d'Arte: Lugano, 1994

Saliga, Pauline; Thorne, Martha: *Building in a New Spain.* Editorial Gustavo Gili: Barcelona, 1992

Sanin, Francisco: *Münster City Library.* (Architecture in Detail) Phaidon Press: London, 1994

Tay, Maggie (ed.): *Architecture of Transportation.* Architectural Design: London, 1994

Teramatsu, Yasuhiro (ed.): *Kansai International Airport Passenger Terminal Building.* In: The Japan Architect, 15, autumn 1994

Tzonis, Alexander; Lefaivre, Liane: *Architecture in Europe since 1968.* Thames and Hudson: London, 1992

Index

Photographic credits
Fotonachweis
Crédits photographiques

The publisher and editor wish to thank each of the architects and photographers for their kind assistance.

p. 2   © Arnaud Carpentier
p. 6   © Santiago Calatrava
p. 9   © Photo: Arcaid/Dennis Gilbert
p. 10   © Photo: Richard Davies
p. 11   © Sir Norman Foster and Partners
p. 12–13   © Photo: Arnaud Carpentier
p. 14/15   © Nicholas Grimshaw & Partners
p. 15   © Photo: Arcaid/John E. Linden
p. 16   © Santiago Calatrava
p. 17   © Photo: Arcaid/Paul Raftery
p. 18   © Photo: Ralph Richter
p. 19   © Photo: Kunsthal Rotterdam
p. 20–21   © Photo: Groninger Museum
p. 22   © Photo: Christian Richters
p. 24–25   © Photo: Alfred Wolf
p. 26   © Photo: Arnaud Carpentier
p. 27–29   © Photo: Alfred Wolf
p. 30–31   © SFMoMA Press Photos
p. 31 bottom   © Photo: Richard Barnes/ SFMoMA Press Photos
p. 32/34   © Axel Schultes
p. 35   © Photo: Hans-Jürgen Commerell
p. 36/37   © Bolles+Wilson
p. 37   © Photo: Christian Richters
p. 38   © Photo: Reinhard Görner
p. 39   © Steidle + Partner
p. 40–41   © Photo: Arnaud Carpentier
p. 43 top   © Photo: Ralph Richter
p. 43 bottom   © Photo: Kunsthal Rotterdam/ Werlemann
p. 45   © Photo: Ralph Richter
p. 48–49   © Photo: Christian Richters
p. 50   © Bolles+Wilson
p. 51   © Photo: Christian Richters
p. 52   © Bolles+Wilson
p. 53   © Photo: Christian Richters
p. 54   © Photo: Richard Barnes/ SFMoMA Press Photos
p. 55   © Paolo Rosselli
p. 56 top   © Photo: Richard Barnes/ SFMoMA Press Photos
p. 56–57   © SFMoMA Press Photos
p. 58 top   © Photo: Richard Barnes/ SFMoMA Press Photos
p. 58 bottom   © SFMoMA Press Photos

p. 59   © Photo: Richard Barnes/ SFMoMA Press Photos
p. 60   © Photo: Arcaid/Paul Raftery
p. 61   © Santiago Calatrava
p. 62–67   © Photo: Arcaid/Paul Raftery
p. 68   © Photo: Arnaud Carpentier
p. 69   © Chemetov/Huidobro
p. 70   © Photo: Jean-Francois Jaussaud
p. 71 top   © Photo: Arnaud Carpentier
p. 71 bottom   © Photo: Jean-Francois Jaussaud
p. 72   © Photo: Jannes Linders
p. 73   © Roos Aldershoff
p. 74–77   © Photo: Jannes Linders
p. 78   © Photo: Arcaid/Richard Bryant
p. 79   © Rudi Meisel
p. 80–81   © Photo: Alfred Wolf
p. 82   © Photo: Richard Davies
p. 83 top   © Photo: Richard Davies
p. 83–84   © Sir Norman Foster and Partners
p. 85   © Photo: Arcaid/Richard Bryant
p. 86/87   © Photo: Ben Johnson
p. 87 top   © Sir Norman Foster and Partners
p. 88   © Photo: Arcaid/John E. Linden
p. 89   © Nicholas Grimshaw
p. 91 top   © Photo: Arcaid/Richard Bryant
p. 91 bottom   © Nicholas Grimshaw
p. 92/93   © Photo: Arcaid/Richard Bryant
p. 94   © Photo: Margherita Spiluttini
p. 95   © Daniel Mayer
p. 96–97   © Photo: Margherita Spiluttini
p. 98   © Photo: Arnaud Carpentier
p. 99   © Rem Koolhaas
p. 100–103   © Photo: Ralph Richter
p. 104   © Photo: Euralille
p. 105   © Photo: Arnaud Carpentier
p. 106   © Photo: Ralph Richter/ Architekturphoto
p. 107   © Vos
p. 109   © Photo: Ralph Richter/ Architekturphoto
p. 110 top   © Photo: Groninger Museum/ John Stod
p. 110 bottom   © Photo: Christian Richters
p. 110/111   © Photo: Ralph Richter/ Architekturphoto
p. 111   © Photo: Christian Richters
p. 112   © Photo: Duccio Malagamba
p. 113   © Hisao Suzuki

p. 114   © Enric Miralles
p. 115   © Photo: Duccio Malagamba
p. 116   © Enric Miralles
p. 117 top   © Photo: Duccio Malagamba
p. 117 bottom   © Enric Miralles
p. 118/119   © Photo: Duccio Malagamba
p. 120   © Photo: Scott Frances/ Esto Photographics
p. 121   © José Rafael Moneo
p. 122   © Photo: Scott Frances/ Esto Photographics
p. 124   © Photo: Arnaud Carpentier
p. 125   © Jérôme Schlomoff
p. 126–129   © Photo: Arnaud Carpentier
p. 130–133   © Photo: Georges Fessy
p. 135 top   © Photo: Hughes Colson
p. 135 bottom   © Photo: Peter Willi
p. 136   © Photo: Hughes Colson
p. 137 1st line   © Photo: Patrick Goetlen
p. 137 2nd line   © Photo: Patrick Goetlen
p. 137 3rd line   © Photo: Patrick Goetlen/ Peter Willi
p. 137 4st line   © Photo: Hughes Colson
p. 138   © Photo: Arcaid/Dennis Gilbert
p. 139   © Michel Denancé
p. 141   © Photo: Arcaid/Dennis Gilbert
p. 142/143   © Skyfront Agency
p. 143 top   © Photo: Arcaid/Dennis Gilbert
p. 144–145   © Photo: Nicolas Borel
p. 146   © Photo: Alfred Wolf
p. 147 left   © Photo: Alfred Wolf
p. 147 right   © Photo: Nicolas Borel
p. 148–149   © Photo: Nicolas Borel
p. 150   © Photo: Hans-Jürgen Commerell
p. 151   © Jan-Peter Böning/Zenit
p. 152   © Axel Schultes
p. 153–155   © Photo: Hans-Jürgen Commerell
p. 156   © Axel Schultes
p. 158   © Photo: Reinhard Görner
p. 159   © Otto Steidle
p. 161 top   © Photo: Reinhard Görner
p. 161 bottom   © Steidle + Partner
p. 162 top   © Photo: Reinhard Görner
p. 162 bottom   © Steidle + Partner
p. 163   © Photo: Reinhard Görner
p. 164   © Photo: Robert César/Archipress
p. 165   © Robert César
p. 167   © Jean-Michel Wilmottte
p. 168–169   © Photo: Robert César/Archipress